江苏省英语专业（本科段）自学考试指定教材配套辅导

英语语言学概论自学指导

主　编　支永碧　王永祥
副主编　王秀凤　李葆春　丁后银

苏州大学出版社
Soochow University Press

图书在版编目(CIP)数据

英语语言学概论自学指导/支永碧,王永祥主编. —苏州:苏州大学出版社,2009.6(2023.3重印)
江苏省英语专业(本科段)自学考试指定教材配套辅导
ISBN 978-7-81137-260-1

Ⅰ.英… Ⅱ.①支…②王… Ⅲ.英语-语言学-高等教育-自学考试-自学参考资料 Ⅳ.H31

中国版本图书馆 CIP 数据核字(2009)第 116326 号

英语语言学概论自学指导
支永碧　王永祥　主编
责任编辑　王　娅

苏州大学出版社出版发行
(地址:苏州市十梓街1号　邮编:215006)
南通印刷总厂有限公司印装
(地址:南通市通州经济开发区朝霞路180号　邮编:226300)

开本 787 mm×1 092 mm　1/16　印张 18.25　字数 456 千
2009 年 6 月第 1 版　2023 年 3 月第 5 次印刷
ISBN 978-7-81137-260-1　定价:48.00 元

苏州大学版图书若有印装错误,本社负责调换
苏州大学出版社营销部　电话:0512-67481020
苏州大学出版社网址　http://www.sudapress.com

修订前言

《英语语言学概论自学指导》主要为参加英语专业(本科段)自学考试和全国研究生入学考试的考生而编写,是《英语语言学概论》(王永祥、支永碧,2007)的配套辅导用书。

自2007年起,《英语语言学概论》被确定为英语专业(本科段)自学考试的指定教材。在此期间,许多参加自学考试的考生希望能再出一本配套的辅导教材。他们中的不少人不仅希望自学考试能轻松过关,还希望和全国其他学生一样将来能通过全国统一的研究生入学考试,继续深造求学。而现有的教材内容和相关练习远远不能满足他们的需求。其一,配套练习尚不够全面,缺少问答题的参考答案;其二,和研究生入学考试真题相比,配套练习的类型也不够全面;其三,参加自学考试的学生往往很难得到老师的亲自授课和指导,而英语语言学理论和概念往往抽象难懂,再加上其他各种原因,不少考生不能轻易地掌握各章的重点、难点。因此,他们迫切需要有一本简单实用的自学考试指南和辅导练习帮助他们解决问题。此外,在英语专业研究生入学考试中,英语语言学是一门必考科目。入学以后,英语语言学也是英语专业研究生的一门必修课。鉴于此,他们希望了解更全面的英语语言学基本理论,多做一些更实用的英语语言学练习和真题,以备将来需要。为了满足广大自考学生和准备参加英语专业研究生入学考试考生的需要,我们在广泛征求了各方面的意见之后,精心编写了本书。本书的编写除了主要参照王永祥、支永碧主编的《英语语言学概论》外,还参考了胡壮麟主编的《语言学教程》(修订版),戴炜栋、何兆熊主编的《新编简明英语语言学教程》,以及其他一些高校使用的语言学教程。

本书第一部分为英语语言学核心理论和概念,主要包括本章主要考点、课文理解与重点内容分析。第二部分为英语语言学概论的十三章单元配套练习。和原教材中的练习稍有不同的是,在第二部分,我们选编了部分自学考试真题和部分高校历年考研真题,以便考生更好地了解本章重点。这样,学生可以更有针对性地进行各章节的学习和复习。虽然该部分略有难度,但对考研和自考的学生都很有帮助。第三部分为英语语言学综合模拟试卷,内容紧扣《英语语言学概论》,针对性很强,适用于英语专业各类考生。第四部分为江

苏省自学考试英语语言学概论部分考试样题及参考答案。

在过去的几年中,许多读者,尤其是我们自己的学生,就本书提出了不少有价值的意见和建议。对此,我们表示特别感谢。为了满足广大读者的需求,我们在苏州大学出版社的关心和支持下,对部分内容进行了修订。南京师范大学博士生导师王永祥教授对第三部分的模拟题和第四部分的样题进行了修改和补充,内容基本更新。苏州科技学院支永碧教授对其他章节的个别概念和理论问题进行了修订和完善。尽管如此,因为时间仓促,水平有限,本书仍可能存在不少问题,欢迎读者批评指正。今后我们将进一步完善本书。

祝参加英语专业自学考试的考生轻松克服《英语语言学概论》的学习难题,祝参加英语专业研究生入学考试的考生在本书的帮助下能轻松通过英语语言学这个难关,实现自己的梦想。

编 者

2014 年 12 月

目录 Contents

第一部分　核心理论与概念

Chapter 1　Language ·· 3
　本章主要考点 ·· 3
　课文理解与重点内容分析 ·· 3

Chapter 2　Linguistics ·· 5
　本章主要考点 ·· 5
　课文理解与重点内容分析 ·· 5

Chapter 3　Phonetics ··· 9
　本章主要考点 ·· 9
　课文理解与重点内容分析 ·· 9

Chapter 4　Phonology ·· 13
　本章主要考点 ·· 13
　课文理解与重点内容分析 ·· 13

Chapter 5　Morphology ·· 19
　本章主要考点 ·· 19
　课文理解与重点内容分析 ·· 19

Chapter 6　Syntax ··· 28
　本章主要考点 ·· 28
　课文理解与重点内容分析 ·· 28

Chapter 7　Semantics ··· 35
　本章主要考点 ·· 35
　课文理解与重点内容分析 ·· 35

Chapter 8　Pragmatics ·· 48
　本章主要考点 ·· 48
　课文理解与重点内容分析 ·· 48

Chapter 9	Discourse Analysis	54
本章主要考点		54
课文理解与重点内容分析		54
Chapter 10	Sociolinguistics	61
本章主要考点		61
课文理解与重点内容分析		61
Chapter 11	Psycholinguistics	68
本章主要考点		68
课文理解与重点内容分析		68
Chapter 12	Linguistic Theories and FLT	78
本章主要考点		78
课文理解与重点内容分析		78
Chapter 13	Schools of Modern Linguistics	79
本章主要考点		79
课文理解与重点内容分析		79

第二部分　单元练习

Chapter 1	Language	83
Chapter 2	Linguistics	94
Chapters 3 & 4	Phonetics and Phonology	107
Chapter 5	Morphology	121
Chapter 6	Syntax	134
Chapter 7	Semantics	147
Chapter 8	Pragmatics	162
Chapter 9	Discourse Analysis	171
Chapter 10	Sociolinguistics	175
Chapter 11	Psycholinguistics	181
Chapter 12	Linguistic Theories and FLT	188
Chapter 13	Schools of Modern Linguistics	191

第三部分　综合模拟练习

语言学概论试卷(一) …… 205
语言学概论试卷(二) …… 212

语言学概论试卷(三)	218
语言学概论试卷(四)	226
语言学概论试卷(五)	232
语言学概论试卷(六)	238

第四部分　语言学全真试题

2014年1月江苏省高等教育自学考试	247
2015年1月江苏省高等教育自学考试	254
References	261
附录Ⅰ　英语语言学主要专业术语汉英对照表	266
附录Ⅱ　江苏省自学考试英语语言学概论考试大纲	275
编者后记	282

第一部分

核心理论与概念

Chapter 1 Language

 本章主要考点

语言的定义(What is language?)
人类语言的识别性特征(What are the design features of human language?)
语言的功能(The functions of language)

 课文理解与重点内容分析

本章介绍语言的基本知识,包括语言的定义、语言的识别性特征和语言的功能。

1. 语言的定义

语言是用于人类交际的任意性的发音的符号系统。该定义有五个要点,即系统、任意性的、发音/声的、符号、用于人类交际。

2. 语言的识别性特征

语言的识别性特征指人类语言区别于任何其他动物交流系统的特点。主要包括:

(1) 能产性:也称创造性,人们能用语言创造新的意义,并立即被从未接触过它的人所理解。创造性归因于语言的二重性和递归性。

(2) 离散性:两个语音具有明显的界限。其中一个替代另一个都会产生意义不同的两个词语,如 pack 中的/p/和 back 中的/b/。语言中的每一个语音都具有离散性特点。

(3) 不受时空限制的属性/位移性:人类语言可以让使用者表达说话时(时间和处所)并不存在的物体、事件和观点。这一特性赋予人们概括和抽象的能力。

(4) 任意性:是语言的核心特征,指符号的形式或声音与意义间没有理据或逻辑关系。任意性有不同的程度。

(5) 文化传递性:语言不是靠遗传,而是通过教与学,由人们接触的文化代代传递的。

(6) 结构二重性:指底层有限的语音结构是上层词、句和语篇结构的组成成分,每层都有自身的组合规则,使语言拥有强大的能产性。

(7) 互换性:指人可以是信息的发出者,也可以是信息的接收者。

3. 语言的功能

按照韩礼德(Halliday)的表述,幼儿语言有如下七个功能:

(1) 工具功能:说话人可以使用语言做事情。

(2) 调节功能:语言可用来控制事件。

(3) 表现功能:语言可用来传达知识、汇报事件、进行陈述、做出说明、解释关系、传递信息等。

(4) 互动功能:语言可用来与周围的人进行交际。

(5) 自指性功能:语言可以用来表达个人的情感并展示个性。

(6) 启发功能:使用语言可以获得知识、了解世界。语言可以用于学习,也可以用于问答、争辩,用于验证假设、推导结论和新奇发现。

(7) 想象功能:语言用于创造想象系统,可以用于文学作品、哲学领域里,也可以是空想、白日做梦和发呆遐想。

成人语言有三大元功能:人际功能、概念功能和语篇功能。

国内著名学者胡壮麟等人在其《语言学教程》中阐述了语言的七大功能:

(1) 信息功能:语言最主要的功能。

(2) 人际功能:语言最重要的社会功能。人们通过它建立和维持在社会中的身份和地位。

(3) 施为功能:主要改变人物的社会地位,使用的语言非常正式,有时甚至成为一种礼节。

(4) 感情功能:用以改变听者的感情。它又可当成表达功能,但表达功能还包括自言自语。

(5) 客气/寒暄功能:指有助于说明、维持人际关系的表达。

(6) 娱乐功能:如婴儿的咿呀学语、歌者的吟唱、对歌等。

(7) 元语言功能:指可以用语言来讨论语言本身。

Chapter 2 Linguistics

 本章主要考点

1. 语言学的定义和语言学的研究范畴(The definition of linguistics and scope of linguistics)
2. 语言学的科学性(Linguistics：the science)
3. 语言学的主要分支学科(Sub-branches of linguistics)
4. 语言学中几组重要的区别性概念(Some distinctions in linguistics)

 课文理解与重点内容分析

1. 语言学的定义

语言学是对语言的科学研究,它研究在各自社会中作为交流系统的各种人类语言的基本原理。语言学家的任务不是学习怎样使用某一特定语言,而是考察和研究每一种语言是如何构造的,一种语言如何产生出以及产生出怎样的方言差异、阶级差异,一种语言是如何变化发展的,儿童是如何习得母语的,以及一个人是如何及应该如何学习外语的,等等。

（1）莱昂斯(lyons)的区分：
普通语言学和描写语言学
共时语言学和历时语言学
理论语言学和应用语言学
微观语言学和宏观语言学

（2）王钢的区分：把语言学分为如下五大范畴：
具体语言学和普通语言学
描写语言学和历史语言学
历史比较语言学和对比语言学
微观语言学和宏观语言学
理论语言学和应用语言学

① "具体语言学"以某一具体语言(如汉语)为研究对象。以英语为研究对象的叫英语语言学。普通语言学探索人类语言的普遍性质和一般规律,它是建立在总结概括具体语言学研究成果的基础之上的。

② "描写语言学"也称"共时语言学","历史语言学"也称"历时语言学"。

③"历史比较语言学"利用语言学中专门的历史比较法研究具有共同来源的所谓"亲属语言"的历史发展。"对比语言学"是对两种以上的语言(不论亲属)通过比较来研究其结构的异同。

④"微观语言学"是对语言系统内部各个方面进行的研究,因此,语音学细分为发声语音学、听觉语音学和声学语音学三个"子分支"。"宏观语言学"位于语言学的外围,包括语言学和其他学科相结合而合成的各门边缘学科。

⑤"理论语言学"研究语言的一般理论,是普通语言学的雅称。"应用语言学"有广义和狭义之分。广义的应用语言学包括把语言应用于解决交际问题的诸方面。狭义的应用语言学专指外语教学(和教学法)的研究。

2. 语言学的科学性

一般说来,语言学研究的科学程序包括以下几个步骤(文秋芳,1995:9):

（1）收集语言数据

（2）根据所得数据建构一个初步规则

（3）通过更多的数据验证初步规则,并做出必要的修正

（4）最后提出一个能够解释或说明有关数据的规则或理论

与此类似,梅德明(2003:2)就语言研究的科学步骤总结如下:

（1）观察语言事实

（2）概括语言事实

（3）提出假设解释语言事实

（4）通过更多的观察检验假设

（5）建构某一个语言理论

语言学成为一门科学有下列要素:穷尽性、一致性、简洁性和客观性。语言学是关于语言的科学,自然应该建立在对语言素材和资料的系统研究上,因为这一研究的宗旨是发现语言的本质特征,挖掘语言的潜在系统。语言学家往往是怀着某种语言假设去从事研究的,在研究中不断地检验、证明或推翻自己既有的假设。为了使其分析具有科学性,语言学家的工作遵循上述四条准则。"穷尽性"指语言学家应收集并分析所有既得资料或数据,并给予充分的解释,不能丢三落四。"一致性"指在分析过程中前后观点要一致,至少不能前后矛盾。"简洁性"指进行复杂的分析或证明当中应力求语言的简洁,不拖泥带水,不冗长乏味。"客观性"指实事求是,一是一,二是二,不凭主观臆断妄加取舍,乱下结论。

3. 语言学的主要分支学科

语言学的主要分支学科有语音学、音位学、形态学、句法学、语义学、语用学等。

4. 语言学中的重要区别

（1）共时和历时研究

"共时研究"也称描写语言学,研究语言在某个时期内相对稳定的系统。"历时研究"也称历史语言学,研究语言在不同时期之内的发展和演变。如谚语研究中的英语发展史,英语词源学等。

（2）语言和言语

语言(langue)一词指一个社会所有成员所共享的抽象的语言体系,言语(parole)指语言的实际运用,即语言的实现。语言是抽象的,言语是具体的,是一定时空中的言语事件;

语言不是任何社会个体所讲的东西,言语却总是自然的言语事件中的有机成分;语言相对稳定、系统,言语却受个人和情景等因素支配。在索绪尔(Saussure)看来,言语是一堆杂乱无章的言语现象或素材,因此它不适于系统的研究,语言学家的任务就是从言语实例中抽取或提炼出语言来,即寻找和发现支配着所有言语实例的语言规则,并使之成为语言学研究的对象。

（3）语言能力和语言运用

根据乔姆斯基(Chomsky)的解释,语言能力(competence)是一个理想的语言使用者对其母语的种种规则的了解和掌握,语言运用(performance)则是这些知识在实际话语行为中的实现。语言能力使人说出并听懂无穷多的句子,并且能够识别语病和歧义。语言能力是相对稳定的,而语言运用常常受制于心理和社会因素。因此,一个说话者的语言运用并非总是与其语言能力相等,有时它们之间有较大的差距。

（4）口头语和书面语

关于语言(口头语言、言语、语言的语音形式)是第一性的,而文字是第二性的这一条语言大原则,语言学界几乎达成了共识。从历史角度看,语言产生的时间比文字产生的时间要早得多。少儿习得母语过程中几乎无一例外地先学说再学写。其次,文字符号只不过是以这种方式或那种方式代表或记录口头语言的语音。与口头语言形式相反,文字只是一些书面符号或代码而已。但它的重要性也不可低估。首先文字可以越过广阔的空间,所以人们能够相互传递信件。其次,文字信息可以跨过漫长的时间,所以今天的人们可以读孔孟之道,可以读《史记》。再次,因为口信经常失真、歪曲,导致间接口头交际的曲解和误解,因此,书信或书面信息更显它的优势。文字材料允许人们反复地阅读,而且百读不改其意。大多数现代语言学家都很重视口头语言形式。这一点与20世纪以及之前的语法学家们把文字材料当作唯一的研究对象的做法是不相同的。

（5）语言行为潜势和实际语言行为

"语言行为潜势"和"实际语言行为"是英国伦敦学派语言学家、系统功能语法创始人韩礼德于20世纪60年代提出来的。他主张从功能的角度研究语言。他发现,一个人在他的生活里有许多事情要做,同样,他有许多话要说,说给许多人听,论及不同的话题,而他每次的语言行为只不过是可供他自由选择的语言项目总库中的一项,这个总体中的每一句话都是潜在的语言行为(即潜势),一旦说出即成为实际语言行为。

（6）横组合和纵聚合关系

横组合关系是一种线性关系,指一个单位和同一序列中的其他单位之间的关系,或共现的所有成分间的关系。处于组合关系的词必须满足一些句法和语义条件。纵聚合关系是一种垂直关系或选择关系,指在结构的某个特殊位置上彼此可以相互替换的成分之间的关系,或者是共现的成分与非共现的成分之间的关系。同一聚合关系中的词语只受句法限制,语义因素不在考虑范围之内。处于聚合关系中的词语有共同的句法特征,但是在语义上不能互相替换。组合与聚合关系就像坐标的两根轴,一起决定语言符号的身份。组合关系也叫水平关系或链状关系,聚合关系也叫联想关系或替换关系。

（7）言语交际和非言语交际

言语交际主要是通过语言手段进行的交际,而非言语交际主要是通过手势、眼神、微笑、面部表情等非言语手段进行的交际。不同的文化中非言语交际的手段不尽相同,如果用错,会导致分歧、误解和交际失败,有时甚至惹怒对方。因此,非言语交际行为和交际手段的重要意义也不容忽视。

(8) 描述性研究和规定性研究,即现代语言学和传统语法之区别

描述性研究指语言研究者只是描述和分析语言事实,规定性研究指语言研究者为人们的所谓的"正确使用"制定种种规约。换言之,如果一位语言学者告诉我们语言中的情况或人们的言语现象,他是在"描述",其研究便是描述性语言学方法;如果他对我们指手画脚地说我们该怎么怎么做,他是在"规定",其研究采取的即是规定性语言学方法。20世纪前的语言研究(传统语法)多半属规定学派,现代语言学研究大多属描述派。

Chapter 3 Phonetics

 本章主要考点

1. 语音学的定义、分支(Phonetics and its sub-branches)
2. 发音器官(Speech organs)
3. 辅音的分类(Classifications of consonants)
4. 元音的分类(Classifications of vowels)
5. 协同发音(Coarticulation)
6. 国际音标(International Phonetic Alphabet)
7. 语音特征(Phonetic features)

 课文理解与重点内容分析

1. 语音学

语音学是对语言的声音媒介的研究,它涉及人类语言中使用的全部语音。语音学从三个不同且又相互联系的角度来研究语音。根据语音产生和感知过程,语音学可分为三个主要领域:发音语音学、听觉语音学和声学语音学。在此我们主要关注的是发音语音学。

首先,它从说话者的角度来研究语音,即说话者是怎样用他的发音器官来发音的。其次,它从听者的角度来研究语音,即声音是怎样被听者辨识的。最后,它还通过研究声波从而研究语音是怎样传播的,声波是语音在空气中从一个人传播到另一个人的物理手段。

2. 发音器官

发音器官指人体参与制造言语的部分,包括肺、气管、喉、鼻、口。人的发音器官位于三个区域或声腔:咽腔——咽喉,口腔——嘴,鼻腔——鼻子。从肺部呼出的气流在这几个声腔以不同的方式发生变化,也可以在到达这几个部位前在喉部变化。这些变化来自于对气流运动的种种干扰。具体地说,这些变化来自以种种方式完全阻断气流或对其进行部分干扰。

3. 辅音的分类

英语的辅音可从四个方面进行分类:
- 软腭位置:口腔辅音和鼻腔辅音
- 声带的振动与否:清辅音和浊辅音
- 发音部位:双唇音、唇齿音、舌齿音、齿龈音、齿龈后音、齿龈硬腭音、硬腭音、软腭音、

声门音
- 发音方式:爆破音、鼻腔音、摩擦音、破擦音、流音、滑音

详见下表:

表 3.1:英语辅音的分类

		发音方式										
		闭止音				摩擦音		破擦音		流音		滑音	
		爆破音		鼻腔音									
		清辅音	浊辅音	清辅音	浊辅音	清辅音	浊辅音	清辅音	浊辅音	清辅音	浊辅音	清辅音	浊辅音
发音部位	双唇音	p	b		m								w
	唇齿音				m̥	f	v						
	舌齿音	t̪			n̪	θ	ð						
	齿龈音	t	d		n	s	z				l		
	齿龈后音							tr	dr		r		
	齿龈硬腭音					ʃ	ʒ	tʃ	dʒ				
	硬腭音	c	ɟ										j
	软腭音	k	g		ŋ								
	声门音	ʔ				h							

4. 元音的分类

英语的元音可从以下六个方面进行分类:
- 软腭状态:口腔元音和鼻腔元音,鼻腔元音以音标上加"~"表示。
- 舌位:前元音、央元音、后元音、高元音、中元音、低元音

舌位详见下图:

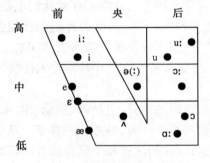

图 3.1:英语元音的分类

高元音:[iː, i, uː, u]
中元音:[e, əː, ə, ɔː]
低元音:[ɛ, æ, ʌ, ɔ, ɑː]
前元音:[iː, i, e, ɛ, ʌ, æ]
央元音:[ə, əː]
后元音:[uː, u, ɔː, ɔ, ɑː]

- 开口度:开元音、半开元音、半闭元音、闭元音

闭元音:[iː],[i],[uː],[u]

半闭元音:[e],[əː]

半开元音:[ɛ],[ɔː]

开元音:[æ],[ʌ],[ɔ],[ɑː]

- 唇形:圆唇元音和不圆唇元音

[uː],[u],[ɔː]和[ɔ]是圆唇元音,其余为不圆唇元音。

- 长短:长元音和短元音

长元音以"ː"表示,如:[uː]。

- 咽部肌肉紧张状态:紧元音和松元音

所有长元音以及短元音[e]都是紧元音,其余为松元音。

除了以上为单元音以外,英语中还有8个双元音,其中3个集中双元音([iə],[ɛə]和[uə]),5个合口双元音([ei],[ai],[ɔi],[əu]和[au])。

5. 协同发音

协同发音:指在实际话语过程中语音持续受邻近音影响,发生同时或重合发音的过程,分为逆化协同发音和重复性协同发音两种。

6. 国际音标

"国际音标"(简称 IPA)是1889年由国际语音协会(成立于1886年)以当时的音标表编制出来的标音系统。它的各种符号来自各种语言。除此之外,还有一些附加符号或变音符用来表示音位变体以及音长、重音和音调的差异。

7. 语音特征

除了传统的描述语音的方法之外,我们也通过语音特征来区分和描述辅音或者元音。在区分语音时,我们常用 + 或 − 值来表示。描述辅音常用的语音特征如下表所示:

表3.2:辅音的语音特征

	p	b	m	w	f	v	θ	ð	t	d	s	z	n	l	tr	dr	r
辅音	+	+	+	−	+	+	+	+	+	+	+	+	+	+	+	+	+
元音	−	−	−	−	−	−	−	−	−	−	−	−	−	+	−	−	+
鼻音	−	−	+	−	−	−	−	−	−	−	−	−	+	−	−	−	−
浊音	−	+	+	+	−	+	−	+	−	+	−	+	+	+	−	+	+
连续音	−	−	−	+	+	+	+	+	−	−	+	+	−	+	−	−	+
前部音	+	+	+	+	+	+	+	+	+	+	+	+	+	+	+	+	+
舌面音	−	−	−	−	−	−	−	−	+	+	+	+	+	+	+	+	+
送气音	−	−	−	−	−	−	−	−	−	−	−	−	−	−	−	−	−

	ʃ	ʒ	tʃ	dʒ	c	ɟ	j	k	g	ŋ	ʔ	h	pʰ	tʰ	kʰ	cʰ
辅音	+	+	+	+	+	+	−	+	+	+	+	+	+	+	+	+
元音	−	−	−	−	−	−	−	−	−	−	−	−	−	−	−	−
鼻音	−	−	−	−	−	−	−	−	−	+	−	−	−	−	−	−
浊音	−	+	−	+	−	+	+	−	+	+	−	−	−	−	−	−

（接上表）

	ʃ	ʒ	tʃ	dʒ	c	ɟ	j	k	g	ŋ	ʔ	h	pʰ	tʰ	kʰ	cʰ
连续音	+	+	−	−	−	−	+	−	−	−	−	+	−	−	−	−
前部音	−	−	−	−	−	−	−	−	−	−	−	−	+	+	−	−
舌面音	+	+	+	+	+	+	+	−	−	−	−	−	−	−	+	+
送气音	−	−	−	−	−	−	−	−	−	−	−	−	+	+	+	+

元音的语音特征如下表所示：

表 3.3：元音的语音特征

	iː	i	e	ɛ	æ	ʌ	ɜː	ə	uː	u	ɔː	ɔ	ɑː
高	+	+	−	−	−	−	−	−	+	+	−	−	−
低	−	−	−	+	+	+	−	−	−	−	−	+	+
前	+	+	+	+	+	+	−	−	−	−	−	−	−
后	−	−	−	−	−	−	−	−	+	+	+	+	+
圆唇	−	−	−	−	−	−	−	−	+	+	+	+	−
紧	+	−	+	−	−	−	+	−	+	−	+	−	+

Chapter 4 Phonology

 本章主要考点

1. 语音学和音位学的定义(Definitions of phonetics and phonology)
2. 音位、音子和音位变体(Phonemes, phones, and allophones)
3. 最小对立体(Minimal pairs)
4. 三种类型的分布(Three types of distribution)
5. 识别音位的四个原则(Principles of identifying phonemes)
6. 区别性特征(Distinctive features)
7. 音位规则(Rules of phonology)
8. 超切分特征(Suprasegmental features)
9. 严式和宽式标音(Narrow and broad transcriptions)

 课文理解与重点内容分析

1. 语音学和音位学的定义以及二者的区别

　　语音学和音位学都是对语音的研究。其英语名称都包含同一个词根 phono-,该词根意思是语音。然而,尽管两者都是对语音的研究,它们在研究方法上和重心上是不同的。语音学具有普遍性的特征,它关心人类语言中使用的全部语音,所有语音是如何发出的,它们为何彼此有所不同,它们具有怎样的语音特征,它们是如何分类的,等等。从另一方面来说,音位学关心的是一种特定的语言语音系统,它旨在揭示一种语言的语音如何形成模式,以及如何被用来在语言交际中表达意思。因此,两者都是语言研究中的既相互区别又相互关联的分支。

　　通过从两个角度审视英语中出现的一些语音,我们可以说明语音学特征和音位学特征的传统差别。我们可以审视一下从语音学角度来看有明显不同的两个语音,它们从音位学角度来看却是同一基本实体的两个变体。两个英语单词 leap 和 peel 中所包含的发音是不一样的,第一个单词中所包含的我们叫作清晰音[l],而第二个单词中所包含的叫模糊音[ɫ]。发清晰音[l]时,舌头升起的部分相当接近上腭的前部,但发模糊音[ɫ]时,舌头升起接近上腭的部分却相当靠后。语音学家们已经辨识了英语中的两个区别相当大的[l]音:

　　他们给这"同一"语音的两个不同变体起了两个不同的名字,并在严式音标中用不同的符号来表示它们。

如果我们从音位学的角度来看这两个语音,我们会说,它们基本上是相同的,因为尽管它们发音不同,但在交际中及在区别单词和意义方面却起着同样的作用。如果一个外语学习者误把 peel 中的模糊音[ɫ]发成清晰音[l],以英语为母语的人并不会因此而误解他,仍能理解其所要表达的意思,只不过觉得发音有点怪。音位学家们发现,[l]音并不是随意地出现在英语单词中的,它们的分布遵循一个精细的互补模式:清晰音[l]通常出现在一个元音之前。音位学是用来研究一种特定语言的语音系统的,所以,我们得出的有关一种语言的语音体系的结论不能被推广用于另一种语言之中。

2. 音子、音位和音位变体

(1) 音子

音子就是一个语音单位或片段。交际过程中可能发出的和听到的语音皆为音子(或因素的组合)。当我们听到 pit, tip, spit 这三个词的时候,我们听到一些音子,其中[p]这个因素有不同的发音方式,如:送气不送气,爆破力的强弱,在元音前面或后面,在长元音或短元音的前面或后面,前面有没有[s],处于重读或轻读音节,等等。这些不同的[p]如果要一一标明和区分,就有必要引用严式标音法的种种"变音符",如在[p]的右上角加上一个小小的[h],应该注意的是,音子可能有辨义的功能,也可能没有。

(2) 音位

音位是音位学的一个单位,它具有辨义的价值。作为一个抽象的语言单位,它不是指具体的某一个音子或语音,它是在一定的语音情景中或环境中由一定的音子来表现或实现的。例如,/p/这个音位在[pit]、[tip]和[spit]这三个词中是由三个不同的音子代表的:第一个/p/送气,爆破力强;第二个/p/送气和爆破力都很微弱;第三个/p/不送气,或者说送气不足。

(3) 音位变体

代表一个音位的音子也可称为"音位变体",或称为一个音位的不同成员(即语音上有一定的差异,但这些差异又不至于大到使一个词几乎成为另一个词或使之产生出新的语义的程度)。上述例词中不同的[p]是/p/这个音位的音位变体。至于一个音位如何由一个音子来表现,或者说,应该使用哪个音位变体,这决定于它的语音情景或环境。不过,音位的选择并非任意,在一般情况下,它是有规律可循的。音位学家的任务就是探寻这些规律。

3. 最小对立体

所谓"最小对立体"指的是两个语音形式(或词)除了一个语音片段之外其余部分完全相同的状态,如 pill 和 bill、pill 和 dill、dill 和 kill 等。以上这些语音形式(或词)形成了一个最小对立集。英语和汉语都有不少最小对立体。它们的存在使得学习者容易辨别哪些是英语音位,哪些是汉语音位。音位学家在研究一种陌生的语言的语音或音位系统时必须着意寻找其最小对立体。

4. 三种类型的分布(对比分布、互补分布和自由变异)

我们能很容易地观察到,从语音学上来看相似的语音之间可能有两种关系:两个相似的语音如果是两个区别性音位,它们可能在意思上形成一个对立,如果是同一音位的变体,它们在意思上就不形成对立。请研究下面单词的发音:

rope[rəup],robe[rəub],pin[pʰin],bin[bin],pot[pʰɔt],spot[spɔt]。

我们发现,有三个语音在语音学上是相似的,即[p],[pʰ],[b],它们有共同的特征"塞音"和"双唇音"。一个重要的语言学问题是去看这些语音在分布上是如何相互联系的。首先,我们会发现,[pʰ]和[b]在词首位置上的互相对立,如在 pin 和 bill 中。我们还发现,它们在词尾位置也互相对立,如在 rope 和 robe 中。所以我们得出结论,/p/和/b/能出现在相同的语音环境中并且意义不同,因此,它们之间的关系是音位对立即对比分布。

另一方面,[p]和[pʰ]从来不对立,它们是同一音位/p/的音位变体,只出现在不同的语音环境中;当发以/p/为首的音时,我们选择了送气的音位变体[pʰ];如果/p/出现在/s/音后,我们就会选择不送气音位变体[p]。因此,同一个音位的两个音位变体之间的关系是互补分布。简单地说,所谓互补分布是指在同一语音环境中出现的两个音并不形成对照或对比,或者说,如果将其中一个代替另一个并不会产生新词或新义,那么我们说这两个音处于自由变异的地位。众所周知,英语的爆破音有时可以失去爆破(如处于爆破音或鼻音之间时)。到底爆破还是不爆破,并不产生新词或新义。它们的区别可以用严式标音法标示出来。这些爆破音与它们的未爆破的音位变体就是一种自由变异的关系。处于自由变异的两个音应该被当作同一个音位看待。例如,在英语中,单词 direct 可以有两种发音方式:/diˈrekt/和/daiˈrekt/,这两个不同的语音 /i/ 和 /ai/处于自由变异的地位。同样的单词有 economics,either,dance 等。

5. 识别音位的原则

要确定两个语音是属于两个独立的音位还是同一个音位的两个音位变体,我们需用下面的四个原则来验证。

(1) 如果两个音处于对比分布,那么它们是两个独立的音位。
(2) 如果两个音总是处于自由变异,则这两个音是同一个音位的音位变体。
(3) 如果语音上相似的两个音处于互补分布,则它们是同一个音位的音位变体。
(4) 如果两个音处于互补分布,但没有语音相似性,则它们肯定是两个不同的音位。

6. 区别性特征

区别性特征就是把两个音位相互区分的特征。因此,区别性特征告诉我们不同的音位是如何相同或不同的。这个概念最初是由布拉格学派的语言学家雅各布森(Jakobson)提出的,在第13章我们还要讨论此重要概念。

7. 音位规则

(1) 序列规则

识别一种语言的音位仅是音位学家们的部分任务。他们还需找出音位组合的方式。一种特定的语言中的语音模式是受规则制约的。音位系统决定了哪些音位能作一个单词的词首、词尾,哪些音位能互相跟从。假若给你四张卡,每一张上面都印有一个不同的英语音位:k,b,l,i,现在让你排列这四张卡,要排出可能出现的所有英语单词,你可能排列出这样的组合:blik,klib,bilk,kilb。你的音位知识告诉你,仅有这些音位排列在英语中是可容许的,而 lbki,ilbk,bkil,ilkb 等不可能是英语单词。

这表明在一种特定的语言中,语音的组合是受规则制约的,这些规则叫作序列规则。英语中有许多这样的序列规则。例如,如果一个单词以[l]或者[r]为首,那么紧随其后的一个语音必须是一个元音。这就是为什么英语中不可能有[lbik]、[lkbi]这样的组合,因为它们违背了音位排序的规则。

此外,如果三个辅音同时出现在单词的词首,语音的组合必须遵从下列规则:

① 第一个音位必须是/s/。
② 第二个音位必须是/p/或/t/或/k/。
③ 第三个音位必须是/l/或/r/或/w/。

这就是为什么英语中所有以三个辅音组合为首的单词都是像 spring [spriŋ], strict [strikt], square [skwεə], splendid [splendid], scream[skri:m]这样的单词。

而且,制约音位模式的规则是随语言不同而不同的。英语中不容许的音位模式在另一种语言中却可能是容许的。例如:软腭鼻音[ŋ]在英语和汉语普通话中从不出现在词首,但在其他一些语言和汉语的一些方言中却可以出现在词首,比如在越南语、上海话及广东话中。

(2) 同化规则

同化规则即通过"模仿"一个序列音位的一个特征使一个语音与另一个语音相似,从而使两个音子变得相似。相邻语音的同化在很大程度上是由发音过程或生理过程引起的。我们说话时倾向于使发音更为简便,这种"马虎"倾向就可能变成语言的规则。

我们都知道,鼻音化在英语中不是一个音位特征,换言之,它并不区别意义。但这并不是说,英语中的元音在实际发音中从不鼻音化,事实上,在一定的语音环境中它们也鼻音化。

同化规则也解释了齿龈鼻音[n]在一些语音组合中的发音变化。这个规则是,在一个单词中,鼻音[n]所处的发音部位和紧随其后的辅音的发音部位变得一样。我们知道,在英语中,前缀"in-"可以加在形容词前使其词义变得与原义相反,如:discreet—indiscreet, correct—incorrect。但前缀"in-"中的[n]音并不总是发成齿龈鼻音。它在单词 indiscreet 中发成齿龈鼻音,因为紧随其后的辅音[d]音是一个齿龈塞音,但[n]音在单词 incorrect 中事实上发成软腭鼻音,即[ŋ],这是因为紧随其后的辅音[k]是一个软腭塞音。因而我们可以看出,当发[n]音时,我们"模仿"了紧随其后的辅音的一个特征。

多数情况下语音同化实际上也体现在有关单词的拼写中。我们知道,possible 的否定形式是 impossible 而不是 inpossible,因为[n]音同化成了[m]音。出于同样原因,plausible, legal, regular 的否定形式是 implausible, illegal, irregular。然而,也有单词,如 input, unproductive, unbeatable 等,同化在这些词的发音中的确存在,但迄今为止在拼写上并没有体现出来。

(3) 省略规则

另一个音位规则是省略规则。它告诉我们什么时候一个语音尽管在拼写中存在,但在发音时却可以省略。我们已经注意到,在单词 sign, design, paradigm 中,尽管其拼写中有字母 g,发音时却没有[g]音。但在其相应形式 signature, designation, paradigmatic 中,字母 g 所代表的[g]音却发音了。这个规则可以这样描述:当[g]音出现在位于词尾的一个鼻辅音前时要省略。鉴于这个规则,在 sign—signature, resign—resignation, phlegm—phlegmatic, paradigm—paradigmatic 这些词中,词根的音位表达将包含音位/g/,但其后如果没有加后缀,根据通常的规则,发音时此音位将被省略。

8. 超切分语音特征

至此我们一直在讨论音位——能区分意义的语音切分成分。但区别性特征可以在由两个或多个音位切分成分所组成的序列中体现出来。出现在切分成分层面之上的音系特征叫作超切分特征,它们是音节、单词和句子等语言单位的音系特征。主要的超切分特征包括重音、声调、语调、连音。

(1)重音

重音根据所存在的语境,可以分为两种:单词重音和语句重音。

当我们说一个词的某一个音节重读时,我们的意思是,发这个音节的音时所用的力气比发其他音节的音时所用的力气要大。因此,重音是个相对的概念:只有两个音节以上的词才有单词重音,不能说单音节词,即只有一个音节的词,有单词重音。

一些语言有固定的单词重音,换言之,单词的重音总是在特定的音节上,比如说第一个音节,或者最后一个音节,或者第二个音节。英语中重音是随意的,并不固定在单词的任何特定的音节上,其位置因词而异,但英语中重音位置能区别意义。

类似的重音变化也出现在复合名词和由相同成分组成的词组中。如前所述,英语复合词的语音特征是,单词重音常在第一个成分上,第二个成分是次重音。例如,复合词 blackbird 由两部分——black 和 bird 构成,发这个词的音时,我们重读第一个成分 black;如果我们重读第二个成分,那就成了 black bird。blackbird 指的是一种特别的鸟,并不一定是黑色的鸟,它和名词短语 black bird 不同,此短语指黑色的鸟。名词短语和复合词的重音是不同的,因为名词词组以 bird 为主要名词,而 black 只是一个修饰语,bird 重读。类似的由重音模式不同而导致的意义不同可以从 greenhouse 和 green house,hotdog 和 hot dog 这两对词和词组上体现出来。a 'greenhouse——一个有玻璃屋顶和四壁且有供热系统的房子,用来种植需要光和热并且怕风的植物;a green 'house——一座绿色的房子;a 'hotdog——一种由面包卷和香肠做成的快餐,a hot 'dog——一只感到热的狗。

单词重音区别意义的作用也可以表现在"-ing"形式加名词的组合中。在英语中,"-ing"形式后加一个名词是常见的,如:dining-room, reading glasses, sewing machine, sleeping baby, swimming fish。尽管形式上是一样的,但是所有这些"-ing"形式加名词的组合有两种类型。一种是"-ing"形式起修饰名词的作用,如:dining-room 是人们用餐的屋子,reading glasses 是人们读书时戴的眼镜,sewing machine 是用来缝纫的机器。这些实际上都是复合名词。两部分是写成一个单词,还是加连字符,或是写成两个独立的词,只是个习惯问题。

但一般来说,发"-ing"形式加名词这类组合形式的音和发其他复合名词一样,单词重音总是在第一个成分上,第二个成分上是次重音,即 'dining-room, 'reading glasses, 'sewing machine。

对另一种"-ing"形式加名词的组合来说,名词实际上是"-ing"形式所指称的动作的发出者。例如,sleeping baby 意思是一个正在睡觉的小孩,而 swimming fish 意思是正在游水的鱼。这些不是复合名词,而是带有"-ing"分词修饰语的名词词组。因此,对这些组合来说,主要重音并不是在第一个成分上,即"-ing"形式上,而是在名词上。"-ing"形式上是次重音:sleeping 'baby, swimming 'fish。比较 swimming 'baby(正在睡觉的小孩)和 'sleeping car(卧铺车),还有 swimming 'fish(正在游水的鱼)和 'swimming pool(游泳池)。

语句重音指句子中某些单词的发音较为用力。一些单词比另一些重要,重要的词发音时用的力较大,以使其显得突出。英语中较为重要的词有名词、动词、形容词、副词和指示代词,这些词发音时通常要重读;另一类词,像冠词、人称代词、助动词、介词、连词通常不重

读。例如,在"He is driving my car"这一句子中,通常重读在主要动词 driving 和名词 car 上,其余的词不重读,但为了强调"他开的车不是自己的,也不是你的,而是我的"这样的事实时,说话者可以重读物主代词 my,虽然物主代词一般情况下是不重读的。

(2)声调

声调指音高变化,这些变化由声带振动频率的不同引起。正如音位一样,音高变化可以区别意义,因此,声调是一个超切分特征。声调区别意义的功能在声调语言中特别重要。英语不是声调语言。我们的母语汉语是典型的声调语言,它有四个声调:阴平,阳平,上声和去声。声调的作用可以通过发同一语音组合 ma 的四个不同声调得到很好的说明:mā (mother), má (hemp), mǎ(horse) and mà(scold)。

(3)语调

当音高、重音和音长依附于一个句子而不是单个的单词时,这些因素合起来叫作语调。几乎在任何一种语言中,语调在表达意义方面都起着重要的作用,在英语这样的语言中尤其如此。英语有四种基本语调,即四音调:降调、升调、降升调和升降调。最常用的是前三种。同一序列的词以不同的语调发出时可能有不同的意义。一般来说,降调表明所说的是直截了当、实事求是的话,升调表示疑问,降升调表示暗示。

(4)连音

另外一个超切分特征是连音。例如:

I scream	/ai + skri:m/	ice cream	/ais + kri:m/
it sprays	/it + spreiz/	it's praise	/its + preiz/
a name	/ə + neim/	an aim	/ən + eim/
grey tape	/grei + teip/	great ape	/greit + eip/
see the meat	/si: + ðə + mi:t/	see them eat	/si: + ðəm + i:t/

连音可能是二语或外语学习者听力理解实践中的一个难点,尤其在上下文语境不清楚的时候。

Morphology

 本章主要考点

1. 形态学的范围（The scope of morphology）
2. 语素的定义（Definition of morpheme）
3. 词根、词缀、自由语素和粘着语素的关系（Interrelations among roots, affixes, free morphemes and bound morphemes）
4. 前缀、后缀和中缀（Prefixes, suffixes and infixes）
5. 屈折和派生词缀（Inflectional and derivational affixes）
6. 词根、词干和词基（Root, stem and base）
7. 语素、语子和语素变体的关系（Interrelations among morphemes, morphs and allomorphs）
8. 空语子和零语子（Empty morph and zero morph）
9. 直接成分分析（IC Analysis）
10. 构词法（Word-formation processes）

课文理解与重点内容分析

1. 形态学的研究范围

形态学研究的是词的内部结构和构词规则。词的构成并不是随意的,而是遵从特定的规则的。形态学的任务就是去发现这些规则。形态学可分为两个分支学种——屈折形态学和词汇/派生形态学。前者研究词的屈折变化,后者研究词的构成。

2. 语素的定义

语素是语言最小的意义单位。句子是由单词构成的,经常被分析到单词,单词经常被看成是最小的语言单位。词可以被进一步分析,即词可以被分成更小的成分。我们把这些处于单词最低一层的、有意义的成分称为"语素"。

3. 词根、词缀、自由语素和粘着语素的相互关系

根据语义,语素可分为词根和词缀；根据结构,语素可以划分为自由语素和粘着语素。请看下列单词：

helper→help-er
roommate→room-mate   quicken→quick-en
frightening→fright-en-ing   disabled→dis-able-d

warmer→warm-er   biology→bio-logy
soliloquy→soli-loquy   assistant→assist-ant
carelessly→care-less-ly   symphony→sym-phony

我们会立刻识别出,其中一些语素是单词,例如:help,room,mate,quick,fright,able。这些词只包括一个语素,它们被称为自由语素。这些语素是独立的意义单位,能够独自自由使用。在上面划分出的其余的语素,像-er,-en,dis-,bio-,-less,-sym 则明显不同。这些语素不能够单独使用。它们被称为粘着语素。

粘着语素是那些不能单独使用,而必须和其他语素——自由语素或粘着语素——结合在一起以形成一个单词的语素。粘着语素包括两类:词根和词缀。词根被看作是词的一部分,它有清楚、明确的意思,但不能单独存在,它必须和另一个词根或词缀组合构成单词。英语中有很多这样的词根。例如,词根"geo-"的意思是"地球,土地",当它和另一个意思是"学问的一个分支"的词根"-ology"组合在一起时,我们就得到 geology 这个单词,其意思是"对地球构造的研究"。

audi-——listening:auditor, audience, auditorium
gene-——life:generate, genetic, genital(生殖的)
semi-——half:semiconductor, semifinal
aqu-——water:aquarium(水族馆), aquatic(水的;水生的)
-loqu-——speech:eloquent, loquacious(饶舌的), soliloquy
-ium——hall:stadium(露天运动场), gymnasium, auditorium, aquarium
-path-——emotion:sympathy, empathy(移情作用)
toler-——endure:tolerate, tolerable
thermo-——heat:thermometer, thermostatic(温度调节装置的), thermonuclear(高热原子核反应的)
manu-——hand:manuscript(手稿), manual(手册), manufacture

词根、词缀、自由语素和粘着语素的关系,可以用下图来形象直观地说明:

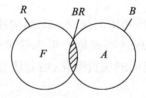

F＝free morphemes(自由语素)   B＝bound morphemes(粘着语素)
R＝roots(词根)   A＝affixes(词缀)
B R＝bound roots

图 5.1:词根、词缀、自由语素和粘着语素的相互关系

4. 前缀、后缀、中缀

词缀是粘着在其他词素(如自由词素)身上的构词成分或因素的统称,可以细分为三类:前缀、后缀和中缀。英语中有许多前缀和后缀,但是中缀为数不多。比如 foot 变成 feet,其中"-ee-"就是中缀,但它实质上只不过是内屈折罢了。我们说英语有许多前缀和后缀,但是与几乎是无限多的自由词素和词汇相比,词缀的数目也是十分有限的。一本词汇学书或

词典不能包容全部词汇,却能囊括全部词缀。还要说明的是不少学者认为英语是不存在中缀的,只有前缀和后缀,但是有些语种存在中缀却是事实,因此我们在这里述及了中缀。

5. 屈折词缀和派生词缀

词缀有两类:屈折词缀和派生词缀。

屈折词缀或屈折语素表明各种不同的语法关系或语法范畴,如数、性、时、体、格、级等。就词尾来说,英语比俄语、法语和德语这些语言都简单,因为在其历史发展中,英语已经丢弃了相当多的屈折词缀。而被保留下来的有:

-(e)s——标示名词的复数

-(e)s——标示现在时的第三人称单数

-(e)d——标示过去时

-ing——标示进行体

-er——标示形容词和副词的比较级

-est——标示形容词和副词的最高级

-'s——标示名词的所有格

派生词缀加在一个原有的单词上以构成一个新词。这是英语中一种很常见的构成新词的方式,这样的方式叫派生法,用派生法构成的新词叫作派生词。能够加上一个派生词缀的原有语素叫作词干。词干可以是一个粘着词根、自由语素或者本身就是一个派生词,例如:

tolerate   词根"toler-" + 词缀"-ate"

quickly   自由语素"quick" + 词缀"-ly"

carelessness   自由语素"care" + 词缀"-less"——→派生词"careless" + 词缀"ness"

根据在新词中的不同位置,词缀又分为两种:前缀和后缀。前缀出现在单词的开头,而后缀用在单词的结尾。

英语中有很多常见的前缀,例如:

dis-: dislike, discontinue, disagree

un-: uneasy, unconscious, unfavorable, unlock

in-: incorrect, indirect

mis-: misinform, mistake, misplace

de-: devaluate(贬值), decentralize, deoxidize(除氧)

over-: overdo, overheat, overpopulate

uni-: unify, unilateral(单方面;单边的), unicorn(独角兽)

前缀改变词干的意思,但通常不改变原词的词性。"be-"和"en(m)-"是例外,它们加在形容词和名词前,会把这些词变成动词。例如:little—belittle, large—enlarge, rich—enrich, body—embody。

后缀加在词干的末尾,改变原词的意思,并且在很多情况下,改变原词的词性。因此,有构成名词的后缀、构成形容词的后缀、构成副词的后缀和构成动词的后缀。例如:

-er: teacher, writer, beginner

-ician: electrician, mathematician, physician

-bility: possibility, solubility, capability

-hood: childhood, manhood
-age: orphanage, anchorage(停泊;抛锚地点), vicarage(牧师住处)
-ary: elementary, secondary
-ful: beautiful, delightful, sorrowful
-en: weaken, darken, deepen
-ize: modernize, nationalize, mechanize
-ly: slowly, highly, dimly, joyfully
-ward: forward, eastward, upward

关于屈折词缀和派生词缀,请参考下面两个表(王永祥、支永碧,2007:60-61):

表 5.1：英语屈折词缀

词缀	语法功能	例句
-s	Third person singular present tense marker	Tom talks.
-s	Plural number marker	The chairs are his.
-ed	Past tense marker	Tom talked.
-ed/-en	Past participle marker / perfect aspect	Tom has talked/it was stolen.
-ing	Present participle marker / progressive aspect	Tom is talking.
-'s	Possessive case marker	John's friend came here.
-er	Comparative degree marker	He is thinner than Tom.
-est	Superlative degree marker	Tom is the tallest in his class.

表 5.2：英语派生词缀

词基	派生词缀	派生词
agree	dis-	disagree
happy	-ly	happily
danger	en-	endanger
use	-ful	useful
teach	-er	teacher
luck	-y	lucky

6. 词根、词干和词基

首先要说明的是不少教材并没有严格区分词基、词干这两个概念,也有的教材将词干、词根、词基混为一谈。尽管它们有些时候可以是同一个词。但我们以为从词缀的角度来区分词干和词基似乎更有利于大家区分两者。在本书中我们这样来界定词干和词基,即:如果打算在一个单词后面加派生词缀,则原来这个单词形式是词基,如果我们打算在一个单词后面添加屈折词缀,则原单词为词干。换句话说,去掉派生词缀得到的词是词基,去掉屈折词缀得到的词为词干。如果去掉词缀后的单词在不改变身份和词义的情况下不能再去任何词缀,则这个词是个词根。在这个意义上,词根可以是个词干或词基,但词干并不一定是词根,词基也不一定是词根。如:derivational 去掉-al,是 derivation,这个词相对于 derivational 来说,是个词基,却绝不是词根。去掉名词性词缀-tion 后,我们得到 derive,此时,这个 derive 既是个词根也是个词基。我们再举 derives 为例,去掉屈折词缀-s 后的单词 derive 既是个词根也可以称为词干。

7. 语素、语子和语素变体的关系

语素是一个抽象概念,是语言的语法系统里最小的有意义的单位,而语子是语素在语言中的具体体现,即语言中用来实现语素的具体形式。语素变体是某一具体的语素的体现形式,语素比它们的语素变体抽象得多。还要说明的是,我们通常将语子和语素变体放在//里,而语素却被放在{ }中。

8. 空语子和零语子

所谓空语子即有形式但无意义的语子,如 r 在 children 中是个空语子,children 可以分析为 child + r + en。所谓零语子则是有意义无形式的语子,我们用符号/∅/来代表零语子,如 work 在 they work in Nanjing 中,可以分析为/wə:k/ + /∅/。

9. 直接成分分析

直接成分分析是一种分析法,用于分析一个语素的层级结构或层级顺序。通过直接成分分析法,我们可以把一个语素分为两个部分,然后再把每一个部分分为两个次部分,一直到不能再分为止。如我们可以把单词 replacements, disapproval 等分析如下:

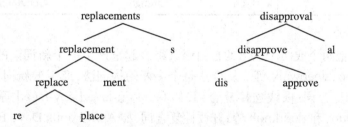

我们称上面的图为树形图,最底端的语素成为最终成分,最上面语素的每一次两分得到的语素都是直接成分,当然,最终成分本身相对于直接坐标语素来说也是个直接成分,如 place 对于 replace 这个坐标语素来说是个直接成分,但对于 replacements 来说则是个最终成分。

10. 构词法

在《英语语言学概论》中,除了新词铸造法和借用法之外,我们还探讨了其他七种常见的构词法,即派生法、复合法、转化法、混合构词法、剪切法、逆构词法和首字母缩略法。下面我们首先对新词铸造法和借用法进行界定和说明。

(1)新词铸造法

通常认为,在人类的最早发展阶段,一种语言的基本词汇是通过新词铸造法产生的。如最早的产品商标名以及早期的 aspirin, nylon 等和较近的 Xeror, Kodax, Clone 等词语的产生方法都属于新词铸造法。

(2)借用法

借用法在英语语言里,尤其在古代英语和中古英语中是个主要而常见的新词来源。借用法一般分为四种类型:

同化词、非同化词、译借词、借义词。

(3) 现在我们来分析七种主要的构词法或构词过程。

① 派生法(derivation)

派生法也称为词缀法,主要通过增加前缀或后缀产生新词,如:

表 5.3：词缀法

词 缀 法		词 基	派生词
前缀法	en-	able	enable
	dis-	obey	disobey
	il-	literate	illiterate
	mis-	fortune	misfortune
	re-	write	rewrite
后缀法	-ly	friend	friendly
	-ism	international	internationalism
	-ness	useful	usefulness
	-less	use	useless
	-en	strength	strengthen

② 复合法

复合法就是把两个或两个以上的自由语素组合起来产生一个新词汇的过程,如 forget-me-not, waterbed, sleepwalk 等。复合法是个多产的构词法,产生的新词称为复合词。一般有三种类型的复合词:横线连接复合词,如 father-in-law, baby-faced 等;固体复合词如 fingerprint, sunburn 和 doorknob 等;开放性复合词,如 April Fool's Day, Boston terrier 等。

③ 转化法

转化法也称为功能转换法或零派生法。在产生新词过程中没有在原单词上增加任何词缀,即词形不变但词性已变。在现代英语里这种构词法经常被使用。例如:

表 5.4：英语语言里常见的转化构词法

转化法	例 句
verb→noun	He **answered** my question at once. →He gave me the **answer** at once.
noun→verb	The **bottle** is full of water. →The soft drinks are **bottled.**
adj.→noun	At that time, my family was very **rich**. →The poor man hates the **rich** very much.
adj.→verb	He wears the **dirty** clothes. →He **dirtied** the water unintentionally.
adv.→verb	He ordered the soldier to come **up**. →They **up** the prices intentionally.
adv.→verb	He put **down** his bag on the floor. →He **downed** a few beers and left the room.
noun→adj.	The **model** is standing there drinking gracefully. →The boy likes the **model** plane very much.

有时一种形式通过转化可以用于多种功能。如 last 可以用于及物动词、非及物动词、名

词、副词、形容词。

ⓐ The food can only last us three days. (vt.)
ⓑ The film lasted two hours. (vi.)
ⓒ He is the last to leave the room. (n.)
ⓓ Who laughs last laughs best. (adv.)
ⓔ Who was the last one to leave the room? (adj.)

④ 混合构词法

混合构词法就是把原来两个单词的部分去掉,把剩余的部分组合起来构成一个新的单词的过程。通常有四类混合构词法,见下表:

表 5.5:英语中常用的混合构词法

类型	混合构词法的种类	例词
1	the 1st part of the 1st word + the 1st part of the 2nd word	teleprinter + exchange = telex modulator + demodulator = modem international + police = Interpol communication + satellite = comsat
2	the 1st part of the 1st word + the 2nd part of the 2nd word	helicopter + airport = heliport breakfast + lunch = brunch smoke + fog = smog motor + hotel = motel news + broadcast = newscast transfer + resistor = transistor glass + asphalt = glasphalt smoke + murk = smurk channel + tunnel = Chunnel smoke + maze = smaze television + broadcast = telecast Spanish + English = Spanglish simultaneous + broadcast = simulcast
3	the 1st part of the 1st word + the whole form of the 2nd word	medical + care = medicare documentary + drama = docudrama parachute + troops = paratroops Motor + town = Motown (nickname for Detroit) Europe + Asia = Eurasia
4	the whole form of the 1st word + the 2nd part of the 2nd word	talk + marathon = talkathon travel + catalogue = travelogue walk + marathon = walkathon air + hotel = airtel

⑤ 剪切法

在讨论剪切法和首字母缩略法之前,我们首先看看缩略法,在词典里,我们经常看到 abbre. 字样,其实就是 abbreviation 的缩写。有时缩略法等同于剪切法,如 prof.(来自 professor),telly(来自 television)等。这些是典型的缩略法例子。

剪切法是这样一种构词过程,它通过删除原词的一个或更多音节来缩短原词(通常是名词)以产生新词,但不改变原词的意义或词性。但要注意的是剪切法往往导致词语的文体变化，从正式变为非正式。通常有四类剪切法，见下表：

表5.6：英语中常见的剪切构词法

类型	剪切法类型	定义	例词 原词	例词 剪切词
1	尾部剪切法	the process of word-formation in which a word is shortened by deleting **the end of the word**	advertisement	ad
			photograph	photo
			automobile	auto
			amplifier	amp
			champion	champ
			microphone	mike
			gymnasium	gym
			facsimile	fax
			condominium	condo
2	首部剪切法	the process of word-formation in which a word is shortened by removing **the beginning of the word**	telephone	phone
			airplane	plane
			omnibus	bus
			parachute	chute
			earthquake	quake
3	首尾部剪切法	the process of word-formation in which a word is shortened by discarding **both the beginning and the end of the word**	influenza	flu
			refrigerator	fridge
			detective	tec
4	短语剪切法	the process of word-formation in which **a phrase is shortened** by dropping the end of the 1st word and the whole of the 2nd	zoological garden	zoo
			popular music	pop
			public house	pub
			permanent waves	perm

⑥ 逆序造词法/逆生法

逆构词法是一种特殊的单词缩短法，它通过删除原词中假定的所谓的后缀来产生新词。可以相当于后缀法的相反形式。如：

baby-sit	from	babysitter
beg	from	beggar
burgle	from	burglar
concord	from	concordance
diagnose	from	diagnosis
difficult	from	difficulty
donate	from	donation

eavesdrop	from	eavesdropping
edit	from	editor

⑦ 首字母缩略法

首字母缩略法是把若干单词的首字母大写形式组合在一起产生新词的过程。通过这种方式产生的新词有两个类型：acronyms 和 initials。前者有一个单独的单词发音而不是以一个个字母发音形式存在，后者是以一个个字母发音而组合起来的单词。如：

ⓐ Acronyms

AIDS	from	acquired immune deficiency syndrome
NASA	from	National Aeronautics and Space Administration
NATO	from	the North Atlantic Treaty Organization
OPEC	from	Organization of Petroleum Exporting Countries
PIN	from	Personal Identification Number
Radar	from	Radio Detecting and Ranging
SARS	from	severe acute respiratory syndrome
TEFL	from	teaching English as a foreign language
TESL	from	teaching English as a second language
TESOL	from	teaching English to speakers of other languages

ⓑ Initialisms

A. D.	from	Anno Domini
ATM	from	Automatic Teller Machine
B. C.	from	Before Christ
C. O. D.	from	cash on delivery
EEC	from	European Economic Community
UFO	from	unidentified flying object
UN	from	the United Nations
VOA	from	Voice of America
WTO	from	World Trade Organization

前面我们讨论了几种常见的构词法，但这里要提醒的是有时一个新单词的产生往往涉及不止一种构词法，如 hard-liner 就有两种构词法的参与，即复合法和派生法。

Chapter 6 Syntax

 本章主要考点

1. 句法学的定义(Definition of syntax)
2. 语法、形态学和句法学的关系(Relation among grammar, morphology and syntax)
3. 三种句法关系:纵聚合、横组合和等级关系(Three syntactic relations: syntagmatic, paradigmatic and hierarchical relations)
4. 直接成分分析、带标记的直接成分分析、短语标记法和括弧法(IC Analysis, labeled IC Analysis, phrase markers, and labeled bracketing)
5. 成分关系和依存关系(Constituency and dependency)
6. 表层结构和深层结构(Surface structures and deep structures)
7. 短语结构规则(Phrase structure rules)
8. 转换规则(Transformational rules)
9. 结构歧义(Structural ambiguity)

 课文理解与重点内容分析

1. 句法学的定义

句法学研究的是词、词组和短语组合成句子的种种规则、规律或方式,它研究句子中各种成分之间的关系。简单地说,句法研究的是语言的句子结构。句法这个术语最初来自希腊语,字面意思是排列。句子是根据一种特定的排列词的方式构成的。排列正确的句子被认为是合乎语法的句子。合乎语法的句子是根据一套句法规则构成的。句法是一个规则系统。

2. 语法、形态学和句法学的关系

布斯曼(Bussmann)(2000:194)认为,语法是关于自然语言形态规则和句法规则的知识和研究。形态学是语法的一部分,是研究词语的内部结构和构词过程的语言学分支学科。句法学也是语法的一个部分,研究词、词组、短语之间的关系及其组成句子的规则、规律和方式,它研究句子中各种成分之间的关系,是语言学的一个分支学科。

3. 三种句法关系：横组合、纵聚合和等级关系

横组合关系指一个单位和同一序列中的其他单位之间的关系，或共现的所有成分间的关系。处于组合关系的词必须满足一些句法和语义条件。

纵聚合关系指在结构的某个特殊位置上彼此可以相互替换的成分之间的关系，或者是共现的成分与非共现的成分之间的关系。同一聚合关系中的词语只受句法限制，语义因素不在考虑范围之内。处于聚合关系中的词语有共同的句法特征，但是在语义上不能互相替换。组合与聚合关系就像坐标的两根轴，一起决定语言符号的身份。组合关系也叫水平关系或链状关系，聚合关系也叫垂直关系、选择关系、联想关系或替换关系。

不同于组合和聚合关系，句子也按照层级顺序来组织，因为句子由小句组成，小句由短语组成，而短语由单词组成。因此，句子内部的层次构成等级结构。句子的等级结构可以通过直接成分分析法、带标记的直接成分分析法、短语标记法和带标记的括弧法来进行分析。

4. 直接成分分析、带标记的直接成分分析、短语标记法、带标记括弧法

句子是一个层级结构。句子里的词首先构成词组。句子与构成要素之间的关系叫作结构体和成分之间的关系。分析这种关系的一个重要方法是直接成分分析法，简称 IC 分析法。直接成分分析法先把句子分析为直接成分——词组（或短语），再把这些直接成分依次切分到各自的直接成分，层层切分，直到最终成分为止。实际操作中，为了方便，通常切分到词为止。直接成分分析法可以用括弧或树形图表示。切分直接成分的标准是替换性：看一个词语的序列，是否可以被一个单词替换而结构保持不变。IC 分析法可以清晰地呈现句子的内在结构，揭示可能的歧义。

由于直接成分分析法不能揭示具有相似或相同结构的句子之间的差异，语言学家们尝试给每一个相应成分加上标记以改进直接成分分析，弥补其不足。这种修改后的直接成分分析法被称为带标记的直接成分分析。如图 6.1 所示：

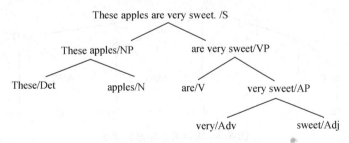

图 6.1：带标记的直接成分分析

虽然带标记的直接成分分析能揭示句子之间的结构差异，但这样的方法太过累赘麻烦，因此，人们再次修改它，将句子层面和短语层面的词语直接用短语标记符号代替，最终成分直接用单词标记。这种修改后的句子分析法叫短语标记法。如图 6.2 所示：

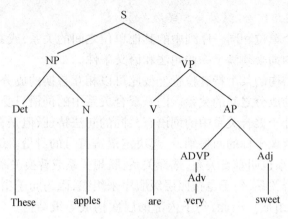

图 6.2：短语标记法

用带标记的括弧来进行句子的等级结构分析,这就是带标记括弧法,如：

[S[NP[Det these][N apples]][VP[V are][AP[ADVP[Adv very]][Adj sweet]]]]

5. 成分关系和依存关系

直接成分分析、带标记括弧法等都是句子的成分结构语法分析法。成分结构分析是一种等级结构句法分析,依据语言形式的分布来揭示不同结构层面的不同成分之间的关系。

还有一种句法分析法叫依存关系句法分析法。它根据语言符号的功能,通过句子结构的各要素之间的依存关系来解释语法关系。依存语法主要关注句子依存结构的描述,也就是描述句子各要素之间的依存关系结构。在依存语法看来,在句子的每两个要素或成分之间,一个是支配要素/成分,另一个则是依存要素/成分。如果一个支配成分依存于另一个支配成分,则形成了一个复杂的等级依存顺序。每一个句子当中,绝对的支配者是动词。如图 6.3 所示：

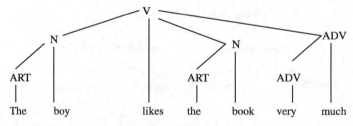

图 6.3：依存关系句法分析法

6. 表层结构和深层结构

句法移位对语法研究的启示是,一个句子结构可以有两个层次的句法表现,一个存在于移位发生前,一个存在于移位发生后。在正规的语言学研究中,这两种句法表现一般被称为深层结构（D-structure 或 the deep structure）和表层结构（S-structure 或 the surface structure）。短语结构规则通过插入词汇在深层结构上生成句子,而应用句法移位规则又把句子从深层结构转化到表层结构。沿着这一转换生成分析方向我可以用下面的图示来概括语法中句法成分的组合：

语法的句法成分：

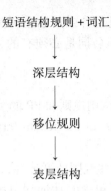

必须要指出的是当我们说一个句子有两个层次的句法表现——深层结构与表层结构时,我们并不是说,一个句子在不同的句法层次上看起来必须是不同的。由于并非所有句子都能发生句法移位,因而一些句子的深层结构和表层结构在不同的表现层次上是完全相同的。

在《英语语言学概论》(王永祥、支永碧,2007:84)里,我们也探讨了句子的动态研究涉及的两个层面,即句子的深层结构和表层结构。深层结构通过短语结构规则来生成,而表层结构由深层结构通过转换规则转换而来。整个动态分析过程如下图所示:

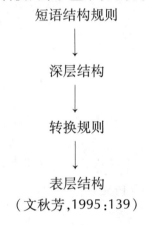

(文秋芳,1995:139)

7. 短语结构规则

既然我们学习了短语划分的四大类别,现在我们看一下短语自身的结构规则:一个句子(S)由一个名词词组(NP)和一个动词词组(VP)组成,如图所示:

让我们把这种组合模式用一个线性算式重写,并把它称为短语结构规则或重写规则:S →NP VP

我们把箭头读作"包含"或"重写为",这样算式中的规则就读作"一个句子包含或可以重写为一个名词词组和一个动词词组"。

NP 至少有七种可供选择的短语结构规则,这就是:N, Det N, Det Adj N, Adj N, Det Ns, Det Adj N PP, Det Adj N PPs。NP 必须包含一个名词(N),其他是可随意选择的。

NP →(Det)(Adj)N(PP)(S)

这个规则可读成"一个名词词组包含或可以重写为一个冠词、一个形容词、一个名词、一个介词词组和(或)一个句子,其中名词是必须有的,其他则是可选成分"。VP 的短语结构规则:

VP→V(NP)(PP)(S)

同样,我们可以写出 AP 的短语结构规则和 PP 的短语结构规则:

AP—A(PP)(S)(curious/curious of the results/curious that no one was there)

PP—P NP(after the English class)

短语结构规则的循环性:由于这些规则的循环性,运用它们可以造出无数句子,这些句子又可以是无限长的。"一个句子所包含的动词词组可以包含另一个句子;一个动词词组可以包含一个句子,而这个句子中又可以包含另一个动词词组;一个介词词组可以包含一个名词词组,这个名词词组后又可以跟另一个介词词组;一个名词词组可以包含一个介词词组,而这个介词词组又可以包含一个名词词组(或)一个句子。"这些规则虽只是语法规则的一部分,却足以解释为什么语言具有创造性,为什么说话人的记忆力是有限的,却能表达并理解无限的句子。这就是说,循环性体现了语言中的句子能够有更多的成分,并且使说话者能够在同一句子中重复一些句法成分。下面是一些常见的短语结构规则:

S→NP AUX VP

NP→(Det)(AP) N

AP→$\begin{Bmatrix} (AP) \\ (ADVP) \end{Bmatrix}$→Adj

ADVP→(ADVP) Adv

VP→V$\begin{Bmatrix} (NP)(PP)(S) \\ (AP) \\ (ADVP) \end{Bmatrix}$

PP→P NP

AUX→Tense (Modal)(Perf)(Prog)

Tense→$\begin{Bmatrix} Present \\ Past \end{Bmatrix}$

Modal→can, may, must, will, shall, etc.

Perf→have-EN

Prog→be-ING

8. 转换规则

转换规则是用来将深层结构转换成表层结构的规则,它一般由两个部分组成:(1)结构描述(the structural description, namely, SD),(2)结构变化(the structural change, SC)。

(1) 常见的转换规则有以下九种:

① T-Affix(词缀转换规则)

② T-Passive(被动转换规则)

③ T-Agent deletion(删除施事者转换规则)

④ T-Negation(否定转换规则)

⑤ T-Do insertion(助动词 do 插入转换规则)
⑥ T-Yes or No question(一般疑问句转换规则)
⑦ T-Wh-word question(疑问词插入转换规则)
⑧ T-Reflexive(反身代词转换规则)
⑨ T-Imperative(祈使句转换规则)

在这些转换规则当中,T-Affix 是必要的转换规则,任何表层结构的产生都必须有 T-Affix 的参与。所有其他的转换规则都是选择性的。

(2) 特别要注意的是,转换规则的顺序很重要:
① T-Reflexive must be applied before T-Imperative.
② T-Passive must be applied before T-Reflexive.
③ T-Passive must be applied before T-Negation.
④ T-Passive must be applied before T-Yes or No question.
⑤ T-Affix is always finally applied.
⑥ T-Agent-deletion is always applied immediately after T-Passive.
⑦ T-Do-insertion is always applied immediately after T-Negation.
⑧ T-Do-insertion is always applied immediately after T-Yes or No question.
⑨ The basic order of transformations for Wh-word questions is:
T-Wh-word insertion→T-Yes or No question→(T-Do insertion)→T-Wh-word switching→T-Affix→Wh-word insertion rule

9. 结构歧义

歧义通常是由于歧义词汇或歧义结构导致的。歧义词汇引起的歧义叫词汇歧义。歧义结构引起的歧义叫结构歧义,通常,我们将结构歧义分为:表层结构歧义和潜在结构歧义。关于结构歧义的例子很多,如:

(1) John is eager to please.

歧义存在于 John 和 to please 的逻辑关系上,John 可以是 to please 的逻辑主语,John is eager to please others,也可以是 to please 的逻辑宾语,John is eager to be pleased。

(2) They decided on the train.

介词 on 可以和 decide 搭配使用,意思是,they chose to take the train,on 也可以和 the train 搭配使用,作句子状语,意思为,They made a decision on the train,他们在火车上做出了决定。

(3) They are cooking apples.

由于 cooking 可以是谓语动词的一部分,带宾语 apple,也可以是表语的一部分,充当 apple 的定语,所以这个句子有两个含义:
第一种含义为 Those people are preparing food by heating apples,第二种含义为:Those are apples for cooking.

(4) Mary hit a man with an umbrella.

这个句子的歧义是由于 with an umbrella 既可以做整个句子的状语,也可以做宾语的定语。Mary 用雨伞打了一个男人,也可以说,Mary 打了一个拿雨伞的男人。

(5) I like Eve as well as Gloria.

这是由于 as well as 引起的结构歧义。
含义1：I like Eve as well as I like Gloria. 我喜欢 Eve 就像我喜欢 Gloria 那样。
含义2：I like Eve as well as Gloria does her. 我像 Gloria 那样喜欢 Eve。
含义3：I like both Eve and Gloria. 我喜欢 Gloria 也喜欢 Eve。
总之，这样的结构歧义不胜枚举，日常生活中，尤其是英语写作中，我们要倍加小心。

Semantics

本章主要考点

1. 语义学的定义(Definition of semantics)
2. 语义学的分支(Sub-branches of semantics)
3. 意义理论(Theories of meaning)
4. 指称/参照、外延、内涵、指称对象、意义、延伸、意图、概念、意涵、字义(Reference, denotation, connotation, referent, sense, extension, intension, concept, implicature, signification)
5. 意义类型(Types of meaning)
6. 意义要素(Elements of meaning)
7. 成分分析(Componential analysis)
8. 语义场(Semantic field)
9. 词汇关系(Lexical relations)
10. 决定句义的要素(Essential factors for determining sentence meaning)
11. 句间意义关系(Sense relations between sentences)
12. 述谓分析、谓词、题元和命题(Predication analysis, predicate, argument, proposition)
13. 语义三角理论(The theory of Semantic Triangle)

课文理解与重点内容分析

1. 语义学的定义

"语义学"就是研究"意义"的学科,即研究语言的意义及其交际功能。哲学家、心理学家和语言学家都对语义学感兴趣。哲学家想了解语言形式与它们所指的客观世界的种种现象之间的关系(如"真假值"问题)。心理学家想通过语言来了解人脑或心理活动。语言学家研究它,是因为人们运用语言形式时大多要表达一定的意义。

2. 语义学的分支

将语义学进行分类是一件非常复杂的事情,根据不同的标准我们可以有不同的分类。笼统地说,我们可以发现这样的分支学科,如操作语义学、框架语义学、自然语义学、词汇语义学、形式语义学、功能语义学、句法—词汇语义学等。但是要进行正确的分类,我们必须有一定的标准。例如：

根据它是否属于语言学范畴，莱昂斯(2000:11)将语义学分为语言语义学、非语言语义学(如哲学语义学、心理语义学和逻辑语义学等)。

根据它在语言中的不同表达层面，文秋芳(1995:210)将语义学分为词汇语义学(lexical semantics)和句子语义学(sentence semantics or sentential semantics)。

从历时角度来说，语义学在不同的历史时期具有不同的研究目标。李福印(2006:22)将语义学的发展历史分为五个阶段：(1) 19世纪末，语义学这个术语开始被人们使用。(2) 从19世纪90年代到20世纪30年代，是历史哲学语义学时期。(3) 从20世纪20年代到20世纪30年代是现代语义学的孕育发展阶段。(4) 在20世纪60年代，现代语义学产生。它的流派结构语义学、生成语义学等很有影响。(5) 自20世纪70年代，现代语义学开始发展，当时典型的流派包括蒙太古语义学、逻辑语义学、认知语义学等。

3. 意义理论

莱昂斯(2000:40)述及了六种可以区分的、具有哲学性的意义理论：

(1) 指称理论(referential theory or denotational theory)

(2) 意念理论(ideational or mentalistic theory)

(3) 行为主义理论(behaviorist theory)

(4) 意义即使用理论(meaning-is-use theory)

(5) 验证性主义理论(verificationist theory)

(6) 真值—条件理论(truth-conditional theory)

李福印(2006:40)还增加了一个语义三角理论(在下文第13个要点我们将详细介绍)。

4. 指称/参照、外延、内涵、指称对象、意思或词义、延伸、意图、概念、意涵、字义中

指称：语言表达(命名、词语符号)与其所表示的客观事物或现象之间的关系，它表现于一定的上下文中。

外延：即语言符号本身固有的、恒定的、抽象的基本意义。是从无数同类事物中抽象出来或概括出来的特征。它不依赖话语语境和使用场景，与内涵意义相对。它是语言体系中语言表达意义的一部分。外延只有词汇意义。要注意的是指称与此恰恰相反，是变化的、依赖话语的，使用场合不同，指称义相应改变。

内涵：与情感联想有关，是词汇意义的一部分，是语言表达的情感成分，是依赖语境的，与语言的弦外之音有关。文秋芳(1995)把内涵分为三种类型：肯定内涵、中性内涵与否定内涵。如：

表7.1：内涵的三种类型

Positive connotation(肯定内涵)	Neutral(中性内涵)	Negative connotation(否定内涵)
stout	fat	corpulent
investigator	detective	spy
decease	die	pegged out
slim	thin	skinny
strong-minded	firm	pig-headed
public servant	government employee	bureaucrat

(引自文秋芳,1995:211)

指称对象:也就是我们所谈论的事物,即语言符号所指的客观事物或现象。

意义或词义:莱昂斯所说的"意义"或"词义"是指这个词在与其他语言词汇中其他词所构成的关系中所占的位置。这纯粹是一种只限于语言词汇系统中词与词之间的语义关系,与客观世界中的事物不发生直接联系。意义或词义除了词汇意义外还常常带有感情色彩,即情感义。而外延只有词汇意义。

内涵、意涵(implicature)或含意(implication)皆指人们的言外之意。意涵往往指人们故意违反格赖斯(Grice)所说的"合作原则"的任一准则而产生的言外之力,一般称为"会话含意"。

延伸:即用语言符号所正确表示的实体类别。

意图:决定语言符号可用性的一套识别性特征。

特别需要说明的是延伸和意图是外延的两个方面,在意义上相互补充。

概念:是客观事物在人们头脑中的印象。换言之,它是在客观事物或现象的基础上概括而成的。它属于思维范畴。概念是意义或词义的基础,而后者是前者在语言中的表现形式,双方相互依存。概念是个抽象的东西,靠词来表达,而词语通过概念来反映客观世界。

字义是指一个词的"词典意义"以及相关联的其他意义,与"价值"(value)相对应。威窦森(H. G. Widdowson)用这两个词说明一些句子只有字义而没有交际价值。如某老师为了教授进行时指着自己的鼻子说:"我正指着鼻子。"这句话有字义,却没有价值。

5. 意义的类型

意义是语言符号与客观世界的一种关联。张维友(1999)认为,意义可以分为词汇意义和语法意义,而词汇意义又可分为概念意义(即外延意义)和联想意义。联想意义又可分为内涵意义、文体意义、情感意义和搭配意义。见下图:

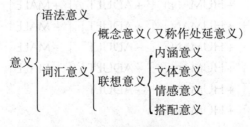

图7.1:意义的分类

(转引自王永祥、支永碧,2007:112)

6. 意义要素

李福印(2006:62)认为,意义的要素主要有五个,它们的关系见下图所示:

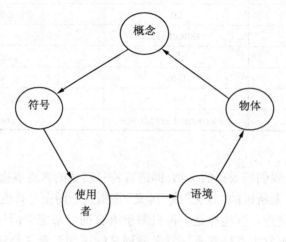

图 7.2:意义的五个要素

7. 成分分析

成分分析是分析词汇的一种方法。成分分析即语义特征分析。词义并非是不可分析的整体,它可以被看作是不同语义特征的复合体,有比词义更小的单位,即所谓的语义特征。结构语义学家们提出:一个单词的意义可以分析为被称作语义特征的意义成分。这一方法和把一个音位分析为更小的叫作区别性特征的成分的方法类似。用加减号来表示某一语义特征在一个词义中是存在或者缺省,这些特征符号通常用大写字母来标示。例如,man 被分析为包含下列特征:

+HUMAN, +ANIMATE, +MALE

成分分析的一个好处是,通过列出某些单词的语义特征,就可能显示这些单词在意义上的联系。例如,man 和 woman 这两个单词有 +HUMAN,+ADULT 和 +ANIMATE 这些共同的特征,但在 MALE 这一特征上不同。而 man 和 boy 有 +HUMAN,+ANIMATE 和 +MALE这些共同特征,但在 ADULT 这一特征上不相同。

换句话说,成分分析能很好地解释和说明涵义关系、解释句子之间的意义关系。语义成分分析是研究"概念上的"词汇语义关系的新尝试,其基本特点是,所有实词的意义都可以分解成一些"语义成分",也就是我们所说的"意义特征"。我们可以分析词语 man、woman、boy、girl、child、person 如下:

(1) man   [+HUMAN] [+ADULT] [+MALE]
(2) woman   [+HUMAN] [+ADULT] [−MALE]
(3) boy   [+HUMAN] [−ADULT] [+MALE]
(4) girl   [+HUMAN] [−ADULT] [−MALE]
(5) child   [+HUMAN] [−ADULT]
(6) person [+HUMAN]

8. 语义场

词语不会孤立地存在。它们总是以某一种方式相互联系着,从而形成语义场。语义场理论是由德国结构主义流派在20世纪30年代所发展起来的。根据这个理论,"一种语言的词汇并非仅仅是一个独立词条的列举,而是组织成一个领域,一个场,在这个场里,词语之间相互联系,并以各种不同的方式互相界定"(Crystal,1985:274)。

下面是一些有关语义场的例子:

(1) vegetable: tomato, pepper, onion, cabbage, spinach, cucumber, etc.
(2) fruit: apple, pear, peach, orange, lemon, mango, pineapple, etc.
(3) color: red, orange, green, yellow, black, blue, white, pink, purple, etc.
(4) get: acquire, receive, obtain, gain, buy, steal, etc.
(5) smell: stink, aroma, perfume, fragrance, scent, etc.

根据语义场理论,一个词语的意义,不是由它自身来决定,而是由它和同一语义场里其他词语的关系来决定,即由它在此种语言里和其他词语的语义关系系统中的位置来决定。

如,汉语词汇"红"(英语词汇 red)的语义在下列句子里的意义是由句子中其他词语的意义来决定和限制的。

(1) 红蛋(red eggs—eggs dyed red to celebrate the birth of a child, and distributed among friends and relatives)
(2) 红白喜事(red and white affairs—weddings and funerals)
(3) 红娘(matchmaker; go-between)

在这些句子里,"红"(red)的意义不是完全相同的,在不同的语境中,"红"的意义受其他词的影响而发生变化,如果不了解汉语文化,外国人很难理解句(1)、(2)、(3)中"红"的真正意义。我们还可以有更多的例子来说明在一种语言的同一语义场里一个词语的意义由它和其他词语的关系来决定。

(4) 开门红(get off to a flying start)
(5) 红道(path of ascent in official hierarchy; career as an official)
(6) 红角(popular actor / actress)
(7) 红人(favorite (with sb in power); fair-haired boy)
(8) 红得发紫([of a person] be extremely popular; be all the rage; [of an official] be at the height of one's power and influence)
(9) 红极一时(enjoy great popularity for a time; be all the rage)
(10) 红粉知己(beautiful woman who is a bosom friend)
(11) 红颜薄命(beautiful women suffer ill fates / are ill-fated)
(12) 看着有些人富起来,他就眼红。(He is green with envy at seeing some people get rich.)

9. 词汇关系

在《英语语言学概论》里,我们分析了萨伊德(Saeed)(2003)关于词汇关系的三个分类,即形式关系(form relation)、意义关系(sense relation)和实体关系(object relation)。下面这个表格能清楚地说明问题:

表7.2：词汇关系的分类

No.	词汇关系	
1	同音(或同形)异义关系	形式关系
2	一词多义关系	意义关系
3	同义关系	
4	反义关系	
5	上下义关系	
6	组成部分和整体的关系	实体关系
7	成员—集体关系	
8	部分—整体关系	

这个表格说明，标记为1、6、7和8的词汇关系不是"意义关系"(sense relation)。我们可以通过三个范畴来阐述词汇关系。下面我们分别来看"形式关系"(form relation)、意义关系(sense relation)和实体关系(object relation)。

(1) 形式关系

需要强调的是不把同音异义或同形异义关系归结为意义关系不太合适。它实际上是一种意义关系，属于词汇关系的第一个范畴。也就是说，同音异义或同形异义现象中涉及的相关词汇其意义之间没有什么关系。它们之间的关系只是通过形体建立起来的。同音异义或同形异义是指意义不同的词有着相同的语言形式的现象，即不同的词发音上或拼写上或者两个方面都相同。同音异义或同形异义关系是一种词汇歧义，涉及两个或两个以上不同词语。当两个或更多的词语具有相同的形体但意义不同时，它们就是同形异义关系。它们具有不同的词源背景。这些词语可以分为三类：完全同音同形异义(absolute/perfect/complete homonyms)、同形异义(homográghs)、同音异义(homophones)。因此，同音异义或同形异义关系可以分为三类关系：完全同音同形异义关系、同形异义关系、同音异义关系。两个单词在发音上相同时，叫同音异义词；两个单词在拼写上相同时，叫同形异义词。注意这两个词 homophone(同音异义词)和 homograph(同形异义词)的构成。词根 homo 的意思是"一样"，phone，graph 的意思分别是"声音"和"形式"。

① 完全同音同形异义的例子有：

ball (spherical object or mass) 和 ball (formal social gathering for dancing)

bank (sloping ground on each side of river) 和 bank (establishment, usually a public company, where money is deposited, withdrawn, and borrowed)

bear (carry) 和 bear (heavy thick-furred mammal)

date (day of month) 和 date (oval stone fruit)

ear (organ of hearing, esp. external part) 和 ear (seed-bearing head of cereal plant)

fair (just, equitable) 和 fair (periodic market)

found (past & past participle of find), found (establish, originate) 和 found (melt and mould metal, fuse materials for glass)

ground (surface of earth) 和 ground (past & past participle of grind)

rose (prickly shrub bearing fragrant red, pink, yellow, or white flowers) 和 rose (past of rise)

sound (sensation produced in ear when surrounding air etc. vibrates) 和 sound (healthy, correct)

② 同形异义的例子有：

bass (/bæs/ common perch) 和 bass (/beis/ lowest adult male voice)

bow (/bau/ incline head or body, esp. in greeting or acknowledgement) 和 bow (/bəu/ weapon for shooting arrows)

sow (/səu/ scatter seed on or in earth) 和 sow (/sau/ adult female pig)

wind (/wind/ air in natural motion) 和 wind (/waind/ go in spiral, crooked, or curved course)

③ 同音异义的例子有：

ad (colloquial word for advertisement) 和 add (join as increase or supplement)

blue (colored like clear sky) 和 blew (past of blow)

dear (beloved) 和 deer (4-hoofed grazing animal, male usually with antlers)

eye (organ or faculty of sight) 和 I (the pronoun used by speaker or writer to refer to himself or herself as subject of the verb)

flower (part of plant from which seed or fruit develops) 和 flour (meal or powder from ground wheat etc.)

meat (animal flesh as food) 和 meet (encounter or (of two or more people) come together)

pair (set of two people or things), pear (fleshy fruit tapering towards stalk) 和 pare (trim or reduce by cutting away edge or surface of)

piece (distinct portion forming part of or broken off from larger object) 和 peace (freedom from or cessation of war)

right (correct, true), rite (religious or solemn ceremony or observance) 和 write (mark paper or other surface with symbols, letters, or words)

rode (past of ride) 和 rowed (past of row)

sea (expanse of salt water covering most of earth) 和 see (perceive with the eyes)

son (male in relation to his parents) 和 sun (the star round which the earth travels and from which it receives light and warmth)

tail (hindmost part of animal, esp. extending beyond body) 和 tale (narrative or story, esp. fictitious)

threw (past of throw) 和 through (from end to end or side to side of)

to (in direction of), two (one more than one) 和 too (to a greater extent than is desirable)

weak (lacking in strength, power, vigor, resolution, or number) 和 week (7-day period reckoned usually from Saturday midnight)

（2）意义关系

在八个词汇关系中,意义关系有四种,即一词多义关系、同义关系、反义关系、上下义关系。

① 一词多义关系

一词多义:有时不同的词有相同或者相近的意义,有时同一单词也有一个以上的意义,这就是我们所说的一词多义,这样的词叫多义词。一个词越常用,它就越可能获得一个以上的意义。现以 table 一词为例,它是英语中非常常用的一个词。

（ⅰ）一张桌子

（ⅱ）一桌人

（ⅲ）放在桌子上的食物

（ⅳ）石板、金属板、木板等

（ⅴ）项目表、表格等

（ⅵ）（机器的）放料盘

（ⅶ）台地、高原

从历史的角度来看,一词多义可以被看作是词义的成长发展或变化的结果。我们假定,table 这一词形最初只有一个意义,很可能指一块石板或木板,这叫作其原始意义。后来它逐渐获得了它现在所指称的其他意义。我们完全可以猜想,当人们学会用木头做家具时,这样做成的家具叫 table。单词 table 就是这样又有了一个新的意义。现在这是单词 table 最常用的意义,而它的原始意义反而变得不常用了。

② 同义关系

同义现象指的是语义的相同或相近的现象。词义相近的词叫同义词。

英语词汇中有两类词:本族语词和借词。本族语词是不列颠群岛本地居民盎格鲁—撒克逊人的言语中最初所用的那些词语,尽管他们实际上是来自欧洲北部的移民。在其漫长的发展中,英语从其他语言中吸收了大量的词语,这些语言主要是欧洲语言,如法语、拉丁语、希腊语、意大利语和德语。很多借词已经被自然化了。在英语中经常发现成对的、甚至三词一组的意义大致相同的词。因为这些同义词的渊源不同,它们之间有细微差别。完全同义词即在任何情况下都可以互换的同义词是罕见的。产生差异的原因可以分为以下几组:

a. 方言同义词——用在不同地域方言中的同义词。这样的同义词是在不同的地域方言中所使用的意义大致相同的词。英国英语和美国英语是英语的两大地理变体。如下:

英国英语（BrE）	美国英语（AmE）
autumn	fall
lift	elevator
luggage	baggage
lorry	truck
petrol	gasoline
flat	apartment
windscreen	windshield
torch	flashlight

方言同义词在英国英语或美国英语本语中也存在。例如,girl 在苏格兰方言中叫作 lass

或者 lasse，liquor 在爱尔兰方言中叫作 whiskey。

b. 文体同义词——在文体上有差异的同义词。有同样意义的词可能在文体上，或者在正式程度上有所不同。也就是说，有些单词往往比较正式，有些比较随意，有些在文体上则是中性的。看下面的例子：

daddy, dad, father, male parent
start, begin, commence
kid, child, offspring
chap, pal, friend, companion
kick the bucket, pop off, die, pass away, decease
room, chamber

c. 情感意义或评价意义有所不同的同义词。有着相同的意义却表达了使用者的不同情感的词语，这些词暗示使用者对他所谈论的事情的态度或倾向。例如，两个词 collaborator（合作者）和 accomplice（同谋者，帮凶）都有"帮助另一个人的人"这样的意思，这时两者是同义的，但其不同在于，帮助别人做好事称为合作者，而在犯罪行为中帮助别人则称为帮凶。

economical, frugal, thrifty, mean, miserly, stingy
He has been a very thrifty person all his life.（他一生节俭。）
Don't you expect a loan from such a miserly man.（不要期望从这么吝啬的人手中借钱。）
like, love, admire, adore, worship
He is a nice man and all the pupils like him.（他为人和气，所有的学生都喜欢他。）
The pop singer is especially worshipped by teenagers.（流行歌手尤其受年轻人的崇拜。）

d. 搭配同义词。同义词在其搭配上各不相同，即能和这些不同的同义词相配的词各不相同。例如，当我们想说某人做了错事或甚至犯了罪，我们可以用 accuse, charge 和 rebuke 这三个词，但它们后面必须跟不同的介词——accuse ... of, charge ... with, rebuke ... for。描述变质不适合食用的食物时，用不同的形容词来修饰不同的食物。如 rotten tomatoes, addled eggs, rancid bacon or butter, sour milk。

e. 语义上不同的同义词。amaze 和 astound 两个词和 surprise 一词的意义非常接近，但却有细微差别，amaze 暗示困惑和迷惑，astound 则暗示难以置信。escape 和 flee 均有逃走之意，不同的是，前者意思是逃离不愉快或者危险的事，而后者意思是匆匆离开。

③ 反义关系

反义关系用以指意义的相反，意义上相反的词叫反义词。我们不应误认为词语只在一方面互相对立，实际上对立可以是多方面的，因而就分出了几种不同的反义词。

a. 分级反义词

一些反义词是级别上的对立，因为一对这样的反义词中间常用其他表示程度的词。意义相反实际上只是程度问题。例如，人们看到"老年的"和"年轻的"两个词，马上就视其为反义词，但它们代表两个极端，在中间还存在着代表年老和年轻的不同程度的其他语言形式，如"中年的"、"成熟的"、"稍老的"。同样，在"热"和"冷"之间也存在着不同程度的既不热又不冷的情况，比如"凉爽"、"温和"和"微温的"。

b. 互补反义词

一对互补反义词具有这样的特征，否定其中一个就意味着肯定另一个。也就是说，是一个非此即彼、非彼即此的问题。例如，一个人要么是"活着的"，要么是"死的"，要么是"男的"，要么是"女的"，没有其他可能性。因此，"活着的"和"死的"是一对互补反义词，"男的"和"女的"也是如此。

c. 关系反义词

在意义上显示出逆向关系的一对词语叫关系反义词。例如，如果 A 是 B 的丈夫，那么 B 就是 A 的妻子。所以"妻子"和"丈夫"是一组关系反义词。"父亲"和"儿子"，"老师"和"学生"，"医生"和"病人"，"买"和"卖"，"让"和"租"，"上面"和"下面"等也是关系反义词。

④ 上下义关系

上下义关系是指一个具有一般性、包容性的词与一个更为具体的词之间的意义关系。意义更具有一般性的词叫上义词，意义更为具体的词叫下义词。同一个上义词的多个下义词叫并列下义词，如：

上义词：flower

下义词：rose, tulip, carnation, lily, morning glory

上义词：animal

下义词：dog, cat, tiger, lion, wolf, elephant, fox, bear

上义词：furniture

下义词：bed, table, desk, dresser, wardrobe, settee

上下义关系是一种包含关系，从意义上来说，上义词包含其所有下义词。如：

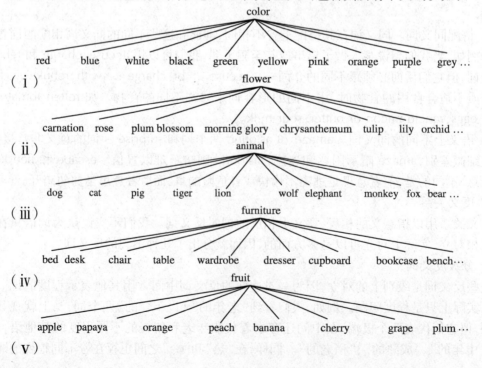

（ⅰ）

（ⅱ）

（ⅲ）

（ⅳ）

（ⅴ）

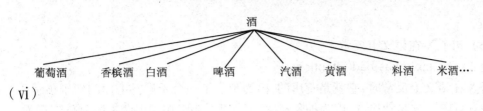

(ⅵ)

(3) 实体关系

实体关系包含三种词汇关系,即组成部分和整体的关系、成员—集体关系、部分—整体关系。

组成部分和整体的关系:如一辆汽车由许多部件组成,包括发动机、轮胎、方向盘、车灯、车刹、座位等(A car is made up of many parts, such as an engine, tyres, a steering wheel, lights, a brake, seats, etc.)。车灯和汽车的关系就是部分与整体的关系。

成员—集体关系:成员和集体关系涉及的全部是可数名词,如:在"Lynne is a girl student of Class 2"句子中,Lynne 是个成员概念,而 Class 2 是个集体概念。Lynne 和 Class 2 构成了一个成员—集体关系,即一个女生和一个班级学生团体的关系。

部分—整体关系:与成员—集体关系不同,它主要涉及不可数名词。也就是说,这个集体由不可数名词组成。如 go out and breathe some fresh air,在这里 fresh air 作为一个部分,区别于集体。

10. 决定句义的要素

决定句子意义的要素有六点:(1) 构成一句话的单个词的意义;(2) 句子的语法功能;(3) 句子中语言形式之间的线性顺序;(4) 音位特征;(5) 等级顺序;(6) 名词的语义功能。

11. 句子间的意义关系

句子间和同一句子的各组成部分间也有一定的关系。

(1) X 和 Y 是同义关系

例如:X:He was a bachelor all his life.
　　　Y:He never married all his life.

从是否真实的角度看,如果 X 是真的,Y 就是真的,如果 X 是假的,Y 也是假的。

(2) X 和 Y 是前后矛盾关系

例如:X:John is married.
　　　Y:John is a bachelor.

从是否真实的角度看,如果 X 是真的,Y 就是假的,如果 X 是假的,Y 就是真的。

(3) X 蕴涵 Y(Y 是 X 的蕴涵)

例如:X:John married a blond heiress.
　　　Y:John married a blond.

蕴涵是一种包含关系。如果 X 蕴涵 Y,X 的意义就为 Y 所包含。

(4) X 预示 Y(Y 是 X 的先决条件)

例如:X:John's bike needs repairing.
　　　Y:John has a bike.

(5) X 是个矛盾句

当句子 X 本身自相矛盾时,它永远是假的。例如:My unmarried sister is married to a

bachelor.

（6）句子X在语义上反常

例如：The table has bad intentions.

当X在语义上反常时，它就是荒唐的，因为预示了一个矛盾。上面的句子预示了"一张桌子能有意图"，这是荒唐的，因为抽象概念"意图"不能跟在无生命主语"桌子"后面。

12. 述谓结构分析、谓词、题元、命题

述谓结构分析是一种分析句子意义的方法。

一个句子的意义不是它所有组成部分的意义的总和，一个句子的意义不能通过把组成它的所有单词的意义相加而得出。例如：

The dog bit the man.

The man bit the dog.

两个句子尽管由完全相同的单词所组成，但在意义方面却大相径庭。因而，句子和单词是不同的，单词的意义是它的所有成分，即其所有语义特征的总和。更重要的是，句子意义包含两个方面，即语法意义和语义。

一个句子的语法意义是指它的语法性，在语法上合乎规范。一个句子的语法性是由它所属的语言的规则所决定的。

The dog are chasing the cat.

He gave the book me.

We will went to Beijing tomorrow.

以上每个句子都违背了一个语法规则。

而一个句子在语义上是否有意义是由被称为选择限制的规则决定的，选择限制即对哪些词项可以和其他哪些词项搭配的限制。一些句子在语法上可能完全合乎规范，即它们完全合乎其所属语言的语法规则。但在语义上可能毫无意义。原因是，它包含了不应放在一起的单词，因而违背了选择限制。例如：

Green clouds are sleeping furiously.

Sincerity shook hands with the black apple.

这两个句子完全合乎语法规则；它们也包含了一个句子所必需的所有语法成分，在一致上和时态上也没有错误，但第一句存在的问题在于，没有人见过绿色的云，云也不会睡，更不会说猛烈地睡了；第二句存在的问题是，诚挚是一个抽象名词，不能实施握手这一行为，也没有人与苹果握手，不用说与一个黑色的苹果了。因而这两个句子都违背了一些选择限制，这就使这两个句子在语义上不合乎规范。

语言学家们提出了不同的分析句子意义的方法。他们的分析基准体系可能有所不同，但他们的目标都是使句子意义抽象化，我们现在简要介绍的是英国语言学家利奇（Leech）提出的述谓结构分析法。对句子进行语法分析时，句子被视为基本单位，它被分析为诸如主谓语和定语这样的语法成分。对句子进行意义分析时句子的基本单位被称为述谓，这是对句子意义的抽象化。这一方法适用于所有句式，包括陈述句、祈使句和疑问句。一个述谓由一个或数个题元和一个谓词组成。一个题元是一个述谓的一个逻辑参与者，与一个句子中的一个或数个名词性成分大体一致。一个谓词是关于题元的陈述，或者说明一个句子的题元间的逻辑关系。比如，"Tom smokes"这一句子的陈述可以说由题元TOM和谓词

SMOKE 构成,这一述谓可以写为 TOM(SMOKE)。因为句子的语法形式不影响其语义述谓,下列所有句子可以说具有同样的述谓:

Tom smokes.

Tom is smoking.

Tom has been smoking.

Tom smoke!

Does Tom smoke?

这是同一语义述谓 TOM(SMOKE)在语法上的多种体现。而一些句子包括的题元(或论元)不止一个。例如,"Kids like apples"这一句子有 kids 和 apples 两个名词性成分,因而它的述谓结构可以写作 KID,APPLE(LIKE)。还有一些句子一个题元(或论元)也没有,包含非人称代词 it 的英语句子,如"It is hot"即是如此。该句中的 it 不能当作一个题元,(BE HOT)是该句述谓的谓词。

根据述谓结构分析理论,一个命题由两个部分组成:即谓词和题元。多数情况下,谓词是动词,但也可能是形容词、介词或名词。

根据一个述谓中所包含的论元的数目,我们把述谓结构分为两位述谓结构(包含两个题元或论元)、单位述谓结构(包含一个题元或论元)和零位述谓结构(没有题元或论元)。

13. 语义三角

语义三角理论是 1923 年由奥格登(Ogden)和理查兹(Richards)提出的一种经典语义理论。语义三角的基本观点是"概念/思想"和"词语/符号"有直接联系,与"所指物/事物"也存在直接关系。但"词语/符号"和"所指物/事物"两者之间的关系要求助于"概念/思想"(用虚线表示)。

由于词语与所指物没有必然联系,所以同一个事物可能或可以用不同的词语来表达,如"钢笔"这个东西在汉语里是"钢笔",在日语里是"万年笔",在英语里是"pen"。从传统的观点来看,词语要通过概念才能与所指物产生联系。所谓意义,就是词语和所指物之间的关系。要建立这种关系,在说话和听话者的心目中必须有一个约定俗成的双方都能理解的概念才行。语义三角理论虽然是论述和解释语义现象的一种经典理论,但是自从它被提出以来,一直受到语义学界的广泛争议和批评。

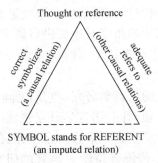

图 7.3:语义三角

(引自 Ogden and Richards,1923:11;cited from Bussmann,2000:425)

Chapter 8 Pragmatics

 本章主要考点

1. 语用学:界定与阐述(Pragmatics: definition and illustration)
2. 指示语及其类型(Deixis and its types)
3. 奥斯汀和塞尔的言语行为理论(Austin's and Searle's speech act theories)
4. 合作原则及其准则(The cooperative principle and its maxims)
5. 会话含意(Conversational implicature)
6. 礼貌原则及其准则(The politeness principle and its maxims)
7. 后格赖斯时期的发展(The Post-Gricean developments)
8. 语用预设(Pragmatic presupposition)

 课文理解与重点内容分析

1. 语用学
（1）定义
语用学研究的是说某种语言的人怎样使用句子去实现成功的交际。由于交际的过程从本质上来说是在一定的语境中表达意义的过程,因而语用学也可以被看作是一种意义研究。在语言学领域,语用学是个较新的分支学科,它在20世纪六七十年代的发展和确立主要是语言学研究,尤其是语义学研究扩大的结果。语境论是把意义研究置于使用语言的环境中。这种观点被看作是从语用学的角度对意义进行研究的最初尝试。事实上,由于定义的标准不尽相同,关于语用学的定义多达14种以上。
（2）语用学与语义学
语用学和语义学都是对意义的语言学研究。它们之间有何区别和联系呢？
从20世纪初以来,有很长一段时间,语言学研究领域占支配地位的观点一直是语言学应当研究语言本身,换言之,语言应作为严格独立自主、内在的系统来研究;研究语言时,任何语言之外的因素均不应考虑。传统音位学对语音的研究,传统句法学对句子结构的研究,传统语义学对意义的研究,都是在上述观念的支配下进行的。语义被看作是某种内在的、固有的东西,换言之,它是语言本身就具有的一种属性。因此,对词的意义和句子意义的研究都是以孤立的方式进行的,根本不考虑它们的使用环境。
但是语言学家发现,如果不考虑语言使用的语境,就不可能对意义进行充分的描述,而一旦把语境因素考虑在内,语义学就又分出一门分支学科——语用学。语义学和语用学的本质区别在于,研究意义是否考虑了语言使用的语境。没有考虑到语境进行的研究就没有超出传统语义学的研究范围;相反,考虑到语境进行的研究就属于语用学的研究范畴。

(3) 语境

语境是语言的语用研究中不可缺少的概念。它一般被理解为说话者和听话者双方所共有的知识;双方在他们所使用的语言方面的知识;双方对世界的认识,包括对世界的总的认识和对正在进行的语言交际所处的环境的具体认识,没有这样的认识,语言交际是难以顺利进行的,不考虑这样的知识,语言交际就不可能从语用角度得到满意地解释。关于语境的要素,下表可以给我们一个形象的说明:

表 8.1: 语境的要素

语境	语言语境	我们所使用语言的有关知识	
		关于语言(使用)环境的知识	
	非语言语境	背景知识	常识
			社会文化习俗
			言语习惯
		共有知识	即交际双方的共享知识
		情景语境	交际的时间和空间
			交际对象和主体
			交际的正式程度
			交际参与者的关系

(4) 句子意义与话语意义

句子是句法概念,句子的意义通常被看作是句子本身所具有的抽象的、内在的属性,对这种意义通常是从述谓结构的角度来研究的。假如我们把一个句子看成是人们在交际过程中实际所说的话,该句子就变成了一个话语,考虑该句子就应该考虑到它实际上被说出(或被使用)时的环境。因而要断定"The dog is barking"是一个句子还是一个话语是不可能的。两种情况都有可能,这完全取决于我们怎样去看待它,怎样去分析它。假如我们把它当成一个语法单位,把它看成是一个孤立的、独立自主的单位,那么我们是把它当成一个句子来对待。假如我们把它看作说话者在一个特定的环境中带着一个特定的目的所说出的一句话,那么我们是把它当作一个话语来对待的。

句子的意义是抽象的,是非语境化的,而话语的意义是具体的,是受语境制约的。话语意义基于句子意义:它是一个句子的抽象意义在特定语境中的具体体现,或简言之,在一个语境中的具体化。

大多数话语是以句子形式出现的,换言之,大多数话语从句法上看是完整的句子,但有些话语则不然,有一些话语甚至不能被复原成完整的句子。例如,"Good morning!"(早上好!),"Hi!"(咳!)和"Ouch!"(哎呀!)都是话语,在交际中都有意义。如果说"Good morning!"尚可被复原成"I wish you a good morning"的话,我们却不知道"Hi!"和

"Ouch!"是来自什么样的完整句子。

2. 指示语及其类型

目前,多数语言学家将指示语划分为五种,即人称指示语、地点指示语、时间指示语、话语指示语和社交指示语。

(1) 人称指示语表示言语事件或言语行为的直接或间接参与者,主要分为三类:第一人称指示语,第二人称指示语,第三人称指示语。人称指示语也即传统语法所指的人称代词。

(2) 时间指示语表示人们通过话语传达信息或实施言语行为的时间关系。时间人称指示信息通常以说话人的话语时间为参照依据。由于语境条件不一样,说话人使用时间指示语表达的指示信息也不一样。要准确获知话语中的特定时间指示信息,我们必须明白说话人使用哪一类时间指示语,以及交际场合和动词时态。

(3) 地点指示语,也称空间指示语,表示人们通过话语传达信息或实施言语行为的地点或空间位置。

(4) 话语指示语或语篇指示语,指在说话或写作过程中选择适当的词汇或结构来传递话语或语篇中的某种指示信息。由于交际涉及一定的时间和地点,所以话语指示语和时间指示语、地点指示语等之间存在密切联系,有时话语指示语本身就是表示时间和地点的指示语。

(5) 社交指示语就是人际交往中与人际关系密切的结构或词语,它们使用的目的在于改变、顺应或调节说话人和听话人之间,或说话人和第三者之间的人际关系,比如各种敬称、称呼语等。

3. 言语行为理论

言语行为理论是语言的语用研究中的一个重要理论。它最初是由英国哲学家奥斯汀(Austin)在20世纪50年代提出的。该理论从哲学上对语言交际的本质作了解释。

在此之前,传统上哲学家对句子的真价值感兴趣,即他们对如何判断句子内容的真假感兴趣;他们认为,一句话要么用来陈述一种事实,要么用来描述事物的一种状态。奥斯汀本人虽是哲学家,却对这一假设表示怀疑,因为他发现,一些句子既不是用来陈述的,也不是用来描述的。它们无法用真假这样的标准来判断:说话者说这些话是为了做某些事,因而他区分了两种不同类型的句子,称之为"叙述句"和"施为句"。叙述句是要么陈述要么描述的句子,因而其内容是可以证实的,相反,施为句是既不用来陈述也不用来描述的句子,其内容是不可证的。奥斯汀为说明这一点所用的四个例子已成为经典。

I do. (我愿意。)

I name this ship Elizabeth. (我把这艘船命名为"伊丽莎白"号。)

I give and bequeath my watch to my brother. (我把我的手表遗赠给我的弟弟。)

I bet you six pence it will rain tomorrow. (明天若下雨我给你六便士。)

"I do"用来回答牧师在主持婚礼的过程中所提出的问题:Do you take this man/woman to be your lawful wedded husband/wife?(你愿意接受这个男子/女子以作为你的合法丈夫/妻子吗?)回答者一说"I do",他或她就算结婚了。奥斯汀因而得出结论说,话语"I do"是用来完成结婚行为的。当被授权为一艘船命名的人,在一艘尚未命名的船的船尾摔碎一瓶香槟,一如习俗所要求的那样,并说"I name this ship Elizabeth"时,该船的名号就确定了,因而"I name this ship ..."是用来完成命名行为的。与此相似,话语"I give and bequeath my watch to my brother"出现在一份遗嘱中,用来完成遗赠行为。当一个人说"I bet you ..."时,他是在打赌。因此,说话者说出这些句子时,他们不是在报告或说明一些事情,而是在做一些事情,换言之,是在完成特定的行为。奥斯汀所举的四个例子都是套式话语。但说话时说话人同时在做某种事情这一观点的适用范围无疑可以被扩大,以包括非规约性行为,如陈述、承诺、请求和建议。因而,这一理论开始被称作言语行为理论。依此理论,我们说话的同时是在实施某种行为。

由于种种原因,奥斯汀放弃了他最初认为叙述句和施为句不同的观点。他认为,陈述与其他许多种行为一样也是一种行为,我们可以用语言去实施行为。他提出另一种模式,用以解释如何通过语言去实施各种行为。根据他的新模式,说话者说话时可能同时实施三种行为:发话行为、行事行为、取效行为。

发话行为是说出词、短语和分句的行为,它是通过句法、词汇和音位来表达字面意义的行为。行事行为是表达说话者的意图的行为,它是在说某些话时所实施的行为。取效行为是通过某些话所实施的行为,或讲某些话所导致的行为,它是话语所产生的后果或所引起的变化,它是通过讲某些话所完成的行为。

You have left the door wide open.(你让门敞开着。)

说话者所实施的发话行为是,他说出了所有的词 you、have、door、open 等,表达了这些词的字面意思。说话者所实施的言外行为是,通过讲这句话,他表达了其意图,即请某人把门关上。

取效行为是话语产生的效果。如果听话者得到了说话者发出的信息,肯定明白了说话者的意图是请某人去关门,说话者就成功地在现实世界引出他所期望的变化,这样一来,言后行为就被成功地实施了。

语言学家对言外行为最感兴趣,因为这种言语行为与说话者的意图完全一致,而且,在对语言交际的研究中,语言学家最感兴趣的是,说话者如何表达他的意图,他的意图又是如何被听话者识别出的。

美国分析哲学家塞尔(searle)对言语行为进行了分类。奥斯汀自己在这方面曾试图做一些工作,但做得不是很成功。

塞尔认为,行事行为可分为五大类。换言之,我们可以用语言实施五大类行为。每一类行为都有一个共同的、普遍的目的。

（1）阐述类:陈述或描述说话者认为是真实的情况。
（2）指令类:试图使听话者做某些事情。
（3）承诺类:说话者自己承诺未来要有一些行为。
（4）表达类:表达对某一现状的感情和态度。
（5）宣告类:通过说话引起骤变。

4. 合作原则及其准则

人们在谈话中会有意无意地遵循这样的合作原则:"使你所说的话,在其所发生的阶段,符合你所参与的交谈的公认目标或方向。"具体表现为四条准则:数量准则、质量准则、关系准则、方式准则。

5. 会话含意

准则的违背除谎言外,其他违背准则的情况实际是在更深的层次上遵守准则。会话含意只有依赖合作原则才能推导出来。

会话含意是一种隐含意义,可以在合作原则及其准则指导下,在词语规约意义基础上,联系语境推导出来。会话含意与言语行为理论中的"言外之力"既相似又有区别。两者都与意义的语境有关,与言外之意有关,不同之处在于会话含意没有对听话人思想行为施行改变或要求的意图,而"言外之力"却有。

会话含意分为一般会话含意和特殊会话含意。

会话含意的特征可包括:推导性、可取消性、不可分离性、非规约性。

6. 礼貌原则及其准则

合作原则有助于说明语句的意义和语句力量之间的关系,但它本身并不能解释人们为什么经常间接地表达意思,礼貌原则是对合作原则的必要补充和补救,可以更好地解释人们为什么在言语交际中要故意违反合作原则。格赖斯理论能够较好地解释话语的言外之意,或特殊会话含意。然而,也还存在某些不足之处,因为在交际中,人们最先考虑的是礼貌问题,它成了一切交际的首要前提,因此,礼貌原则实际上具有更大的约束力。利奇效仿格赖斯把礼貌原则划分为六个准则:策略准则(tact maxim)、宽宏准则(generosity maxim)、赞扬准则(approbation maxim)、谦虚准则(modesty maxim)、一致准则(agreement maxim)、同情准则(sympathy maxim)。

7. 列文森(Levinson)的数量、信息和方式原则

数量原则包括:(A)说话人准则,不要让你的陈述在信息上弱于你所知道的程度,除非较强的陈述与信息量原则相抵触;(B)听话人推论,相信说话人的陈述已经是就他所知所做的最强陈述。

信息原则包括:(A)说话人准则,最小化准则,即"尽量少说",只提供实现交际目的所需的最小语言信息量;(B)听话人推论,扩展规则,扩充说话人所说话语的信息内容,找出最具体的理解,直到认定说话人的发话意图。

方式原则包括:(A)说话人准则,不无故使用冗长、隐晦或有标记的表达形式;(B)听话人推论,如果说话人使用了冗长或有标记的表达形式 M,他的意思就与他本来可以用无标记的表达形式 U 所表达的意义不一样,即说话人是在设法避免 U 带来的常规性的联想和信息量含义。

8. 关联理论:后格赖斯主义

每一个话语交际行动,都传递一种假定:该行动本身具备最佳关联性。

9. 语用预设

(1) 定义

语用预设的概念最早由斯塔奈克(Stalnaker)于1970年提出,之后有很多学者对其进行了阐释。概括起来主要有三种观点:第一种从说话人的态度出发,把预设定义为命题态度;第二种从言语交际功能出发,把预设看作是交际双方的共有知识,或者说是话语的背景知识;第三种从言语行为的角度出发,把预设看作是实施有效言语行为的条件。无论是发话人的态度、交际双方的共有知识、还是话语适切的条件,它们都是包括了发话人、受话人及和语境因素有关的适用于话语交际的概念,因为话语交际的过程就是发话人、受话人和

语境相互作用的过程。所以,语用预设的概念可以定义为:语用预设都是在具体的语境下,说话人为了交际的需要,或故意设置的假设,或对受话人知识状态做出的假设,抑或是交际双方认为想当然的信息,它是交际过程中使得言语行为有效的条件。

(2) 特征

① 共知性

就成功的交际来说,语用预设总表现为交际双方都可理解、都可接受的那种背景知识。这种背景知识可以是现实世界的知识,也可以是信念世界的知识(如小说中的人物等),或者也可以是一种普遍的世界知识(战争是残酷的等)。语用预设的共知性是在具体语境中话语被理解的基础,是交际双方进行话语交际的前提。

② 适切性

适切性是语用预设的又一大特征。语用预设是实施一个言语行为所需要的恰当的条件,或是使一句话具有必要的社会合适性必须满足的条件。

③ 主观性

语用预设具有主观性,是指带有断言性质的语境假设,本身并不具备必然的真实性或正确性。斯塔奈克认为,语用预设不但同语境有关,而且跟说话人有关。语用预设不是命题之间的关系,而是说话人和命题之间的关系。这里说的"主观性"就是发话人想当然认为真的命题。

④ 隐蔽性

语用预设的隐蔽性是指语用预设的部分是隐含的,它不表现在说话人所说出的话语中,而是以隐含的形式存在于说话人的话语里。有时,一旦听话人不留神就会把说话人预设的"断言"看作是真实的而加以接受。语用预设常常表现为发话人的隐含信息,需要听话人的推断。在交际中,语用预设的认同要求听话人在说话人的"话里"获得"话外"之意。语用预设在话语交际中表现出这样那样的特征,主要是出于发话人交际的某些需要。发话人的态度、信念和意图等都影响着他对受话人所作出的假设。但是,预设作为一种信息,受话人至少可以根据语境推断出来。它不表现在话语之内,却包含在话语之中。它的共知性和适切性是表现在话语交际中的最主要的特征。这些特征都影响着话语交际的顺利进行。

Chapter 9 Discourse Analysis

 **本章主要考点**

1. 语篇、语篇性、话语和语境(Text, texture, discourse and context)
2. 话语分析/会话分析(Discourse analysis/Conversation analysis)
3. 批评话语分析/积极话语分析(Critical discourse analysis/Positive discourse analysis)
4. 衔接与连贯(Cohesion and coherence)
5. 话轮/话轮转换(Turn/Turn-taking)
6. 前置语列(Pre-sequence)
7. 相邻语对和优先应答(Adjacency pairs/Preferred second parts)
8. 照应/替换/省略/连接/重复/搭配(Reference/substitution/ellipsis/conjunction/reiteration/collocation)

 课文理解与重点内容分析

1. 语篇、语篇性、话语和语境

关于text,语言学家感到很难用定义把它明确下来,对这个问题至今仍然是众说纷纭,未能达成共识。

韩礼德和哈桑(Hasan)认为,"text"一词在语言学里指任何口头或书面的、长短不限的、构成一个统一整体的段落(passage)。text 是使用中的语言单位,不是像小句或句子一样的语法单位,不能用长度来确定它。text 可以是一个词、一个句子,也可以是一个长篇巨著,是不受句子语法约束的,在一定语境下表达完整语义的自然语言。text 不是由句子组成的,而是由句子体现的,也就是说 text 与句子的关系是体现关系,句子是用于体现 text 的。韩礼德和哈桑指出:"一个 text 最好是看作一个语义单位,即不是形式单位,而是意义单位。"

夸克等人认为:"text 是在实际运用中具有恰当连贯性的一段语言。这就是说,该 text 在语义和语用上与现实世界中的实际语境'相一致',而且它在内部或语言上也具有连贯性。"

侯易(Hoey)(1991)给 text 的定义是:"text 可清晰地表示一个或多个作者和一个或多个读者之间相互独立的、有目的的互动,其中作者控制着互动并生产大部分或所有的语言。"布朗（Brown）和尤尔（Yule）则认为"text 是交际行为的文字记录"。伯格兰德（Beaugrande）和德斯勒（Dressler）(1981) 在其专著 Introduction to Text Linguistics 中，把 text 定义为"满足语篇性七个标准的交际性产物"。他们同时认为，如果这七个标准中的任何一个被认为是没有得到满足，该 text 就不具备交际性，不具备交际性的 text 则视为"非语篇"。这七个标准是：衔接性（cohesion）、连贯性（coherence）、目的性（intentionality）、可接受性（acceptability）、信息性（informativity）、情景性（situationality）和篇际性（intertextuality）。总之，语篇（text）是言语作品，是语言实际交际过程中的产物。无论以何种形式出现，语篇都应该合乎语法、语义连贯，包括与外界在语义和语用上的连贯，也包括语篇内在语言上的连贯。语篇是有效交际的基本单位（胡曙中，2005：4—6）。伯格兰德和德斯勒（1981）认为，语篇语言学至少应该与三个方面有着密切的联系：(1) 语篇；(2) 参与者；(3) 广义的情境。正是这三个方面决定了语篇应该满足上文所说的七个标准，这七个标准就是语篇性（texture）。

话语和篇章是两个容易混淆的概念。首先，从地域上讲，美国学者倾向于使用"话语"，与之对应的是"话语分析"，欧洲学者习惯用"篇章"说法，与之对应的是"篇章语言学"，实际上指的是同一个内容。但在语言学文献的描述中，话语和语篇的侧重点有所不同。首先，我们经常区分书面语篇（written text）和口头话语（spoken discourse）。换句话说，话语是交际话语（interactive discourse），而书面语篇指的是非交际独白（non-interactive monologue）。比如提到学术论文，我们指的是对观众所做的报告或发表的成品。另一个区别是话语通常较长，而语篇可能很短，如韩礼德和哈桑（1976）提到的"No smoking!"也可构成语篇。范·迪克（Van Dijk）(1977) 认为语篇是一个抽象的理论构体，话语是它的具体体现，二者的关系就如同句子（sentence）与话语（utterance）的关系一样。布朗和尤尔（1983）认为，话语是一个过程，是说话者或作者在某个语境中用来表达自己的意思或实现自己的意图的词、短语和句子，而语篇是成品，可以是书面的，也可以是口头的。威窦森（1979：50）则把话语定义为句子组合的使用；系统语言学家斯泰纳（Steiner）和维尔特曼（Veltmen）(1988) 把话语解释为"作为过程的语言"，强调其动态的性质；克拉申（Krashen）(1998) 从社会语言学的角度把话语定义为讲话方式、阅读方式和写作方式，同时也是某一话语社区的行为方式、交际方式、思维方式和价值观念。正如李悦娥、范宏雅（2002：4—5）所说，上述这些观点从不同侧面反映出话语的本质，同时也表明话语分析的定义也因为语言学家不同的着眼点而不尽相同。

语境是语言的语用研究中不可缺少的概念。它一般被理解为说话者和听话者双方所共有的知识；双方在他们所使用的语言方面的知识；双方对世界的认识，包括对世界的总的认识和对正在进行的语言交际所处的环境的具体认识，没有这样的认识，语言交际是难以顺利进行的，不考虑这样的知识，语言交际就不可能从语用角度得到满意解释。关于语境的要素，请参阅《英语语言学概论》一书第八章表 8.1。

2. 话语分析/会话分析

话语分析这一术语是由美国结构主义语言学家哈里斯（Z. S. Harris）于 1952 年在美国《语言》（Language）杂志第 29 卷发表的一篇题为《话语分析》的文章中首次使用的。从此，它作为现代语言学的专门术语被广泛使用。现在人们普遍认为，话语分析是从 20 世纪 60 年代中期开始成为一个独立的研究领域的。它的出现是人类对语言认识不断发展的必然结果,体现了语言研究从形式到功能、从静态到动态、从词语、句子分析到话语、语篇分析、从语言内部到语言外部、从单一领域到跨学科领域的过渡。(李悦娥、范宏雅,2002:1)

那么究竟何为话语分析呢? 其实,不同的学者往往从不同的角度定义它。如,有些语言学家从话语分析的研究对象和内容上来定义它。斯塔布斯(Stubbs)(1983:1)认为话语分析是对"自然发生的连贯的口头或书面话语的语言分析"。因此,它的分析单位是大于句子的或从句的语言单位,如口头话语或书面语篇,而且这些语言序列是连贯的。同时他强调分析社会语境下语言的使用,即"自然发生的"话语。而辛克莱尔(Sinclair)和库尔德(Coulthard)认为话语分析是话语语法学。和威窦森与韩礼德一样,他们认为,话语分析是对语篇和话语连贯的研究。

还有一些语言学家从话语功能角度定义话语。威窦森(1979:52)认为话语分析是对"句子用于交际以完成社会行为的研究",强调话语的交际功能;布朗和尤尔认为话语分析是对使用中的语言分析,它不仅是探索语言的形式特征,更是对语言使用功能的研究。

也有一些语言学家从社会语言学的角度定义话语分析。如范·迪克(1980)和韩礼德(1978)指出话语分析是一种社会分析方法,解释人类如何理解彼此的话语。美国社会语言学家拉波夫(1969:54)指出话语分析就是制定规则"把所做与所说或所说与所做联系起来",强调话语规则的先决条件,指出必须满足一定条件话语才能被看作是某种特定的交际行为。

由此可见,话语结构形式、话语规则、话语模式等都是话语分析研究的不同侧面。话语分析的定义无外乎两个层次:话语分析是对超句单位结构的静态描写;话语分析是对交际过程意义传递的动态分析(李悦娥、范宏雅,2002:5)。

话语分析的主要任务基本上有两个方面,一方面,话语分析要通过日常话语语料分析揭示超句话语和社会交际的结构;另一方面,话语分析要揭示谈话双方在语境中理解意义的过程。前者研究的是一个静态的话语成品,旨在阐述话语结构规则,后者研究的是一个动态的话语过程,旨在揭示谈话双方在语境因素作用下理解话语含义的交际过程。

话语分析的最主要的研究方法是:(1)记录、转写并分析日常会话语料;(2)分析研究观察和记录下来的交际行为模式。第二种方法可以称之为人类学的研究方法。

那么何为会话分析呢? 会话分析是语用学的重要领域,甚至可以说是最重要的领域(姜望琪,2003:208)。会话分析的主要内容包括会话结构、话轮换转、前置语列、相邻语对和优先应答等。会话分析和话语分析有很多共同的研究内容和研究任务,但也有一些不同的研究对象和研究方法。国内学者黄国文和徐珺对话语分析和会话分析进行了较为全面而系统的研究。

3. 批评话语分析/积极话语分析

批评语言学的语篇分析方法是福勒(Fowler)、霍奇(Hodge)、克莱斯(Kress)和特鲁(Trew)等在1979年出版的《语言与控制》(*Language and Control*)一书中首次提出的,旨在通过对公众语篇的分析来揭示意识形态对语篇的影响和语篇对意识形态的反作用(辛斌,2005;戴炜栋等,2002)。辛斌(2005)在其专著的前言中分析指出,批评语言学也叫批评话语分析,是20世纪80年代初首先在英国兴起的有关语篇分析方法的学科。它的方法论主要建立在以韩礼德为代表的系统功能语言学上,同时兼容其他语言理论中有关的概念和方法。它在分析中特别强调对语篇生成、传播和接受的生活语境和社会历史背景的考察,并把注意力主要放在发现和分析语篇中那些人们习以为常、却往往被忽视的思想观念上,以便人们对它们进行重新审视。批评语言学一出现便迅速得到西方语言学界的重视。在过去的二十几年里,研究语言、权力和意识形态关系的队伍不断壮大。目前它在英国、美国、荷兰、奥地利和澳大利亚等国方兴未艾,形成语篇分析的研究热潮。这些研究从不同角度,运用不同方法,通过分析语篇的语言特点和它们生成的社会历史背景来考察语言结构背后的意识形态意义,并进而揭示语言、权力和意识形态之间复杂的关系。批评语言学认为语篇是说话者在形式结构和意识形态意义两方面进行选择的结果。批评语言学是在当代西方人文科学领域中普遍存在的反唯科学主义和反唯理主义的背景下产生的。实证主义把科学或科学知识视为纯粹客观的东西,实证主义科学只限于所谓的"客观"描写和呈现"事实",它忽视了这样一个简单的事实,即科学是由科学家进行的,而科学家跟任何其他人一样具有自己的观点、兴趣和意识形态。今天,语言对社会过程具有重要的干预作用这一思想在人文科学中已为人们所普遍接受(辛斌,2005)。批评式语篇分析是建立在语言学理论基础上的语篇分析模式。它通过描述、阐释、说明三个分析步骤,对语篇进行分析,揭示语篇中所隐含的意识形态领域的控制和统治关系。近年来批评语言学引起了我国语言学界的重视,出现了不少研究成果。目前批评话语分析新动态主要体现为新的研究思路初见端倪,新的理论逐渐引入批评话语分析研究;研究方法不断得到丰富,研究内容、研究对象逐渐趋向多样化;英、汉语篇的批评性分析对比研究日益得到重视;在重视英语语料的同时,汉语语料的本土化研究初步得到加强;国内批评话语分析和积极话语分析的对比研究已经起步,正在努力与国际接轨(支永碧,2007)。

积极话语分析是由以马丁为代表的韩礼德学派所倡导的。他们认为,功能语法的理论如评价理论等不仅可以用来批判也可以用于建设,即进行他们所谓的积极话语分析。2005年7月在悉尼召开的第29届国际系统功能语言学大会的主旨是"希望的话语:和平、和解、学习和改变",目的是使批判性思考更多地朝着积极的话语分析方向进行,即更着力研究如何将我们的世界变得更美好,以及系统功能语言学者如何为此做出贡献。我们可以看出,在这个主旨中,马丁等学者对于评价理论的应用既抱存和批评话语分析相同的社会关怀,又更多地着眼于建设性的改变(胡壮麟等,2005:332)。

4. 衔接与连贯

衔接被笼统地定义为"所有连接语言单位和模式的方法"。衔接的主要手段有词汇法和韵律。衔接指的是表层语篇的语言成分即人们听到或看到的实在语词,在一个序列中、在语言的语法规则基础上有意义地相互连接的方式(Beaugrande & Dressler,1981:3)。韩礼德和哈桑在《英语的衔接》(*Cohesion in English*)(1976)里对衔接进行了界定。他们认为,"当话语中的某个成分的解释取决于话语中另一个成分的解释时,就出现了衔接"(ibid:4)。衔接决不仅仅提供叙述的连续性,它还由此构成语篇的语义整体。实质上,衔接是个语义概念,体现语篇的语言成分之间的语义关系。根据韩礼德和哈桑(1976,1985)的划分,衔接手段大致可分为语法衔接和词汇衔接两种。前者包括照应(reference)、省略(ellipsis)、替代(substitution)和连接(conjunction),后者则包括词汇重述(reiteration)、同义(synonymy)、下义(hyponymy)和搭配(collocation)等。这里,值得注意的是隐性衔接语篇的衔接常可以借助语篇的显性表述来实现,如照应、替代、省略、连接词和词汇连接等。有时,语篇的衔接也可以借助语篇的隐含意义,即蕴涵在语篇显性表述之内的含意来实现。

前者我们称之为显性衔接,后者称之为隐性衔接。显性衔接的语篇,形式标记明显,句与句之间的语义关系脉络分明,转承清晰。隐性衔接的语篇,无形式标记,句与句之间的语义关系含而不露,隐晦曲折。在语篇营造过程中,显性衔接是主要的语篇接应手段,但隐性衔接也是建构连贯语篇不可缺少的方式。这主要是语言的节俭原则和合作原则使然。显性衔接是实现语篇连贯的主要手段,隐性衔接是实现语篇连贯不可缺少的方式。二者相间使用,相互补足,促成整个语篇连贯性的建立(牛保义,1998:1—5)。另外,我们需要注意汉英语篇含意衔接。含意性是指在任何一段话语里,都可以从中感知到一些潜存于词语里的语义之外的隐性表述。这些隐性表述同话语中由语言单位的概念意义传递的显性表述有补足、延伸、限定、阐发、待释等关系,两者共同实现话语的相对完备表达。含意性是一种构架谋篇手段,即借助含意实现语篇衔接,达到语言的"简约性",增强语言的"审美性"。语篇建构中,一般含意衔接是指用句子语词的隐含意义或语句的逻辑事理关系连接句子和语篇。特殊含意衔接是指通过对特定的语境知识的阐释和发挥实现句子或语篇的衔接。语篇含意衔接主要借助语篇显性表述所隐含的常规关系或者是结合特定的语境信息对常规关系的阐释发挥实现的。因此,实质上,语篇含意衔接的作用是用常规关系的具体内容嫁接句子中的语义空缺部分。含意作为一种衔接手段,也就是用语句字面的词义和寓意,用对语句内藏事理和语词内涵外延的领悟去衔接语句和构筑语篇。研究语篇的衔接,也就是探究作者如何利用语词的词义和寓意、语句的逻辑事理和语词的内涵外延发展语篇的,也就是从更深的层次去解读语篇(牛保义,1999:35—42)。

"连贯"指的是语篇世界的组成成分互相影响和互相关联的方式(Beaugrande & Dressler,1981:4)。在 Beaugrande 和 Dressler 看来,连贯甚至比衔接更为重要。连贯不仅仅是语篇的一个重要特征,更是语篇使用者之间认知过程的结果。信息组织的起承转合,与衔接有关,而将不同概念有机地组合起来,形成一个语义整体,并在情景语境中行使恰当的功能,靠的是连贯。"连贯这一概念已经描绘出把语篇当作人类活动这一门学科的实质。一个语篇本身并没有什么意义,而是要依靠语篇所描述的知识与人们头脑中存储的世界知识的相互作用才有意义。"(Beaugrande & Dressler,1981:6)其实,篇章的连贯性是一个相当复杂的问题,受多种因素的影响。除了结构的衔接之外,语义、语用和认知原则及篇章的主题与类别都是影响篇章连贯性的重要因素。因此,在分析一个篇章的连贯性时,必须全面考虑这些因素的影响(武果,1987:20—23)。主题连贯性实质上就是根基于英语话语的这种自然信息结构。发话人在组织话语时,尽量将表示已知信息的语言单位放在句子前部,让表示未知信息的成分尽可能出现在句子较后的位置上,从而每句话里的新信息都成为接下来要传达的新信息的出发点或背景知识,如此循环交替,不断把意义向前铺展,直到把话说完(辛斌,1989:24—29)。话题对衔接具有宏观上的限制作用,衔接手段能够有效加强语篇的连贯性,但前提是语篇中话题的发展必须具有一定程度的统一性和逻辑性(辛斌,1998:6)。连贯反映了人类的认知规律,它的产生条件是关联、连接、一致、顺序和层级,其中顺序与层级是充分必要条件。现有连贯理论和阐释模式的描写力大于解释力,根源在于未能充分考虑连贯的顺序与层级性问题。语篇连贯可分为形式连贯和功能连贯。形式连贯主要通过词汇语法衔接手段在语篇的表层来实现,其手段是显性的。功能连贯则没有表层衔接语符,其连贯的实现建立在逻辑-语言和社会符号层面上。隐含连贯需要语言内外部的语境、世界知识、言语行为、合作原则、共有知识和想象等手段来实现。语篇连贯是一个语义概念;语篇衔接机制的范围应该扩大到所有语义联系机制,包括结构性衔接、话语语义结构、外指性衔接机制和隐性信息衔接等,它不仅表示语篇成分和部分之间的语义联系,还要最终形成一个语义整体;语域使语篇与语境相联系,使语篇的衔接与连贯联系;连贯是语篇的衔接机制和情景语境相互作用产生的总体效应。它还有层级性、连接性、整体性和功能性等突出特点。此外,我们还需关注"人际意义连贯",它主要体现为语篇内人际意义的衔接性和语篇外语域在话语基调和话语方式上的一致性。把体现衔接关系的衔接机制与体现人际意义的语言项目结合起来,可以获得相邻对、语气并列、主语链、态度词汇衔接、极性/情态/语态重复、语调模式等人际衔接机制。而语篇外人际连贯则主要是由社会角色、交流角色、语言角色与语篇的一致性来实现的。由此,可以构建一个由情景语境、语义和词汇语法、语音三个层面组成的人际连贯分析框架,并就一语篇进行人际连贯的实例分析(杨才英,2005)。

5. 话轮/话轮转换

话轮是萨克斯(Sacks)等人提出的理论概念,是人们日常会话的基本结构单位。话轮是指在会话过程中,说话者在任意时间内连续说的话,其结尾以说话者和听话者的角色互换或各方的沉默等放弃话轮信号为标志(李悦娥、范宏雅,2002:22)。萨克斯等人(1974:696—701)认为话轮转换系统对一切会话来说都存在,并且是一个基本的言语转换机制。话轮转换系统包括话轮构造部分、话轮分配部分及话轮转换规则。

6. 前置语列/预示语列

前置语列或预示语列是指为了探明某些具体言语行为能否实施而采用的语列。下面就是一个前置语列或预示语列:

甲:你周末打算做什么?

乙:没有什么特别的事。有事吗?

甲:那干吗不跟我们一起出去郊游?

这里,乙已经明白了前置语列的用意,于是便问甲"有事吗",知道甲还有下文。

7. 相邻语对和优先应答

相邻语对指一类话语常常配之以某一特定类型的答话这一语用现象,如在一个会话结构中或话轮转换过程中,问题后面往往跟着回答,提议后面往往跟着采纳或拒绝,劝告后面往往跟着认可,抱怨后面往往跟着道歉或辩解。这种两两相对的语句被称为相邻语对。相邻语对的其中一个问题是可能出现的第二部分的范围可能很大。对一个问题,可以做出许多反应,都不是对问题的回答,但都可以充当第二部分。所谓"优先应答"指的是一句问话之后、第二部分全部的话语总库中的较正常的、较一般的、不太特别的选择项。如:

甲:考及格了吗?

乙:及格了(没有及格、60 差一分、倒数第三,等等)。

乙的答话中前两项为优先应答,后面两项较特殊,较具体,是相邻语对中的非优先应答。

8. 照应/替换/省略/连接/重复/搭配

(1) 照应是一种语义关系,它指的是语篇中一个成分做另一个成分的参照点,也就是说,语篇中一个语言成分与另一个可以与之相互解释的成分之间的关系。如:

The dictionary is very expensive. I bought it yesterday.

此例中，It 与 the dictionary 构成照应关系。

（2）省略指的是把语言结构中的某个成分省去不提。它是为了避免重复，使表达简练、紧凑、清晰的一种修辞方式。如：

Tom bought some potatoes. Mary some sweet peas.

此例中"Mary some sweet peas"在结构上不完整，省略了谓语动词成分，因为 bought 在上下文中出现过，采用省略的表达方式就可以避免不必要的重复。

（3）连接是指在一个结构里将两个分句连在一起。如：

I love Mary and Mary loves me.

需要注意的是，英语连接性词语中，除了 but, so, and 之类的连接词之外，其余均可以纳入连接性修饰状语（conjunctive adjuncts）的语法范畴。为了便于分析研究，韩礼德和哈桑（1976）将连接成分划分为四种类型，即加合（additive）、转折（adversative）、因果（causal）和时间（temporal）。但后来他们（1985）进一步发展和完善了语篇中连接成分的分类方法，采用了以逻辑语义为切入点的更为合理、更为科学的三分法，弥补了早些时候无法将某些连接成分归类的缺陷。这三类连接词是详述（elaboration）、延伸（extension）和增加（enhancement）。

（4）替代指的是用替代形式来取代上文中的某一个成分。在语法和修辞上，替代被认为是为了避免重复而采用的一种重要的语言手段。如：

My axe is too blunt. I must bought a sharper one.

此例中，one 替代了 axe，避免了重复。

（5）重复指的是语篇中某一个或某几个词再次或多次出现。但韩礼德和哈桑（1976）所说的复现（reiteration）是一个含义比较宽泛的概念，既包括重复即某一个或某几个词项在同一个语篇或语段中两次或多次出现，也包括同义词的使用，条件是指代对象不变。参照的标准不同，对重复的分类也就不同。朱永生等（2001:105—109）从重复语言单位之间的距离、重复涉及的语言单位等级（rank），及讲话者的人数这三点将重复进行了划分。

（6）搭配，简单说来，指的是一个词或某些词一起使用（即共现）的倾向性。它实质上是句法上讲究的"横组合关系"。需要提出的是，不少语言学家都曾经对属于"搭配"类型的语义关系作过专门的论述和分析，但由于各自的着眼点不同，他们为"搭配"所下的定义和划定的范畴自然也不尽一致。

Chapter 10 Sociolinguistics

本章主要考点

1. 语言和社会的关系(Relationships between language and society)
2. 社会语言学和语言社会学的区别(Differences between sociolinguistics and sociology of language)
3. 言语社团(Speech community)
4. 言语变体(Variety)
5. 口音和方言(Accent and dialect)
6. 地域方言(Regional dialects)
7. 社会方言(Social dialects)
8. 个人方言(Idiolect)
9. 语言与性别(Language and gender)
10. 语域(Register)
11. 正式级别和说话风格(Scales of formality and styles of speaking)
12. 语码转换和混合语码(Code-switching and code-mixing)
13. 双言和双语现象(Diglossia and bilingualism)
14. 禁忌语和委婉语(Taboo and euphemism)

课文理解与重点内容分析

1. 社会语言学

社会语言学是语言学的一个分支,它研究社会语境中的语言。鉴于语言是社会中人与人之间进行交际的首要工具,社会语言学家关心的是在不同言语社区中的语言变异和语言使用的社会意义,这些言语社区包括地域群体、民族群体和社会群体。社会语言学家还关心非语言因素对语言使用的影响,这些因素包括年龄、性别、职业和社会地位等。

2. 语言变异

作为一种社会交际工具,语言从来就不是同一群体的人所使用的同一体系。既然语言运用在本质上是一种社会现象和一种依赖语境的行为,语言使用在不同的言语社区中,不同的地域群体中,不同的社会群体中,甚至在不同人之间都有所不同。社会语言学的目的就是探索在种种言语社区中和不同社会情景中的语言变异和语言使用的本质。

3. 言语社团

社会语言学研究中,说话者被当作是社会群体的成员。分离出来用于任何特定研究的社会群体称作言语社团。因而,言语社团就被定义为一个社团(人数小到一个家庭,大到一个国家)使用同样的语言或语言的某种变体的一群人。言语社团的重要特点是,这个群体的成员必须以某种适当的方式与其他社团成员进行语言交流。这些成员不仅可能对语言规范持相同态度,而且可能使用紧密联系的语言变体。

4. 言语变体

社会语言学家尤其对三类言语变体或方言感兴趣,它们是地域性变体、社会方言及被称为语域的功能性言语变体。方言作为语言学中的一个术语,没有高低、优劣之分,它仅指一种语言的一种独特形式。因此,语言学家把所谓的标准英语也叫作一种方言。

尽管方言通常被认为是有地域性和社会性的,语言学家也用方言指那些不能用地域、社会阶层和民族等标准来划分的语言变异。更确切地说,在这种情况下,方言仅仅指说话者个人在说或写某种语言时所表现出的某种独特的差异。对个人言语形式的研究表明,讲某种地方语言变体的每个人的言语都有独有的特征。

5. 地域变异

地域变异是取决于说话者所来自的特定地区的语言变异。语言的地域变异是最易辨别和界定的。

语言变异会出现在发音、词汇或句法这些方面,尤其是在发音方面,语言地域性变异的最显著的语言特征就是地域口音。口音是一种发音方式,该方式能使听话者知道有关说话者的地域背景或社会背景方面的信息。应把它与方言区分开,后一术语描述语法、词汇和发音等方面的综合特征。

通常,使用同一种语言但说的是该语言的不同地域方言的人交流起来很困难。这种困难主要在于许多语音的发音方式不同。这种困难还在于用词和对话语理解的不同。解决这种交际困难的一种方法是被称为语言规则的语言标准化。这个术语的意思是,某些权威机构,如一个国家的政府或政府机构,选择一种特定的语言变体,并跨越地域在全国推广它,包括推广它的发音体系和拼写体系。

6. 社会变异

尽管来自某一特定地理区域的一个人说话带着一种口音,他的言语中也可能包含一些与地域变异毫无关系的特点。两个在同一个城镇出生、长大的,并讲同样地区方言的人,其讲话方式可能会因为一些社会因素而有所不同。如果他们属于不同的社会群体的话,情况尤其如此。

无论意识到与否,他们的社会背景,都会影响他们对适合其社会身份的语言特征的选择。因此,人们的社会方言是根据与各自可界定的社会群体相关的语言差异界定的,这些社会群体甚至生活在同一个地区。

语言的社会变异产生了社会方言,社会方言又可以分为更小的语言类别,这些类别不仅显示了说话者的性别和年龄特征,也显示了他们在社会经济、教育、职业及民族等方面的背景。

7. 文体变异

除了与说话者所来自的地域和社会特征有关的不同说话者之间的言语差异之外，还有一些言语差异是说话者本人的言语在不同的言语情景中所具有的：言语情景即在什么情况下，为了什么目的，谁与谁讲什么。因此，尽管大多数人仅会说一种地域方言，一个有社会群体意识的说话者却必须使用多种文体的言语，这些文体被称为语域。

根据交际情景的类型，一个人的口头语和书面语中的文体会发生变异，变异区间是从随便文体或口语体到正式文体或文雅文体。文体（风格）也可以指一个人一直在使用的口头语或书面语，或指在一个特定的时期内的说话或写作方式，例如，狄更斯的风格、海明威的风格。

使用一种特定语域的可能是一个群体，他们有相同的职业，如都是医生、教师或律师，或有相同的志趣，如都是集邮者或足球迷等。

一个语域时常通过以下几个方面和其他语域区分开：一些有特色的词，以一种独特的方式去运用词或词组，而且有时会使用特殊的语法结构，例如，科技用语或法律用语就包含有特殊的语法结构。

8. 个人言语变异

言语变体并不限于一般的、有系统的分类，如地域方言或社会方言。语言使用既是有系统的，又是无系统的，它不仅受内部变异的影响，也受外部变异的影响。一个说话者的语言运用是庞杂的而非均一的。社会语言学家们认识到，一个人所讲的语言是易变的，一种语言的任何可辨别的方言本身都以这样或那样的方式受制于相当大的内部变异。没有哪两个使用同一种语言或方言的人是以完全相同的方式使用他们的语言或方言的。一个人说话时，他在一种特定语言的总的体系内来表达，但他实际上所说出的是他自己独特的语言体系。这种个人方言被称为个人习语。

因此，个人习语是说话者的个人方言，它以这样或那样的方式综合了涉及地域变异、社会变异和文体变异的各方面特征。从比较狭窄的意义上来说，个人方言也包含音质、音调、言语节奏这样的因素，这些因素都构成了个人言语中的可识别特征。我们能根据不同的人所具有的独特言语模式来辨别这些人，这些言语模式也是个人身份的一些最基本的特征。从比较严格的意义上来说，使用一种语言的每一个人都有其独特的个人习语，使一个人与众不同的因素中就有他或她独特的个人习语。

9. 标准语与非标准语

标准语是语言中一种享有最主要位置的方言。标准语为政府和司法部门采用，也用于新闻媒介和教育机构——包括外语或第二语言的教学场所——所教授的也是标准语。标准语之外的语言变体被称为非标准语，或本地话。

指定某一变体为标准语是由历史和社会政治原因促成的，与特定语言变体的任何假定的语法成分所固有的语言优越性毫无关系。认为一种语言的标准变体"正确，合乎逻辑，纯正"是怀有偏见的。认为一种方言比另一种方言更具有表现力是一种社会观，它反映出一种社会政治评价，而不是语言学评价。

另一方面，与其他一种或多种本地话相比，一种特定方言的标准化不一定是由蓄意的政府政策造成的，而是由社会传统和文化传统造成的，比如说，首都城市的语言或统治阶级的语言的标准化就是如此。

（1）通用语

通用语是一种语言变体，它在有多种语言背景的人群的交际中起媒介作用。正因为如此，通用语必定是一种为了各种目的而进行社会接触的人所使用、约定的"共同语"。通用语这一术语起源于一种混杂语（hybrid language），这种混杂语由意大利语、西班牙语、希腊语、阿拉伯语和土耳其语混合而成，为中世纪时地中海东部地区的商人所使用。

通用语这一术语可以广义化，以用来指作为贸易或交际媒介的其他任何语言。因此，任何语言都可以作为通用语。

一种通用语也可能是世界通用的。英语就是这样一种国际通用语，它被用在很多需要一种共同语的社会和政治生活中。

（2）洋泾浜语

洋泾浜语是一种语言变体，它通常被使用其他语言的本族者作为一种交际媒介来使用。

尽管许多洋泾浜语已经不复存在了，然而，在世界的某些地区，一些洋泾浜语仍然被作为一种有效的交际工具。世界上使用洋泾浜语的具体人数尚不清楚，大约在600万到1,200万之间。以英语为基础的洋泾浜语大约有60种，其中一些至今仍在使用。

作为一种接触语言，一种洋泾浜语可能包含两种或两种以上语言的重要语法特征。洋泾浜语以两种或两种以上语言的语言特征为基础，它在词汇方面通常体现出受较高级的或起支配地位的语言的影响，在音系、有时在句法方面通常体现出受较低级语言的影响。作为一种简化语言，洋泾浜语的词汇萎缩，这些词汇最为常见的是源自于处于支配地位的语言。像格、时态、语气和语态这些语法特征在洋泾浜语中通常没有。洋泾浜语的特色是屈折语素，例如，名词后没有显示它的复数形式的词尾，动词后没有表示动词时态或与主语一致的词尾。另外，系动词be的各种形式在洋泾浜语中通常不存在，介词通常也只有少数几种，但它们可以起多种作用。

尽管洋泾浜语是简化语言，其语法特征是简化了的，但它们像任何人类语言一样是受规则制约的。

（3）克里奥尔语

克里奥尔语最初是一种洋泾浜语，后来它发展成为某个言语社区的本族语。也就是说，当一种洋泾浜语逐渐被一个地区的全体居民作为主要语言使用，并且孩子们也把它作为第一语言来学习时，这种洋泾浜语就被称为克里奥尔语。

克里奥尔语是充分发展的语言，在各个方面都和其他语言一样完善。与洋泾浜语相比，它有更多的词和范围更广泛的语法特性。当一种洋泾浜语成为克里奥尔语，并超越其作为商贸语言的作用时，它的词汇和语法被相当大地扩展，并开始具有在本质上和复杂性方面都与其他人类自然语言的规则相对等的规则。尽管洋泾浜语和克里奥尔语都来源于一些独特的、受高度制约的本地话，但在某种情况下，克里奥尔语已获得标准语这样的显赫地位。例如，美拉尼西亚洋泾浜语现在已成为新几内亚的官方标准语。

10. 双言和双语现象

尽管居住在同一地区的大多数人一直都只讲一种地区方言或民族方言，但另一些人必须经常交替地讲一种语言的两种方言或两种不同的语言，这种现象也是很正常的。对于这些人来说，熟练地使用两种或多种语言变体是为了满足不同社会交际的需要。当一个地区的人讲两种不同的地区方言或民族方言时,被称为双言现象或双语现象的社会语言情景就出现了。

(1) 双言现象

双言现象这个术语是由弗格森在1959年最先使用的,指一种类似于双语现象的社会语言情景,它通常用来描述在一个言语社区内同时存在两种不同的语言变体这样一种社会情景,其中每一种变体都有它特殊的社会作用,并适用于特定的情景。通常,一种是较标准的变体,称作高层次变体,它被用于较为正式或严肃的场合,另一种是没有地位的变体,称为低层次变体,它被用在口语或其他非正式场合中。

通常,高层次变体被看作是称为古典语言的文学标准语,而低层次变体一直是一种本地土话。在某些情况下,只有受过教育的阶层才能用这两种语言变体。然而,对于一个用两种语言变体的人来说,使用哪一种语言变体可能不是由他的社会地位决定的,而是由他所处的交际情景决定的。由于社会文化原因,高层次变体被许多人当作是更正确、更纯正的语言,这反映出他们对更口语化的低层次变体的社会偏见。

双言现象并不是一个普遍现象。例如,它很少出现在像英国、美国这样的讲英语的国家。在这些国家里,尽管标准英语和种种非标准的本地话可能会同时存在,而且在标准英语中也存在正式英语和口语化英语这样的功能性变体,但这些社会方言和功能方言之间的区别并不类似于有双言现象的言语社区中的高层次变体和低层次变体之间的区别。一个人得在标准语和非标准本地话或地区方言之间进行转换是单语社区中的普通语言现象,因而不能被当作是双言现象。

(2) 双语现象

双语现象指个人或社会群体,如一个特定地区或国家的居民,使用两种标准语的语言情景。

在双语社区中,社区成员在日常生活中使用两种语言。一个社区只有当足够多的社区成员使用两种语言时才能被称为双语社区。典型的双语社区是民族聚居区,它的大多数居民或者是移民或者是第二代移民。

双语现象也出现在有相当多的人口讲另一种语言,因而需要不止一种标准语的国家里。这些国家可能指定两种官方语,以便在全国或某些区域使用,从这种意义上来说,这些国家是双官方语国家。

然而理想的双语现象是不常见的,因为能在各种情景中熟练地使用双语的人很少见。对于大多数双语者来说,无论他们是童年时同时习得两种语言,还是先习得一种语言然后再习得另一种,他们接近理想的双语现象,因为他们能够在相当多的情景中同样熟练地使用两种语言。对于那些一前一后地掌握两种语言的双语者来说,通常他们能更为熟练地使用其中一种语言。他们讲那种用得不是很熟练的语言时,在潜意识里可能会有一个从用得熟练的语言向另一种语言翻译的过程。

不管接近理想的双语现象的具体情况有何不同,在大多数双语社区中有一点是一致的,即在不同的被称为语用范围的言语情景中,两种语言间存在一个相当清楚的功能区分。在双语社区中,一种语言可能用于某些语用范围,而另一种语言用于其他语用范围。例如,一个常见的语用范围就是"家语用范围",家不仅是一个交谈主题,也是一个实际场所。因此,一个居住在美国的讲双语的波多黎各人可能会把西班牙语当作家里的语言,即在家里用西班牙语来和其他家庭成员谈论家事。同时可能会在办公室这样的"工作语用范围"使用英语,或在家里谈论与"家语用范围"无关的话题时使用英语。

一个双语者在和另一个双语者交谈时经常会交替使用两种语言,这种言语情景叫作代码切换。

11. 禁忌语和委婉语

禁忌语指在"上流"社会中一般被禁止使用的一些词语或表达方式,淫秽的、猥亵的和骂人的词语都是禁忌语,它们被完全避免使用,或至少在同时有男女同伴的情况下避免使用。

在社会语言学中,禁忌语,或更确切地说是语言禁忌,指所有禁止使用特定的词项指称一些物体或行为的情况。由于语言使用以特定的社会背景为语境,所以语言禁忌起源于社会禁忌。当一种行为是禁忌时,提及这种行为也成为禁忌。禁忌词语和表达方式反映出特定文化的特定社会习俗和观点。

由于语言禁忌反映社会禁忌,某些词语更可能被避免使用。在许多文化中,与性、性器官和身体自然功能相关的词构成了禁忌语的一大部分。在最极端的情况下,有些语言没有指"性交"这种普通而又普遍的行为的本族词,而在交际中需要用词来表达此行为时则依靠外来词汇。其他语言有一组描写这种生理行为的词,其中大多数词被当作是禁忌语而避免在公共场合使用。

像许多社会一样,在英语言语社区中,最明显的禁忌词语与其说是与宗教有关的词,不如说是与性、性器官和排泄物有关的词。英语中像 prick、cock 和 cunt 通常被视为下流词语。

大多数说英语的人避免使用像 tits、fuck 和 balls 这样的词,一些人甚至认为像 breast、intercourse 和 testicles 这样的词也属于禁忌语。描写排泄物的词,如 shit、fart 和 piss,通常不能从受过教育的人那里听到。而且,避免使用禁忌语体现了社会态度、情感和价值判断,与语言本身无关。

委婉语来源于希腊词 euphemismos,该词的意思是"用好词来说话"。那么,委婉语就是说话者或写作者担心较为直截了当的措辞可能是粗野的、令人不悦的或无礼时,而用来取而代之的温和、迂回的或不太无礼的词语或表达方式。

在许多文化中,人们避免使用与死亡有关的直截了当的词语,因为这是人人都恐惧并且不愿意提到的话题。这就产生了很多与死亡主题有关的委婉语。例如,在讲英语的社会中,人们不是 die 而是 pass away,或者只是 kick the bucket。一个从事葬礼服务的 undertaker 获得了一个更委婉的称呼 funeral director。有些人甚至不想提到身体上的疾病,对于他们来说,他们从不 sick(生病),而只是感觉 indisposed(不舒服)。

通常,当讲英语的人不得不提到去厕所这一话题时,他们用一种兜圈子的方式来表达,即说成 do their daily duties 或 perform their bodily function。许多有关排泄的表达语同样被视为禁忌语而需要用委婉语来代替,因此,shit 用 poop 代替,piss 成了 pee,而 fart 则被 break wind 代替。在普通英语谈话中,委婉语的使用使"文雅的"说话者能够避免使用较粗陋的口语话词项,这些人喜欢用 limb 代替 leg,用 rooster 代替 cock,用 bosom 代替 breast,用 make love 代替 have sexual intercourse,等等。

尽管使用委婉语有消除贬义暗示的作用,然而遗憾的是,像这样的分离作用不会维持太久。通常，当人们意识到一个词的委婉语形式中的负面含义时，就不得不找寻一个新的委婉语来代替它。经历了这种连续被取代的过程的一个例子是 concubine（妾）这个词，它后来变成 mistress，然后是 unmarried wife，接着又变成 common-law wife。

　　尽管委婉语的生命期限是短暂的，但作为分离一个词的暗示意义和它的负面含义的一种方法，它至少对某些社会群体的说话者来说是有意义的。只要有避免使用禁忌语的必要，就有使用委婉语这种替代方式的必要。几乎所有的说话者偶尔都会使用委婉语。委婉语成了说话者在社会交际中所用的"文雅"词汇中的一个必不可少的部分。

Chapter 11 Psycholinguistics

 本章主要考点

1. 心理语言学(Psycholinguistics)
2. 语言理解和语言产生(Language comprehension and language production)
3. 语言习得理论(Language acquisition theories)
4. 第一语言习得(First language acquisition)
5. 第二语言习得问题(Issues on second language acquisition)
6. 关键期假说(The critical period hypothesis)
7. 萨丕尔—沃尔夫假说(Sapir-Whorf hypothesis)
8. 影响二语习得的个人因素(The individual learner factors affecting SLA)

 课文理解与重点内容分析

1. 心理语言学

心理语言学研究语言和心脑的关系。

2. 语言理解和语言产生

(1) 语言理解

影响词语识别的一个最重要的因素是词语在某语篇或语境中的出现频率。人们理解句子结构时一开始构建的是最简(或者说最不复杂)的句法结构。篇章作为语境,会影响词和句子的意义,并能确定歧义。语言理解往往要求寻求言外之意,必然用到推论。综合知识,即大脑储存的意义信息包,在语言理解中起重要作用。

(2) 语言产生是一种有目标的活动。谈话中的口误表明,说话者在开始讲话之前就有"预先计划",能说明这一点的证据有以下几种典型错误:首音互换(或"舌头打滑")、预期错误、交换错误。

3. 语言习得理论

语言学家们已达成了这样的共识,习得第一语言的能力是全人类都具备的一个基本遗传特性,即人们在习得第一语言的能力方面无高低之分。

(1) 语言习得的生物基础

语言习得是全人类均具备的通过遗传而得来的能力。可以说,人生来就具备一种天赋,或一种生物机制,这使他们至少能习得一种语言。因而,语言发展与人的发育和成熟过程中的其他方面生理发展,如四肢与器官的发育和成熟相似。在语言习得方面的这一生物或先天论的意思是说,人类生来就具备习得语言与运用语言的独特的神经系统,正如鸟儿生来就具备能学会其特有的鸣叫的生物机制一样。

儿童只要能习得某种人类语言,他就能本能而轻松地习得任何人类语言,认识到这一点有着重大的语言学和社会政治意义:语言不存在优势之分,所有生理和心理健全的人都具有相同的语言习得能力。说一种语言优于另一种语言是没有任何生物学根据的。我们的语言天赋使我们能够习得我们所接受的任何语言,这种天赋使耳聋的儿童也能学会手语。

(2)语言习得即语法规则的习得

语言习得主要是语言的语法体系的习得。将儿童习得一种语言简单地看作是语言的具体表达方式的内在化是一种误导。事实上,儿童习得的不是一些具体的话语,而是一系列使他们能够说话并理解口头语的规则、条件和要素。语言技巧的习得包含的不是单词、句子的简单记忆,而是语法规则的习得。从理论上来说,人的大脑不可能储存一种语言的所有词汇与表达方式。

语言习得主要是语言的语法规则的习得,但并不意味着必须习得一种语言的语法体系的所有规则。儿童习得的是一些一般的原则,这些原则使口头语能合乎语法的基础。

(3)语言输入与交流的作用

人的习得语言的能力是由遗传决定的,但这种先天遗传并不是语言发展的充分条件。原因是,要最终习得语言必须给儿童提供适当的环境,使儿童可以接触到语言信息并有机会用输入的语言进行交流。儿童要习得语言,必须具有收发语言的语音信号的生理功能,同时为了使他们的语言天赋能发挥出来,他们还必须有机会不断听到语言信息,并与其他语言使用者进行交流。

(4)语言教学的作用

语言学家们已经发现,对绝大多数儿童而言,语言发展是本能地进行的,几乎不需要成人刻意的传授。他们在不断地教育他们的孩子说合乎语法规则的句子,但在自然的环境中,很少有父母去更正孩子违背语法规则的话语,更不会有意地去教授正确的语言形式。事实上,父母向儿童传授语法规则徒劳无益。

这并不是说,从儿童咿呀学语到能流畅地说话这一语言发展过程中,语言教学全然无效。父母及其他人对儿童进行的有意识的教导中有一部分对其语言有一定的影响。有意识地教儿童正确的语言形式对他们所起的作用不大。

(5)纠错与强化的作用

研究人员已经发现,纠错与强化并不像人们以前所认为的那样是儿童语言发展的主要因素。例如,许多父母纠正儿童语病的笑话似乎都说明了纠错的无效性。即使人们试图对儿童的语病加以纠正,并用较为含蓄的方式重复正确的语言形式,儿童仍继续使用他们自己造出的语言形式。据发现,强化通常出现在儿童的发音与转述事实方面,而不是句子的语法方面。

(6)模仿的作用

全盘否定模仿在人们习得母语中的作用是错误的。许多儿童很少重复他们所听到的话语,一些年轻的语言学习者却的确对模仿加以选择性的运用。例如,在学习一些词汇时,

他们模仿已知的结构中的新词,或模仿包含有熟悉的单词的新结构。这种选择性模仿说明,儿童不是鹦鹉学舌般地模仿成人语言,而是对之加以有限的利用提高自身的语言技能。结论是,模仿与刻意的语言教学一样,在儿童的语言学习中所起的作用大。

4. 第一语言习得

儿童对语言体系这一社会交际工具的掌握不是一蹴而就的。语言是在人的发展的一个特定成长期以明显的阶段性而习得的。语言习得进程的生物基础与诸如拿东西、坐立、行走等一些运动技能的发展过程的生物基础相同,这一进程与幼儿大脑的发育成熟及其侧化进程密切相关。

(1)前语言阶段

婴儿最早发出的多种声音不能算是早期的语言。无论身处何种语言社区,新生儿发出的诸如哭喊或低语等声音听起来都是相同的。这些声音全部是应激性的,即对饥饿和不适产生无意识的反应,当婴儿希望被抱或感觉不适时,也会发出这些声音。

婴儿在三个月大之前,最早发出可辨别的声音是"咕咕"声,常由软腭辅音如/k/和高位元音/u/构成。在三四个月时开始发出如/da/、/ma/、/na/、/ba/等类似语音的声音。到了六个月他们能坐时,已能发出一些不同的元音和辅音了。

婴儿在咿呀学语阶段发出的语音和音节仍是无意义的,尽管他们此阶段发出的声音比早期的吵闹声更像语言。婴儿的咿呀学语尤其是早期学语,与婴儿所处的特定语言环境无关。这一阶段婴儿发出大量不同的语音,其中许多是其家人言语中所没有的。事实上,即使生来就聋的孩子也能发出同样的声音,和有听觉的孩子相似。另外,父母都是聋哑人的但有听觉的孩子也能发声。人们还注意到,即使是早期由于生理原因不能学语的孩子,一旦生理功能恢复,也能正常发音。所有这些都说明,婴儿咿呀学语并不依赖听觉与声音的输入。

当婴儿十个月或十一个月大开始站立时,他们能开始运用发音功能以表达情感或加强语气,从而试着开始语言习得这一重要过程。这就是第一语言发展阶段的开始。

(2)独词句阶段

在儿童接近一岁或一岁初的某个时间,咿呀学语阶段逐步被语言最早的可辨识阶段所取代,此阶段通常被称为独词句阶段。在这个阶段,儿童明白语音与意义是相关联的。他们开始反复使用母语中相同的一串语音去指代同样的事物。

儿童发出的一个词也可以被称为独词句,因为它们能够表达概念或论断,起到成人语言中一句话的作用。因此,儿童可能通过说 dada(爸爸)来表达"I saw daddy's hat",说 more 来表达"Give me more candy",说 up 来表达"I want up"。

独词句有时表现出语义扩展过度或扩展不足的情况。非常典型的是,儿童会用相同的词来描述外貌相似的事物。

(3)双词句阶段

在儿童一岁至两岁期间,他们的话语逐渐增长。独词句阶段结束的确切时间因不同儿童而相差很多。一般而言,双词句阶段大概开始于儿童一岁半到两岁期间。

在这个阶段,儿童所说的双词句的组合方式是多样的。最初,这些双词句像是两个独词句的并置,其中每个独词句都有各自的语调。此后不久,儿童开始组成具有明确句法和语义关系的真正双词句。

儿童的双词句能通过词序表达许多不同的语法关系。例如,在 Baby chair,Daddy hat,Me going,Doggie bark 中,所有者出现在被持有者之前,主语出现在谓语前。同时,儿童还使用双词句表明特定的概念关系。

除此之外,这一阶段的语言开始出现句型的区别,如否定句、祈使句和疑问句。这是结构语言的开始。很明显,儿童已经开始掌握其母语语法的更多特征。

(4) 多词句阶段

当儿童的话语超过两个词后,则出现两词、三词、四词、五词或更长的话语,此阶段被称为多词句阶段。在这个阶段,话语最显著的特征不再是单词的数量,而是单词顺序的不同。如:

Cathy build house.　　　　Cat stand up table.
Daddy like this.　　　　　He play little tune.

儿童早期的多词句有一个典型的特点,即缺少屈折语素和大多数的功能词,如不定式标志 to、冠词 the、助动词 can、系动词 be 的不同形式等。存在于多词句中的通常只是一些传达主要信息的实词。由于这些言语与电报中的电文风格相似,所以这个习得阶段的言语经常被称为电报式言语。

尽管电报式言语缺少起语法作用的语素,但它们也不是随意攒到一起的,而是遵循一定的句法组合规则。

在这一阶段,儿童话语没有语序错误。他们的话语可能会出现错误的词尾,但却应用了成人的语序。到这一阶段,儿童已明显地习得了一些造句能力。在语序不同的各种语言中,儿童几乎能与成人一样运用不同的语序模式。

随着这类电报式言语的增多,儿童言语中开始出现一些语法性语素。他们开始使用屈折语素来表示语法功能,如加上语素"-s"表示第三人称动词或名词复数,加"-ed"表示过去式。同时,儿童言语中也开始出现一些简单的介词,尤其是那些表示位置的 in,on 和 up 等。

5. 第二语言习得

第二语言习得是个具有概括性的术语,是与第一语言习得相对而言的,它指第二语言的习得过程,此外,也可以用于指一门外语或其他语言的习得(如第三或第四种语言)。因此,第二语言习得主要是研究人们在习得第一语言后是如何习得或学习其他语言的。在第二语言习得文献中,语言学家们常将第一语言称为本族语或母语,将第二语言称目标语。

第二语言习得与第一语言习得有一些相似之处,青少年或成人在习得第二语言时遇到的一些问题则是儿童在第一语言习得过程中所不存在的。人们认识到,当成人过了习得语言的关键时期——正如某些语言学家所认为那样——其语言官能已失去了灵活性,以至于难于习得一门新语言的特征,因而,无论习得环境多么优越,没有多少成人似乎能在第二语言的各个方面达到本族语的精通程度。因此,第二语言习得研究的一个关键的问题,就是第二语言习得与第一语言习得相似及不同的程度。同时,第二语言习得的研究者还对成人习得第二语言的过程中所遇困难的根源,及可促进其第二语言习得的方法极为感兴趣。

(1) 习得与学习

大多数第二语言习得者的一个主要难点,可以用美国第二语言习得学者斯蒂芬·克拉什(S. D. Krashen)对习得与学习的观点加以说明:他提出语言习得与语言学习是不同过程的假设,从而把二者进行了对比。

克拉什认为,习得指的是在日常交际环境中通过自然地运用第一语言能力而逐步地、下意识地发展这种能力。而学习则被定义为在学校环境中有意识地积累第二语言知识的过程。

语言学家已有这样的共识,儿童不需要专门的学习就能习得母语。克拉什则认为,第二语言的能力一般是通过学习而获得的,但也可以在一定程度上被习得,这种习得取决于学习者所处的语言环境与所接受的语言输入。人们在把一个规则内在化(习得)前可以学习它,但学习了规则不一定就意味着以后能习得它。

(2) 转移与干扰

无论学习者是有意识还是无意识地学习目标语,他们总是带着第一语言的知识去学第二语言。学习者在学第二语言的过程中总是下意识地运用第一语言的知识,这种现象被称为语言转移。

语言转移可为正向转移也可为负向转移。不言而喻,任何两种语言的语法和其他体系都既存在着相似,也存在着不同。如果第一语言与目标语的模式相同或相似时,就很可能出现正向转移。相反,当第一语言的模式与目标语中相应的模式不同时,出现的则是负向转移,即人们常说的干扰。干扰曾一度被认为是第二语言学习者所遇困难和所犯错误的主要根源,理由是,当第一语言与第二语言之间存在着差异时,学习者的第一语言知识会干扰第二语言的学习。

语言学家们提出一种被称为对比分析的研究方法。这种对比分析方法的理论基础是,通过找出本族语与目标语的不同来预测学习者在学习某种第二语言时会遇到的难题和可能犯的错误。根据这种方法,有人提出了这样的假设,学习第二语言时所犯错误主要是由负向转移或母语干扰所导致的。

根据对比分析理论,第二语言学习的关键在于掌握第一语言与第二语言体系的差异。这种观点对于第二语言教学有着重大的启发意义。第二语言教学的主要任务在于将本族语与目标语体系加以对比,对学习者可能遇到的难点与可能犯的错误做出预测,然后根据这些预测确定在教学和教材编写中需特别处理的语言点,并确定使用何种强化方法来克服干扰导致的学习困难。

用实际调查去验证对比分析假设,结果发现,有相当大比例的语法错误无法用母语干扰加以解释。事实上,通过对比分析预测的错误常常不会出现,而许多实际错误,如 goed 和 foots,不是由于语言的负向转移而是由于过度概括而导致的。

这些经验性研究的重要价值在于,它改变了人们对学习者所犯的错误的态度。认为学习者的语言错误是有害无益的,因而必须被根除,这样的传统观念被放弃了。对学习者语言错误的认可反映了对第二语言习惯的看法的一个根本性转变。第二语言习得不再被视为克服旧的语言习惯而形成新语言习惯的过程,而是构建和修改交际规则的过程。有关语言学家认为,第二语言学习者的言语错误很可能只是语言发展错误,因而不应被简单地视为学习正确形式时所出现的失败,而是表明语言习得过程正在进行。诸如过度概括造成的发展错误,常常是由于学习者试图构建和检验目的语的一般性交流规则而引起的。

(3) 错误分析与第二语言的自然发展轨道

由于不同的第一语言会导致不同的困难,所以人们会本能地认为,第一语言不同的学习者会以不同的方式来学习第二语言。

另一种相反的观点认为,由于负向转移不再像以往那样被认为是第二语言习得的主要因素,学习者在习得第二语言时遵循着一条普遍轨道。根据这种观点,所有学习者,无论其第一语言是什么,都以类似的轨道来学习第二语言的语法。

　　与此相关的一个问题是,第一语言习得与第二语言习得的轨道是否相同,即在习得方面第二语言是否等同第一语言。根据它们等同的假设,第二语言习得与第一语言习得过程由于学习者采用的方法相似而非常相似。这种假设通过对学习者的错误的分析得以检验。这种错误分析方法表明,不同的第二语言学习者在习得新语言时其方法具有惊人的相似性。第二语言学习者所犯的许多语言发展错误表明,不同的第二语言学习者在学习方法上的相似性体现了第二语言习得与第一语言习得一样,都有一条自然发展轨道。一些语素和纵向研究的结果也表明,第二语言学习者遵循着大致相同的发展轨道,尽管由于自身的一些因素与学习环境的不同,他们的语言发展轨道也存在一些细微的差别。

　　(4) 第二语言习得是一个创造性构建过程

　　在这一过程中,学习者构建了一系列内在的表达方式,这种表达方式组成了学习者对目标语的过渡性知识,此种知识被称为语际语或中继语言,即学习者在第二语言习得的某一阶段所说的语言。第二语言习得研究中与此相关的一个要点就是第二语言学习者语际语的实质与发展。

　　具体地说,语际语包含一系列与本族语和目标语相关并相似的语言体系。是既介于本族语和目标语之间,又不同于它们的语言体。它反映了学习者从第一语言能力向目标语语言能力的过渡。作为一种实实在在的语言体系,语际语是第二语言训练、母语干扰、对目标语语言规则的过度概括以及学习者的学习和交际策略的综合产物。

　　学习者能充分接触适当的语言并有机会用语言输入进行交流,他们的语际语就会逐步向目标语语言能力方向发展。但是,大多数第二语言学习者却达不到最终目的,也达不到本族语的语言能力。对这种学习中止的一种解释是,学习者的语际语在未达到目标语言能力时,就发生了僵化,此时其内在化的规则体系与目标语语言体系所包含的规则不尽相同。据认为,学习者语际语的僵化现象是导致错误的语言形式的主要原因。

　　(5) 语言输入的作用

　　很明显,学习者只有接收到第二语言输入并有机会纳入输入信息时,才能进行第二语言习得。第二语言研究者与教师感兴趣的问题之一就是,语言输入在语言习得中能起多大的作用。

　　(6) 正规教学的作用

　　大多数成年人通过正规教学来学习第二语言。正规教学就是教师在课堂上设法提高学习者对目标语语言规则的特点的认识,从而帮助他们学习第二语言。

　　有关正规教学对第二语言习得的影响所做的研究表明,正规教学对一种特殊的语言学习任务,如自然随意的对话,影响不大,但却有助于学习者完成其他学习任务,如有准备的发言、写作或职业考试。接受正规教学较多的学生比接受正规教学较少的学生在水平测试中得分要高。

　　另一方面,我们应当注意,正规教学有着强烈的滞后性:即使从中获得的第二语言知识不能立即应用于自然随意的交谈,学习者以后经常进行口头交际,将会发现它的有用性。

(7) 学习者的个人因素

许多因素都能影响第二语言习得。习得速度及最终的成功不仅取决于最佳的语言输入与教学,而且还受到学习者个人因素的影响。学习者在习得第二语言知识时,没有统一的方式,这一点已成定论。可能影响第二语言习得方式以及和学习者自身有关的因素有许多。引起第二语言习得研究者注意的学习者的个人因素有年龄、领悟力、学习动机、个性以及认知方式。

① 第二语言习得的最佳年龄

第一语言习得的最佳时期是青春期前的最初几年,但第二语言习得的最佳年龄却并非总是遵循"年龄越小越好"这一准则。已有证据显示,青少年在学习第二语言时比儿童速度更快、效果更好。第二语言习得的最佳年龄是在青少年时期前期这一论断是有道理的,因为在这一年龄段,学习者的认知技巧发展很快,同时他们的语言习得官能还保持有一定的灵活性,这些条件有利于掌握一种新语言的特点。

② 学习动机

语言学习动机可以从学习者总体学习目标或方向角度加以释义。成人是出于交际的需要学习第二语言的。他们学习第二语言的目的可能是功能性的(即把语言当作一种工具来达到某种目的,例如,获得一份渴望的工作或通过一次重要的考试),也可能是社会性的(即将自己融入第二语言社区中)。因此,当学习者的学习目的是功能性时,这种动机称为工具性学习动机,学习目的是社会性时,则称为介入性学习动机。

在某些情况下,介入性学习动机更能促进学习者成功地习得第二语言,但从长期角度看,工具性学习动机发挥的作用更大。如果目标语是外语(用于有限的环境,如学校),介入性学习动机可能会对学习者有所裨益;如果目标语是第二语言(作为学习者所处社区的一种主要交流方式),那么工具性学习动机的作用更大。

③ 语言文化移入

与介入性学习动机相关的一个问题是,不同学习者适应第二语言社区的文化风俗的过程在多大程度上有所不同,这个适应过程被称为语言文化移入。

语言是文化最显著的一种表现,一门新语言的习得被视为与学习者对目标语社区的认识相关,这一点是语言文化移入这一概念的基础。根据语言文化移入的观点,第二语言习得涉及、也取决于对社区文化风俗的习得。有关语言学家们假设,当学习者适应了第二语言社区文化习俗时,就更有可能成功地习得该语言。因此,学习者适应目标语社区的文化风俗的程度以及学习者与目标语的文化风俗所保持的社会及心理距离的程度,将决定学习者与目标语的接触量,从而影响学习者将外在的语言输入转化为内在的语言纳入的成功程度。

④ 学习者的个性

有的语言学习者比较外向,而有的则较内向。人们凭直觉往往会假定,外向型个性会有助于语言习得。这种观点认为,外向型成年学习者学习语言更快,因而比内向型学习者学习更为成功。有人提出,外向型学习者更易与其他的第二语言使用者沟通,因而可以获得更多的语言输入。同样,外向型课堂学习者能通过更多地使用第二语言而受益。

而研究结果只证实了这一假说的部分内容。外向与精通第二语言之间没有任何举足轻重的联系。但人们已认识到,通过经常接触目标语,并用其进行交流,外向型学习者的确可能比非外向的学习者的口语更为流畅。

6. 关键期假说

关键期指的是在人一生中大约从两岁到青春期这一时期。在这一时期内,大脑处于准备习得某一语言的最佳状态,学习语言既容易又快,且不需要刻意的教导。

我们知道,没有哪个儿童一出生就能够完全会说话。一般认为,大脑的侧化过程可能与儿童的语言学习能力有关,因为第一语言习得的关键期与大脑的侧化期一致。伦尼伯格(Lenneberg)认为,关键期的结束与侧化过程的完成相一致,语言中枢通常位于大脑左半球。根据他的观点,在此之前,两个半球在一定程度上都涉及语言,而且如果其中一个半球受伤,另一个可以取而代之。在有关专著中,这种神经的适应性被称为大脑弹性。

儿童的大脑有相当大的弹性,这一观点可以由以下两点来证实。第一,据研究,左脑受伤的青春期前的儿童能把语言中枢转到右脑,能再次习得失去的语言技能,而且这些技能相对而言几乎没什么损失。因此,比起其他儿童,青春期前患失语症的儿童可以更快、更完全地康复。

第二,我们知道,儿童易于学好第二语言,而他们的父母学一种新语言往往是努力了数年也无法完全掌握。这一点常被用来证实下面的观点:语言习得和侧化过程大致同时开始,而且就语言要点而言,到侧化过程终结的时候,语言习得通常也完成了。还有一点事实也可以说明这个观点:在侧化完成的年龄之后,习得语言变得越来越难。

因此,如果一个孩子出于任何一种原因,比如没有语言环境,而没有在关键期习得语言,那么,以后他或她不可能成功地学会一种语言。然而,除非是有了实证,这样的观点都只是假设。要为关键期假说做一个理想的实验,很可能必须要在完全无法接触语言的环境中养大一个孩子,然后观察他在关键期之后才接触语言是否还能正常学习。而这样的实验是违背社会道德的,因而不可能付诸实施。

7. 萨丕尔—沃尔夫假说

萨丕尔(Sapir)—沃尔夫(Whorf)假说主要探讨语言系统中的语法、语义范畴与思维模式的关系,包括两个部分:(1)语言决定论,即个人的思维完全由母语决定,因为他只能根据其母语中编码设定的范畴和区别定义来认识世界;(2)语言相对论,语言结构有无限的多样性,一种语言系统中的范畴类别和区分定义为该语言系统独有,与其他语言系统中的范畴类别和区分定义不同。这一假说逐渐演化为强式理解和弱式理解。强式理解认为,不同的语言类型决定人们以不同的方式认识世界;弱式理解则认为,语言类型在一定条件下可能对人们认识世界的方式产生某种影响,但不是决定性影响。

沃尔夫首先提出,所有高层次的思维都依赖于语言。说得更明白一些,就是语言决定思维,这就是语言决定论这一强假设。由于语言在很多方面都有不同,沃尔夫还认为,使用不同语言的人对世界的感受和体验也不同,也就是说与他们的语言背景有关,这就是语言相对论。简而言之,萨丕尔—沃尔夫假说这种强假设提出,我们所说的语言决定了我们感知世界的方式和思维的本质。沃尔夫部分地是以他所观察到的多种美洲印第安人语言之间的许多不同为基础来阐述他的观点的。

沃尔夫还从语言的其他部分中找到了论证他的观点的论据。他指出,当我们来看更抽象一点的概念,如时间、持续期间、速度时,各语言间的区别就变得更复杂了。例如,沃尔夫认为,霍皮语缺少一种时间概念,他的根据是,霍皮语中没有与英语相对应的形式。他认为,鉴于这种语言上的巨大差异,一个说霍皮语的物理学家和一个说英语的物理学家很难彼此理解对方的思维。

由萨丕尔—沃尔夫假说的这种强假设可以得出这样的结论,即根本没有真正的翻译,学习者也不可能学会另一种文化区的语言,除非他抛弃了他自己的思维模式,并习得说目的语的本族语者的思维模式。

这里我们必须说明一下人们对萨丕尔—沃尔夫假说的批判。

沃尔夫所举的那些作为他的假设的基础的例子表明,他太注重各种语言的表层结构。实际上,所有语言,包括语言中的词汇语义和句法部分,从根本上说都体现人的共性。所有正常人生来都具有同样的语言天赋和一般的认知能力。鉴于语言被看作是一个用于交际的任意体系,某种语言的词汇符号和句法规则不会使说该种语言的人感受世界的方式和说另一语言的人有根本性的不同。

(1) 词与意义

词的符号和意义之间的关系具有相当大的任意性。怎样称呼一种自然现象或物体,如雪,对于一个概念体系来说并不是最重要的。对雪有很多种称呼并不意味着其概念上的任何重大不同。英语中只有一个单词指称雪并不意味着说英语的人不能感知不同类型的雪。例如,有经验的滑雪者对不同类型的雪就很敏感。对某一领域非常精通的任何人都必然会有较大的词汇量来描述这一领域里的事物。

人们普遍接受了这一观点:语言中的词汇只是一些无意义的标签,语言使用者用它们来引起情绪上的或行为上的反应,传递信息或引导听者的注意力。词和短语的意义在很大程度上依赖于语境。词句的语境变了,它们的要旨和意义也随之发生改变。

(2) 语法结构

沃尔夫不仅过分依赖于词的字面意义用法,而且还过分依赖于语法结构。语言的句法系统与使用该语言的人的感知系统之间并没有萨丕尔—沃尔夫假说所声称的那种互相依赖的关系。语言的很多语法特征都纯粹是语言结构的表层现象。

(3) 翻译

对萨丕尔—沃尔夫假说的另一批判来自于语言间可以有成功的翻译这一事实。这一批判基于这样的逻辑:如果两种语言有完全不同的概念体系,那么把一种语言翻译成另一种语言就是不可能的;如果翻译是不可能的,说一种语言的人就无法理解另一种语言。而我们可以用英语来解释如霍皮语这样的语言的概念上的独特性,这一事实可以证实翻译批评的论点。沃尔夫认为,霍皮语的概念体系是无法用英语的概念体系来理解的,而他却用英语描述了霍皮语的概念体系。具有讽刺意义的是,他用一般说英语的人都能理解的语言对其作了描述,而且,他用英语准确而又成功地描述了霍皮语的概念,这实际上证明霍皮语和英语是可以用同一标准来衡量的。

我们承认,由于语言不同,不同文化之间有概念上的差异,但这并不是说,这种差异大到了双方都不可能互相理解。一种语言可能要用很多词来表达另一种语言用一个词所能表达的概念,但最终这种委婉曲折的方式也能表达清楚意义。

(4) 第二语言习得

对萨丕尔—沃尔夫假说的另一种批判来自第二语言习得的著述。与翻译批判观点相似,第二语言习得的批判观点也是不仅在逻辑上有道理,而且有事实证明。这也就是说,如果不同语言有不同的概念体系,那么说某种语言的人就会因为没有所需要的概念体系而无法学会另一种语言。然而,由于人们可以学会完全不同的语言,因而这些语言不应该有不同的概念体系。

类似的更为有力的论据取自于双语现象。世界上有许多能够成功地使用双语的例子。虽然他们对两种语言都很精通,而这两种语言在渊源上也没有关系,他们却并不具有两种不同思维体系的"双重头脑"。与单语者一样,双语者和多语者对客观世界有着统一的概念——感知体系。

(5)语言与世界观

语言体系并不一定能影响一个人对世界的看法。一方面,说同一语言的人对世界可能有不同的看法,包括政治观点、社会观点、宗教观点、科学观点和哲学观点都可能有所不同。另一方面,说不同语言的人也可能有相似的政治观点、社会观点、宗教观点、科学观点和哲学观点。另外,一种语言也可以描述对世界的多种不同的看法,这一点在成功的翻译作品中被表现得很清楚。

Chapter 12 Linguistic Theories and FLT

 本章主要考点

1. 不同的语言观及其对外语教学的意义(Various linguistic views and their significance in foreign language teaching)
2. 语言学习理论(Language learning theory)

 课文理解与重点内容分析

1. 不同的语言观及其对外语教学的意义

(1) 传统语法强调语言的正确性、文学上的优雅,偏爱书面语和拉丁语模式。教科书以优秀作家的作品作为语言典范,注重语言细节,讲究语言规范,存在很多语法禁忌;教学方法包括对大量定义、规则和解释的介绍,采用以教师为中心的语法翻译法,教和学的行为主要是语法和翻译的学习。

(2) 结构主义语言学开始描写人们在日常交际中使用的口语,但关注的焦点仍是语法结构。受行为主义观点影响,认为语言学习是在"刺激-反应"链条的基础上形成某种习惯。教学方法是一套能使学习者自动形成语言形式的训练技巧。

(3) 转换—生成语言学把语言视为内在的规则系统,认为语言习得是建立和验证假设的过程。但因其形式化和抽象化,目前在语言教学领域的作用还比较有限。

(4) 功能语言学把语言看作社交中实施各种功能的工具,学习语言是用一整套与句子形式有直接关系的语言功能来表达意思。成人语言有三种元功能:概念功能、人际功能、语篇功能。语言教学中,发展了以意念功能为基础的教学大纲。

(5) 交际能力理论认为语言学习应培养言语行为能力,有效地参与交际活动,强调话语发生的语境。这种理论带动了以意念功能为基础的教学大纲的发展,尤其是交际教学大纲的发展。

2. 语言学习理论是从语言学习角度概括语言学和语言学习的关系。语法和语言学习是探讨二语教学中怎样教授语法的问题。输入信息和语言学习重点是语言输入说。这一理论认为:学习者掌握语言是他们理解了输入信息的结果。正在学习一种语言的二语学习者或外语学习者构建的介于目标语言和学习者母语之间的语言系统就是中介语,跟目标语相比还不完善,但又不仅仅是学习者对母语的翻译。

Chapter 13 Schools of Modern Linguistics

 本章主要考点

1. 索绪尔与结构主义语言学(Saussure and Structuralism)
2. 布拉格学派(The Prague School)
3. 哥本哈根学派(The Copenhagen School)
4. 美国结构主义(The American Structuralism)
5. 乔姆斯基和转换生成语法(Chomsky and TG Grammar)
6. 伦敦学派和系统功能语法(The London School and Systemic-Functional Grammar)

 课文理解与重点内容分析

1. 索绪尔与结构主义语言学

索绪尔认为,语言是用声音表达或交流思想的符号系统。符号是形式和意义的联合,是表示者和被表示者的结合。符号是语言事实的核心,研究语言必须从符号本身的特性入手。他区分了几组重要的概念:能指与所指,语言与言语,共时研究和历时研究,连锁关系与选择关系,把研究引向语言的本质,确立了语言学作为一门科学所要研究的对象(刘润清,2002:83)。索绪尔是结构主义的创始人,他的学说标志着现代语言学的开端,在不同程度上影响了20世纪各个语言学流派。

2. 布拉格学派

布拉格学派实践了共时语言学研究,最重要的贡献是从"功能"角度看待语言,音位学说以及对语音学和音位学的区分。最重要的三个观点:(1)强调共时语言研究,但并设有将其与历时语言研究分离;(2)强调语言的系统性,认为要想正确评价语言中的任何成分,就必须明确该成分与其他成分之间的关系;(3)把语言视为一种"功能",是用来完成一系列基本职责和任务的工具。

3. 哥本哈根学派

在布拉格学派语言学家研究语言学理论的同时,以丹麦哥本哈根为中心,诞生了结构主义三大流派之一的另一个语言学流派——哥本哈根学派。该学派成立于1931年,在欧洲结构主义的传统基础上继承和发扬了索绪尔的结构主义理论,在现代语言学史上具有重要地位。哥本哈根学派人数不多,主要代表人物是叶尔姆斯列夫(Hjelmslev)。

哥本哈根学派继承了索绪尔关于语言是一个符号系统,语言是形式而不是实体等观点,并进一步加以发展,从而形成了一个与布拉格学派极不相同的结构主义学派,有人称之为语符学(glossematics)。语符学强调语言学理论的本质和现状以及语言与描述之间的关系。同时也区分了系统和过程,即对任何一个过程来说,都有一个相应的系统,在这个系统里,过程可以得到描述。语符学的主要特征之一是强调研究关系而不是物质对象。物质对象可以被看作是功能性的。

哥本哈根学派的特点是偏重纯理论研究,具体语言分析方面的著述很少。

4. 美国结构主义

早期有鲍阿斯(Baos)和萨丕尔的理论,后来是布龙菲尔德(Bloomfield)的理论。该理论从行为主义语言观出发,认为儿童的语言习得是"刺激—反应—强化"的过程,成人对语言的使用也是"刺激—反应"的过程,其著名的公式是:S⟶r……s⟶R。其中,S指外部刺激,r指语言的替代反映,s指语言的替代性刺激,R指外部的实际反应。

后布龙菲尔德时期语言学以直接的观察为中心,系严格彻底的经验主义,发明设计了一套"显形发现程序",用计算机处理原始的语言数据,以此形成一套完整的语法。

5. 转换生成语法

乔姆斯基(Chomsky)1957年出版的《句法结构》标志着转换生成语法的形成。转换生成语法使用被称为"评价过程"的"假设—演绎"的方法,与布龙菲尔德的发现程序相对,已历经五个发展阶段:古典理论、标准理论、扩展的标准理论、修正的扩展的标准理论、最简方案。生成语法一词简明地表示"一套用来给句子进行结构描写、定义明确严格的规则系统",认为任何一种语言的说话者都掌握并内化了一种有生成能力的语法,帮助表达他的语言知识。生成语法力图揭示个别语法与普遍语法的统一性,探索语言的普遍规律,以期揭示人类的认知体系和人的本质。其"天赋假设"认为语言是某种天赋,儿童天生具有学习语言的能力——"语言习得机制"。儿童生来就有基本的语法关系和语法范畴的知识,这种知识是一种通用的、普遍性的知识。

6. 伦敦学派

伦敦学派专门用来称呼独具英国特色的语言学研究。弗斯(Firth)使语言学在英国完全成为一门公认的科学。弗斯主要受人类学家马林诺夫斯基(Malinowski)影响,而他又影响了他的学生韩礼德。三人都强调"语言环境"和语言"系统"的重要性。因此,伦敦学派也被称为系统语言学和功能语言学。

韩礼德的系统功能语法由系统语法与功能语法两部分组成,两者密不可分。系统语法的特点是:(1)非常重视语言的社会学特征;(2)把语言视为一种行"而不是"知,区分了语言行为潜势和实际语言行为;(3)比较重视描述某一特定语言或某一语言的各种变体的特点;(4)用渐变群的形式描述了语言不同侧面的特点;(5)通过对语篇的分析和统计数据来验证自己的假设;(6)把"系统"作为核心的范畴。功能语法提出语言的三种元功能:概念功能、人际功能、语篇功能。

第二部分

单元练习

Chapter 1 Language

1. Define the Following Terms

1) discreteness
2) design features
3) arbitrariness
4) duality
5) displacement
6) cultural transmission
7) the imaginative function of language
8) the personal function of language
9) the heuristic function of language
10) language

2. Multiple Choice

Directions: In each question there are four choices. Decide which one would be the best answer to the question or to complete the sentence best.

1) Which of the following words is entirely arbitrary?
   A. tree   B. crash   C. typewriter   D. bang

2) The function of the sentence "Water boils at 100 degrees Centigrade" is _____.
   A. interrogative   B. directive   C. informative   D. performative

3) In Chinese when someone breaks a bowl or a plate the host or the people present are likely to say *sui sui ping an* (every year be safe and happy) as a means of controlling the forces which the believers feel might affect their lives. Which function does it perform?
   A. Interpersonal.   B. Emotive.   C. Performative.   D. Recreational.

4) Which of the following properties of language enables language users to overcome the barriers caused by time and place, due to this feature of language, speakers of a language are free to talk about anything in any situation?
   A. Interchangeability.   B. Duality.
   C. Displacement.   D. Arbitrariness.

5) Study the following dialogue. What function does it play according to the functions of language?
   —A nice day, isn't it?
   —Right! I really enjoy the sunlight.
   A. Emotive.   B. Phatic.   C. Performative.   D. Interpersonal.

6) Unlike animal communication systems, human language is _____.
   A. stimulus free
   B. stimulus bound
   C. under immediate stimulus control
   D. stimulated by some occurrence of communal interest

7) Which of the following is the most important function of language?
   A. Interpersonal function.   B. Performative function.
   C. Informative function.   D. Recreational function.

8) In different languages, different terms are used to express the animal "狗", this shows the nature of _____ of human language.
   A. arbitrariness   B. cultural transmission
   C. displacement   D. discreteness

9) Which of the following disciplines are related to applied linguistics?
   A. Statistics.   B. Psycholinguistics.
   C. Physics.   D. Philosophy.

10) _____ has been widely accepted as the father of modem linguistics.
    A. Chomsky   B. Saussure   C. Bloomfield   D. John Lyons

3. Word Completion

Directions: Fill in the blanks with the most suitable words.

1) Design features, a framework proposed by the American linguist Charles Hockett, refer to the _____ properties of human language that distinguish it from any animal system of communication.

2) _____ refers to the phenomenon that the sounds in a language are meaningfully distinct. For instance, the difference between the sounds /p/ and /b/ is not actually very great, but when these sounds are part of a language like English, they are used in such a way that the occurrence of one rather than the other is meaningful.

3) In any language words can be used in new ways to mean new things and can be combined into innumerable sentences based on limited rules. This feature is usually termed p_____ or c_____.

4) Language has many functions. We can use language to talk about language itself. This function is m_____ function.

5) Cultural transmission refers to the fact that language is c_____ transmitted. It is passed on from one generation to the next through teaching and learning, rather than by i_____.

6) One general principle of linguistic analysis is the primacy of _____ over writing.

7) The _____ function refers to the use of language to communicate knowledge

about the world, to report events, to make statements, to give accounts, to explain relationships, to relay messages and so on.

8) The _____ function refers to language used to ensure social maintenance. Phatic communion is part of it. The term phatic communion introduced by the anthropologist Bronislaw Malinowski refers to language used for establishing an atmosphere or maintaining social contact rather than for exchanging facts.

9) Language is a system of arbitrary _____ symbols used for human communication.

10) Language has two levels. They are _____ level and _____ level.

11) Language is a _____ because every language consists of a set of rules which underlie people's actual speech or writing.

12) The _____ function refers to language used in an attempt to control events once they happen.

13) The design features of language are _____, _____, _____, _____, _____, _____ and _____.

14) By saying "language is arbitrary", we mean that there is no logical connection between meaning and _____.

15) The four principles in the linguistic study are _____, _____, _____ and _____.

4. True or False Questions

Directions: Decide whether the following statements are true or false. Write "T" for true and "F" for false in the bracket before each of them.

1) (   ) The relation between form and meaning in human language is natural.
2) (   ) When language is used to get information from others, it serves an informative function.
3) (   ) The reason for French to use "cheval" and for English to use "horse" to refer to the same animal is inexplicable.
4) (   ) Most animal communication systems lack the primary level of articulation.
5) (   ) Language change is universal, ongoing and arbitrary.
6) (   ) Language is a system of arbitrary, written signs which permit all the people in a given culture, or other people who have learned the system of that culture, to communicate or interact.
7) (   ) In theory, the length of sentences is limited.
8) (   ) The relationship between the sounds and their meaning is arbitrary.
9) (   ) Linguistic symbols are a kind of visual symbols, which include vocal symbols.
10) (   ) Linguistic symbols are produced by human speech organs.
11) (   ) Every language has two levels: grammatically meaningless and sound meaningful.

12) (   ) Such features of language as being creative, vocal, and arbitrary can differentiate human languages from animal communicative systems.

13) (   ) Duality is one of the characteristics of human language. It refers to the fact that language has two levels of structures: the system of sounds and the system of meanings.

14) (   ) Language is a means of verbal communication. Therefore, the communication way used by the deafmute is not language.

15) (   ) Arbitrariness of language makes it potentially creative, and conventionality of language makes a language be passed from generation to generation. As a foreign language learner, the latter is more important for us.

5. Glossary Translation

1) personal function   2) heuristic function
3) ideational function   4) interchangeability
5) 控制功能   6) 表现功能
7) 文化传递性   8) 分离性
9) 区别性特征   10) 不受时空限制的属性
11) interactional function   12) instrumental function
13) imaginative function   14) 寒暄功能
15) 元语言功能   16) personal function
17) performative function   18) 娱乐功能
19) 信息功能   20) 人际功能

6. Answer the Following Questions

1) What are the functions of language? Exemplify each function.
2) Explain what the term "duality" means as it is used to describe a property of human language.
3) Is language productive or not? Why?
4) What is language?
5) What are the major design features of language? Please explain three of them with examples.

Answers

1. Define the Following Terms

1) discreteness

Discreteness refers to the phenomenon that the sounds in a language are meaningfully

distinct. For instance, the difference between the sounds /p/ and /b/ is not actually very great, but when these sounds are part of a language like English, they are used in such a way that the occurrence of one rather than the other is meaningful. The fact that the pronunciation of the forms *pad* and *bad* leads to a distinction in meaning can only be due to the difference between the sounds /p/ and /b/ in English. Each sound in the language is thought of as discrete. It is possible to produce a range of sounds in a continuous stream which are all generally like the sounds /p/ and /b/.

2) design features

Design features refer to the defining properties of human language that tell the difference between human language and any system of animal communication. They are discreteness, arbitrariness, duality, productivity, displacement, cultural transmission and interchangeability.

3) arbitrariness

Arbitrariness means that there is no logical connection between meaning and sounds. A dog might be a pig if only the first person or group of persons had used it for a pig.

Language is therefore largely arbitrary. But language is not absolutely arbitrary, because there are cases where there are or at least seem to be some sound-meaning association, if we think of echo words, like "bang", "crash", "roar", which are motivated in a certain sense. Secondly, some compounds are not entirely arbitrary either. For instance, "snow" and "storm" are arbitrary or unmotivated words, while "snowstorm" is less so. So we can say "arbitrariness" is a matter of degree.

4) duality

Linguists refer "duality" of structure to the fact that in all languages so far investigated, one finds two levels of structure or patterning. At the first, higher level, language is analyzed in terms of combinations of meaningful units (such as morphemes, words etc.); at the second, lower level, it is seen as a sequence of segments which lack any meaning in themselves, but which combine to form units of meaning. According to Hu Zhuanglin et al., language is a system of two sets of structures, one of sounds and the other of meaning. This is important for the workings of language. A small number of sounds can be grouped and regrouped into a large number of semantic units (words), and these units of meaning can be arranged and rearranged into an infinite number of sentences. (For example, we have dictionaries of words, but no dictionary of sentences!) Duality makes it possible for a person to talk about anything within his knowledge. No animal communication system enjoys this duality, or even approaches this honor.

5) displacement

Displacement, as one of the design features of the human language, refers to the fact that one can talk about things that are not present, as easily as he does things present. In other words, one can refer to real and unreal things, things of the past, of the present, of the future. Language itself can be talked about too. People can use language to describe something that had occurred, is occurring, or is to occur. But a dog could not bark for a bone to be lost. The bee's system has a small share of "displacement", but it is an unspeakable tiny share.

6) cultural transmission

Cultural transmission refers to the fact that language is not biologically transmitted from generation to generation, but the details of the linguistic system must be learned anew by each speaker. It is true that the capacity for language in human beings (N. Chomsky called it "language acquisition device", or LAD) has a genetic basis, but the particular language a person learns to speak is a cultural one rather than a genetic one like the dog's barking system. If a human being is brought up in isolation he cannot acquire language. The wolf-child reared by the wolves turned out to speak the wolf's roaring "tongue" when he was saved. And it was difficult for him to acquire human language.

7) the imaginative function of language

The imaginative function refers to language used to create imaginary system, whether these are literary works, philosophical systems or utopian visions on the one hand, or daydreams and idle musings on the other hand. It is also language used for sheer joy of using language, such as a baby's babbling, a chanter's chanting, a poet's pleasuring.

8) the personal function of language

The personal function refers to language used to express the individual's feelings, emotions and personality.

9) the heuristic function of language

The heuristic function refers to language used in order to acquire knowledge and understanding of the world. The heuristic function provides a basis for the structure of knowledge in the different disciplines. Language allows people to ask questions about the nature of the world they live in and to construct possible answers.

10) language

Language is a system of arbitrary vocal symbols used for human communication.

2. Multiple Choice

1)—5) A C C C B   6)—10) A C A B B

3. Word Completion

1) defining   2) Discreteness
3) productivity or creativity   4) metalingual
5) culturally, instinct/inheritance 6) speech
7) representational   8) interactional
9) vocal
10) grammatically meaningful, sound meaningless
11) system   12) regulatory

13) arbitrariness, duality, productivity, cultural transmission, interchangeability, discreteness, displacement.

14) sound

15) exhaustiveness, economy, objectivity, consistency

4. True or False Questions

1)—5) F F T F F   6)—10) F F T F T   11)—15) F F T F T

5. Glossary Translation

1) personal function：人际功能

2) heuristic function：启发功能

3) ideational function：概念功能

4) interchangeability：互换性

5) 控制功能：regulatory function

6) 表现功能：representational function

7) 文化传递性：cultural transmission

8) 分离性：discreteness

9) 区别性特征：design features

10) 不受时空限制的属性：displacement

11) interactional function：互动功能

12) instrumental function：工具功能

13) imaginative function：想象功能

14) 寒暄功能：phatic function

15) 元语言功能：metalingual function or metafunction of language

16) personal function：自指性功能

17) performative function：表达功能

18) 娱乐功能：recreational function

19) 信息功能：informative function

20) 人际功能：interpersonal function

6. Answer the Following Questions

1) What are the functions of language? Exemplify each function.

According to Wang Gang (1988：11), the functions of language can be mainly embodied in three aspects. i) Language is a tool of human communication; ii) Language is a tool whereby people learn about the world; iii) Language is a tool by which people create art.

As a matter of fact, different linguists have different terms for the various functions of language. The British linguist M. A. K. Halliday uses the following terms to refer to the initial functions of children's language:

A. Instrumental

The instrumental function of language refers to the fact that language allows speakers to get things done. It allows them to control things in the environment. People can cause things to be done and to happen through the use of words alone. An immediate contrast here is with the animal world in which sounds are hardly used in this way, and, when they are, they are used in an extremely limited degree. The instrumental function can be primitive too in human interaction. Performative utterances such as the words which name a ship at a launching ceremony clearly have instrumental functions if the right circumstances exist; they are acts, e. g. *I name this ship* Liberty Bell.

B. Regulatory

The regulatory function refers to language used in an attempt to control events once they happen. Those events may involve the self as well as others. People do try to control themselves through language, e. g. *Why did I say that? / Steady! / And Let me think about that again.* Language helps to regulate encounters among people. Language provides devices for regulating specific kinds of encounters and contains words for approving or disapproving and for controlling or disrupting the behavior of others. It allows us to establish complex patterns of organization in order to try to regulate behavior, from game playing to political organization, from answering the telephone to addressing in foreign affairs. It is the regulatory function of language that allows people some measure of getting control over events that occur in their lives.

C. Representational

The representational function refers to the use of language to communicate knowledge about the world, to report events, to make statements, to give accounts, to explain relationships, to relay messages and so on. This function of language is represented by all kinds of record-keeping, such as historical records, geographical surveys, business accounts, scientific reports, government acts, and public data banks. It is an essential domain of language use, for the availability of this material guarantees the knowledge-base of subsequent generations, which is a prerequisite of social development.

D. Interactional

The interactional function refers to language used to ensure social maintenance. Phatic communion is part of it. The term phatic communion introduced by the anthropologist Bronislaw Malinowski refers to language used for establishing an atmosphere or maintaining social contact rather than for exchanging facts. A greeting such as "How are you?" is relatively empty of content, and answers like "Fine" or "Very well", "Thank you" are equally empty, because the speaker is not interested in the hearer's health, but rather to demonstrate his politeness and general attitude toward the other person when he gives a conversational greeting.

E. Personal

The personal function refers to language used to express the individual's feelings,

emotions and personality. A person's individuality is usually characterized by his or her use of personal function of communication. Each individual has a "voice" in what happens to him. He is free to speak or not to speak, to say, as much or as little as he pleases, and to choose how to say what he says. The use of language can tell the listener or reader a great deal about the speaker or writer—in particular, about his regional origin, social background, level of education, occupation, age, sex, and personality.

Language also provides the individual with a means to express feelings, whether outright in the form of exclamations, endorsements, or curse, or much more subtly through a careful choice of words. Many social situations display language used to foster a sense of identity: the shouting of a crowd at a football match, the shouting of names or slogans at public meetings, the reactions of the audience to television game shows, the shouts of affirmation at some religious meetings. For example, the crowds attending President Regan's pre-election meetings in 1984 repeatedly shouted "*Four more years*!" which united among those who shared the same political views.

F. Heuristic

The heuristic function refers to language used in order to acquire knowledge and understanding of the world. The heuristic functioning provides a basis for the structure of knowledge in the different disciplines. Insofar as the inquiry into language itself, a necessary result is the creation of a metalanguage, i. e. a language used to refer to language, containing terms such as sound, syllable, word, structure, sentence, meaning and so on.

G. Imaginative

The imaginative function refers to language used to create imaginary system, whether these are literary works, philosophical systems or utopian visions on the one hand, or daydreams and idle musings on the other hand. The imaginative function also allows people to consider not just the real world but all possible worlds—and many impossible ones. Much literature is the most obvious example to serve this function as an account of Robinson Crusoe in the deserted island. The imaginative function enables life to be lived vicariously and helps satisfy numerous deep artistic urges.

2) Explain what the term duality means as it is used to describe a property of human language.

Language is organized at two levels or layers—sounds and meaning—simultaneously. This property is called duality, or "double articulation". In terms of speech production, we have the physical level at which we can produce individual sounds, like /n/, /b/, and /i/. As individual sound, none of these discrete forms has any intrinsic meaning. When we produce those sounds in a particular combination, as in *bin*, we have another level producing a meaning, which is different from the meaning of the combination in *nib*. So, at one level, we have distinct sounds, and at another level, we have distinct meanings. This duality of levels is, in fact, one of the most economical features of human language, since with a limited set of distinct sounds we are capable of producing a very large number of sound combinations (relatively finite words and infinite number of sentences) which are distinct in meaning. No animal communication system has duality, or ever comes near to possessing it.

3) Is language productive or not? Why?

A. Language is productive or creative. This means that users can understand and produce sentences they have never heard before. Every day we send messages that have never been sent before, and we understand novel messages. Much of them we say and hear for the first time; yet there seems no problem of understanding. For example, the sentence "A red-eyed elephant is dancing on the hotel bed" must be new to you and it does not describe a common happening in the world. Nevertheless, nobody has any difficulty in understanding it.

B. Productivity is unique to human language. Most animal communication systems appear to be highly restricted with respect to the number of different signals that their users can send and receive. For example, gibbon calls are not productive, for they draw all their calls from a limited repertoire, which is rapidly exhausted, making any novelty impossible. Bee dancing is used only to indicate food sources, which is the only message that can be sent through the dancing.

C. The productivity or creativity of language partially originates from its duality, because of which the speaker is able to combine the basic linguistic units to form an infinite set of sentences, most of which are never before produced or heard. The productivity of language also means its potential to create endless sentences. It is the recursive nature of language that provides a theoretical basis for this possibility.

4) What is language?

A. It is very difficult to give this question a satisfactory definition. However, most linguists would accept a tentative definition like this: language is a system of arbitrary vocal symbols used for human communication. B. Language must be a system, since elements in it are arranged according to certain rules; they cannot be combined at will. If language were not systematic, it could not be learned or used consistently. C. Language is arbitrary in the sense that there is no intrinsic connection between the word *pen* and the thing we use to write with. The fact that different languages have different words for it (钢笔 in Chinese for instance) speaks strongly for the arbitrary nature of language. D. This also explains the symbolic nature of language: words are associated with objects, actions, ideas, etc. by convention. E. We say language is vocal because the primary medium for all languages is sound, no matter how well developed are their writing systems. All evidence shows that writing systems came much later than the spoken forms and that they are only attempts to capture sounds and meaning on paper. F. The term "human" in the definition is meant to specify that language is human specific; that is, it is very different from the communication systems other forms of life possess.

5) What are the major design features of language? Please explain three of them with examples.

A. Displacement is one of the defining properties of human language, which refers to the fact that human language can be used to talk about things that are present or not present, real or not real, and about matters in the past, present or future, or in far-away places. In other words, language can be used to refer to contexts removed from the immediate situations of its users. This phenomenon is thought of as "displacement", which can provide its users with an opportunity to communicate about a wide range of subjects, free from any barriers caused by separation in time and space. That is, the feature of displacement can enable us to talk about things and places whose existence we cannot even be sure of. We can refer to mythical creatures, demons, fairies, angels, Santa Claus, and recently invented characters such as superman. This feature is unique to human language. No animal communication system possesses it. Some animal calls are often uttered in response to immediate changes of situation. For instance, during the mating season, in the present of danger or pain, animals will make calls. Once the danger or pain is missing, their calls stop.

B. Discreteness refers to the phenomenon that the sounds used in language are meaningfully distinct. For example, the difference between the sounds /b/ and /p/ is actually not very great, but when these sounds are part of a language like English, they are used in such a way that the occurrence of one rather than the other is meaningful. The fact that the pronunciation of the forms *pack* and *back* leads to a distinction in meaning can only be due to the difference between the sounds /p/ and /b/ in English. This property of language is described as discreteness. Each sound in the language is treated as discrete. It is possible, in fact, to produce a range of sounds in a continuous stream which are all generally like the /p/ and /b/ sounds. However, that continuous stream will only be interpreted as being either a *p* sound, or a *b* sound (or, possibly, as a non-sound) in the language. We have a very discrete view of the sounds of our language and wherever a pronunciation falls within the physically possible range of sounds, it will be interpreted as a linguistically specific and meaningfully distinct sound.

C. Language is a system. It is organized into two levels simultaneously. We have distinct sounds at the lower level (sound level), which is seen as a sequence of segments which have no meaning in themselves. At the higher level, we have distinct meanings (meaningful level). Language is analyzed in terms of combination of meaningful units. Then the meaningful units (such as morphemes, words, etc.) at the higher level can be arranged and rearranged into an infinite number of sentences. The organization of language into two levels, one of sounds, the other of meaning, is known as duality or double articulation. This unique feature of language enables its users to talk about anything within their knowledge. No animal communication system possesses the feature of duality.

Chapter 2 Linguistics

1. Define the Following Terms

1) syntagmatic relation *vs* paradigmatic relation
2) langue *vs* parole
3) competence *vs* performance
4) descriptive linguistics *vs* historical linguistics
5) theoretical linguistics *vs* applied linguistics
6) descriptive linguistics *vs* prescriptive linguistics
7) synchronic linguistics *vs* diachronic linguistics
8) macrolinguistics *vs* microlinguistics
9) comparative historical linguistics *vs* contrastive linguistics

2. True or False Questions

Directions: Decide whether the following statements are true or false. Write "T" for true and "F" for false in the bracket before each of them.

1) (   ) Prescriptive linguistics is more popular than descriptive linguistics because it can tell us how to speak correct language.
2) (   ) Competence and performance refer respectively to a language user's underlying knowledge about the system of rules and the actual use of language in concrete situations.
3) (   ) The antithesis of langue and parole was created by Chomsky. （中国矿业大学,2004）
4) (   ) Cockoo in English is onomatopoeia. （中国矿业大学,2004）
5) (   ) Synchronic linguistics is concerned with the study of language development through time. （中国矿业大学,2004）
6) (   ) Prescriptive linguists are concerned with how languages work, not with how they can be improved. （中国矿业大学,2004）
7) (   ) Linguistics tries to answer the basic questions "What is a language" and "How does a language work". （南京师范大学,2002）
8) (   ) Onomatopoetic words are found in almost all human languages, which

shows the arbitrary nature of languages. (中国矿业大学,2002)

9) (   ) Each language contains two systems rather than one, a system of sound and a system of meaning. (中国矿业大学,2002)

10) (   ) Cultural transmission refers to the fact that the details of the linguistic system must be learned anew by each speaker. (中国矿业大学,2002)

11) (   ) Phatic function refers to language used to exchange information and ideas. (中国矿业大学,2002)

12) (   ) Speakers of all languages are capable of producing and comprehending an infinite set of sentences, which accounts for syntactic universality. (中国矿业大学,2002)

13) (   ) Halliday's linguistic potential is similar to the notions of parole and performance.

14) (   ) By diachronic study we mean to study the changes and development of language.

15) (   ) Langue is relatively stable and systematic while parole is subject to personal and situational constraints.

16) (   ) In language classrooms nowadays the grammar taught to students is basically descriptive, and more attention is paid to developing learners' communicative skills.

17) (   ) Saussure's exposition of synchronic analysis led to the school of historical linguistics.

18) (   ) Applied linguistics is the application of linguistic principles and theories to language teaching and learning.

19) (   ) Semantics is the study of the meaning of words and sentences.

20) (   ) A diachronic study is concerned with the historical development of a language over a period of time.

21) (   ) A paradigmatic relation is a relation between a linguistic element in an utterance and linguistic elements outside that utterance, but belonging to the same sub-system of the language.

22) (   ) General linguistics aims at developing a theory that describes the rules of a particular language.

23) (   ) English linguistics is a kind of descriptive linguistics.

24) (   ) Competence is more concrete than performance.

25) (   ) Descriptive linguistics attempts to establish a theory which accounts for the rules of language in general.

26) (   ) Langue is more abstract than parole and therefore is not directly observable.

27) (   ) General linguistics deals with the whole human language.

28) (   ) All the English words are not symbolic.

29) (   ) All sounds produced by human speech organs are linguistic symbols.
30) (   ) Descriptive linguistics studies one specific language.
31) (   ) Morphological knowledge is a native speaker's intuition about how a sentence is formed.
32) (   ) Phonetics is the science that deals with the sound system.
33) (   ) A diachronic study of a language is concerned with a state of a language at a particular point of time.

3. Multiple Choice

Directions: In each question there are four choices. Decide which one would be the best answer to the question or to complete the sentence best.

1) _____ made the distinction between competence and performance.
   A. Saussure   B. Chomsky   C. Bloomfield   D. Sapir
2) Findings in linguistic studies can often be applied to the solution of some practical problems, the study of such applications is known as _____.
   A. anthropological linguistics   B. computational linguistics
   C. applied linguistics   D. mathematical linguistics
3) _____ refers to the abstract linguistic system shared by all the members of a speech community.
   A. Parole   B. Langue   C. Speech   D. Writing
4) Which of the following is not the major branch of linguistics?
   A. Phonology.   B. Pragmatics.   C. Syntax.   D. Speech.
5) _____ deals with language application to other fields, particularly education.
   A. Linguistic geography   B. Sociolinguistics
   C. Applied linguistics   D. Comparative linguistics
6) Which branch of linguistics studies the similarities and differences among languages?
   A. Diachronic linguistics.   B. Synchronic linguistics.
   C. Prescriptive linguistics.   D. Comparative linguistics.
7) _____ has been widely accepted as the forefather of modern linguistics.
   A. Chomsky   B. Saussure
   C. Bloomfield   D. John Lyons
8) The study of language as a whole is often called _____.
   A. general linguistics   B. sociolinguistics
   C. psycholinguistics   D. applied linguistics
9) The study of language meaning is called _____.
   A. syntax   B. semantics
   C. morphology   D. pragmatics
10) The description of a language at some point in time is a _____ study.

A. synchronic   B. diachronic
C. descriptive   D. prescriptive

4. Word Completion

Directions: Fill in the blanks with the most suitable words.

1) _____ refers to the abstract linguistic system shared by all the members of a speech community.
2) _____ is the actual realization of one's linguistic knowledge in utterances.
3) Modern linguistics is _____ in the sense that the linguist tries to discover what language is rather than lay down some rules for people to observe.
4) The description of a language as it changes through time is a _____ study.
5) Linguistic potential is similar to Saussure's langue and Chomsky's _____.
6) The four principles in the linguistic study are _____, _____, _____ and _____.
7) _____ is the branch of linguistics which studies the form of words.
8) The branch of general linguistics which is named _____ studies the internal structure of sentences.
9) In Saussure's view, the relationship between signifier (sound image) and signified (concept) is _____.
10) _____ is an umbrella term which covers a variety of different interests in language and society, including the social functions of language and the social characteristics of its users.
11) The distinction between langue and parole is made by the Swiss linguist F. de Saussure. The distinction between competence and performance is made by the American linguist _____.
12) The writing system of English is known as the sound writing system while that of Japanese as _____ writing system.
13) According to John Lyons, _____ linguistics deals with language in general and _____ linguistics is concerned with one particular language.
14) In F. de Saussure's term, _____ refers to the system of language and _____ refers to the speaker's speech.
15) _____ is the science that deals with the sound system.
16) Syntax studies two kinds of rules: _____ rules and _____ rules.
17) Langue or competence is _____ and not directly observable, while parole or performance is _____ and directly observable.
18) A _____ relation refers to the sequential characteristic of speech.
19) _____ knowledge is a native speaker's intuition about the sounds and sound patterns of his language.
20) _____ knowledge is a native speaker's intuition about how a word is formed.

21) _____ knowledge is a native speaker's intuition about whether a sentence is grammatical or not.

22) _____ knowledge is a native speaker's intuition about the meaning of language, including meaning of words and meaning of sentences.

23) _____ is the study of speech sounds of all human languages.

5. Answer the Following Questions

1) What is the difference between general linguistics and descriptive linguistics?
2) What is the difference between synchronic and diachronic linguistics? Is it easy to draw a sharp line between them if we look at language closely?
3) What distinguishes prescriptive studies of language from descriptive studies of language? Comment on the merits and weaknesses of descriptive grammar and prescriptive grammar.
4) What are the four principles for the scientific analysis of language?
5) Point out three ways in which linguistics differs from traditional grammar.
6) What are the main differences between "competence" and "performance"?
7) What is the major difference between Saussure's distinction of langue and parole and Chomsky's distinction of competence and performance? What should be studied in linguistics in your opinion and why?
8) Explain "speech and writing", and cite two or more examples.

Answers

1. Define the Following Terms

1) syntagmatic relation *vs* paradigmatic relation

Essentially the relations between linguistic elements are of two dimensions, usually syntagmatic and paradigmatic. Syntagmatic or sequential relations are those holding between elements forming serial structure, or "strings" as they are sometimes called. In syntax, the horizontal relationship between elements shows how a form (X) combines with others (W + X + Y) in a serial combination. It refers to the linear ordering of the words and the phrases within a sentence. Paradigmatic relations are those holding between comparable elements at particular places in structures. The vertical or substitutional relationship shows how other different forms (Xa, Xb, Xc) can function in the same place in structure in a paradigmatic relation.

2) langue *vs* parole

Saussure refers "langue" to the abstract linguistic system shared by all the members of a speech community and refers "parole" to the actual or actualized language, or the realization of langue. Langue is abstract, parole is specific to the speaking situation; langue is not actually spoken by an individual, parole is always a naturally occurring event; langue is relatively stable and systematic, parole is subject to personal and situational constraints. For Saussure, parole is a mass of confused facts, thus not suitable for systematic investigation. What a linguist ought to do, according to Saussure, is to abstract langue from instances of parole, i. e. to discover the regularities governing all instances of parole and make them the subject of linguistics. The langue-parole distinction is of great importance, which casts great influence on later linguists.

3) competence *vs* performance

According to Chomsky, "competence" is the ideal language user's knowledge of the rules of his language, and "performance" is the actual realization of this knowledge in utterances. The former enables a speaker to produce and understand an indefinite number of sentences and to recognize grammatical mistakes and ambiguities. A speaker's competence is stable while his performance is often influenced by psychological and social factors. So a speaker's performance does not always match or equal his supposed competence.

Chomsky believes that linguists ought to study competence, rather than performance. In other words, they should discover what an ideal speaker knows of his native language.

Chomsky's competence-performance distinction is not exactly the same as, though similar to, Saussure's langue-parole distinction. Langue is a social product and a set of conventions for a community, while competence is deemed as a property of the mind of each individual. Saussure looks at language more from a sociological or sociolinguistic point of view than Chomsky since the latter deals with his issues psychologically or psycholinguistically.

4) descriptive linguistics *vs* historical linguistics

Linguistic study can be divided into descriptive linguistics(synchronic linguistic study) and historical linguistics(diachronic linguistic study). The former refers to the description of a language at a particular point of time in history while the latter, a diachronic study of language, studies the historical development of language over a period of time.

5) theoretical linguistics *vs* applied linguistics

The former copes with language and languages with a view to establishing a theory of their structures and functions and without regard to any practical applications that the investigation of language and languages might have, whereas the latter is chiefly concerned with the application of the concepts and findings of linguistics to all sorts of practical tasks, including language teaching.

6) descriptive linguistics *vs* prescriptive linguistics

A linguistic study is descriptive if it only describes and analyzes the facts of language, and it is prescriptive if it tries to lay down rules for "correct" language behavior. Linguistic studies before the 20th century were largely prescriptive because many early grammars were based on "high" (literary or religious) written records. Modern linguistics is mostly descriptive, however, which believes that whatever occurs in natural speech (hesitation, incomplete utterance, misunderstanding, etc.) should be described in the analysis, and not be marked as incorrect, abnormal, corrupt, or lousy. These, with changes in vocabulary and structures, need to be explained also. The distinction lies in prescribing how things ought to be and describing how things are. To say that linguistics is a descriptive science is to say that the linguist tries to discover and record the rules to which the members of a language community actually conform and does not seek to impose upon them other rules, or norms, of correctness, which are in the scope of prescriptive linguistics.

7) synchronic linguistics *vs* diachronic linguistics

Synchronic linguistics takes a fixed instant (usually, but not necessarily, the present) as its point of observation. In contrast, diachronic linguistics is the study of a language through the course of its history; therefore, it is also called historical linguistics.

The description of a language at some point of time (as if it stopped developing) is a synchronic study (synchrony). The description of a language as it changes through time is a diachronic study (diachrony). An essay entitled "On the Use of THE", for example, may be synchronic, if the author does not recall the past of THE, and it may also be diachronic if he claims to cover a large range or period of time wherein THE has undergone tremendous alteration.

8) macrolinguistics *vs* microlinguistics

Macrolinguistics falls on the verge of linguistics. It includes the following disciplines: philosophical linguistics, sociolinguistics, psycholinguistics, etc. Lyons has the same distinction.

Microlinguistics concentrates on the study of all the interior aspects of a language system. Traditional linguistic study describes language system from two aspects—lexicon and grammar. Dictionaries and grammar books are products of such researches and studies.

9) comparative historical linguistics *vs* contrastive linguistics

Comparative historical linguistics draws on the special historical comparison in linguistics to study the historical development of some related languages (languages originating from a uniform ancestry). It is in fact a special part of historical linguistics. Thanks to the development of historical comparative linguistics in the 19th century, linguistics comes to be an independent discipline. Contrastive linguistics focuses on structural similarities and differences of two or more languages (relevant or unrelated) by means of comparison and contrastive study. This study belongs to descriptive linguistics. It can help people have a deep understanding of the properties and universal characteristics of different languages and thus exerts great influence on foreign language teaching.

2. True or False Questions.

1)—5) F T F T F   6)—10) T T F T T   11)—15) F F F T T
16)—20) T F T F T   21)—25) F F T F F   26)—30) T T T F T
31)—33) F F F

3. Multiple Choice

1)—5) B C B D C   6)—10) D B A B A

4. Word Completion

1) Langue
2) Performance
3) descriptive
4) diachronic
5) competence
6) consistency, economy, objectivity, exhaustiveness
7) Morphology
8) syntax
9) arbitrary
10) Sociolinguistics
11) Chomsky
12) syllabic
13) general, descriptive
14) langue, parole
15) Phonology
16) phrase structure, transformational
17) abstract, concrete
18) syntagmatic
19) Phonological
20) Morphological
21) Syntactic
22) Semantic
23) Phonetics

5. Answer the Following Questions.

1) What is the difference between general linguistics and descriptive linguistics?

The former deals with language in general, i.e. the whole human language whereas the latter is concerned with one particular language. The former aims at developing a theory that describes the rules of human language in general while the latter attempts to establish a model that describes the rules of one particular language, such as Chinese, English, French, etc. General linguistics and descriptive linguistics are dependent on each other. In the first place, general linguistics provides descriptive linguistics with a general framework in which any particular language can be described, studied and analyzed. Very often, it may supply several different frameworks for descriptive linguists to choose from. Depending on their different views on language, they may follow one model exclusively or combine two or more models. In the second, the resulting descriptions of particular languages, in turn, supply empirical evidence which may confirm or refute the model(s) put forward by general linguistics. In other words, general linguistics and descriptive linguistics are complementary to each other despite their different objects of study and different goals.

2) What is the difference between synchronic and diachronic linguistics? Is it easy to draw a sharp line between them if we look at language closely?

Synchronic linguistics takes a fixed instant (usually, but not necessarily, the present) as its point of observation. In contrast, diachronic linguistics is the study of a language through the course of its history; therefore, it is also called historical linguistics.

Synchronic/diachronic perspective toward language is one of Saussure's most central ideas expressed in the form of pairs of concepts. The former sees language as a living whole, existing as a "state" at a particular moment in time; the latter sees it as a continually changing medium. In this view, it is always necessary to carry out some degree of synchronic work before making a diachronic study: before we can say how a language has changed from state X to state Y, we need to know something about X and Y. Correspondingly, a synchronic analysis can be made without referring to history. This can be illustrated as Saussure did using an analogy with a game of chess. A state of the set of chessmen is like a state of language. "The respective value of the pieces depends on their position on the chessboard just as each linguistic term derives its value from its opposition to all the other terms." On the other hand, the value of each piece also depends on the convention—the set of rules that exists before the game begins. This is like the set of rules that exists in language. A state of the game of chess is momentary just like a state of language change. When one piece is moved, the game passes from one state of equilibrium to the next. This corresponds closely to the situation of language between states. To study this static state is called synchronic linguistics. The moving of one piece is like one type of change in language. The consequence of one move can be very big or small; the same is true with language changes. The player of a chess game is solely concerned with the momentary positions of the pieces; he does not need to remember the previous moves so as to decide the next move. A player who knows the history of the game does not necessarily have more to say about the next move than a man who has just come to the game, ignorant of what has happened before. Similarly, a speaker of a language can learn the language well without knowing its historical states. We can describe a state of a game without bothering the techniques both players have used to bring about the state. Likewise, we can describe the state of a language without knowing its history.

3) What distinguishes prescriptive studies of language from descriptive studies of language? Comment on the merits and weaknesses of descriptive grammar and prescriptive grammar.

The distinction lies in prescribing how things ought to be and describing how things actually are. The essence of prescriptivism is the notion that one variety of languages has an inherently higher value than others, and this ought to be imposed on the whole of the speech community. Although prescriptivism is still with us, descriptivism wins more and more understanding. It proposes that the task of the grammarian is to describe, not prescribe—to record the facts of linguistic diversity, and not to attempt the impossible tasks of being language police and trying to stop language from changing, or imposing on members of a language community the so-called norms of correctness.

Weakness of prescriptive grammar (Merits of descriptive grammar): A. The reason why present-day linguists are so insistent about the distinction between the two is simply that traditional grammar was very strongly normative in character, e.g. "You should never use a double-negative", "You should not split the infinitive" etc. People realize nowadays the facts of usage count more than the authority stipulated "standards". We can appeal neither to logic nor to Latin grammar when it comes to deciding whether something is or is not correct in English. B. Prescriptivism is an individual attitude. The related social attitude that goes to the extreme of prescriptivism is purism, which is something we should guard against. Pure prescriptive grammar will lead to artificial claims that are hard to maintain in light of the facts. While prescriptivists would prefer the use of the subjunctive past after if (If I were you, etc.), it is very difficult to claim that everyone who uses "was" is wrong, especially as they are the majority in spoken language. While there are still traditionalist grammarians claiming that they are right and half the population is wrong, most have modified their approach and talk of this form as preferable, or describe it as formal register. C. The prescriptive attitude seems to ignore the fact that English has evolved over the centuries into what it is today whereas the descriptive attitude seems to be more sensitive to anything that goes on to a certain extent. A language is a living creature. There is no fixed form for any language. No one speaks Shakespearean medieval English today. However, no one says the British today speaks the incorrect English. It will and should change over time.

4) What are the four principles for the scientific analysis of language?

The four principles to make a scientific study of language are exhaustiveness, consistency, economy, and objectivity.

A. Exhaustiveness: the linguist should gather all the materials relevant to his investigation and give them an adequate explanation. Language is extremely complex; he cannot attempt to describe all aspects of language at once, but to examine one aspect at a time.

B. Consistency: there should be no contradiction between different parts of the total statement.

C. Economy: other things being equal, a shorter statement or analysis is preferred to a longer or more involved one. The best statements are the shortest possible, which can account most fully for all facts.

D. Objectivity: a linguist should be as objective as possible in his description and analysis of data, allowing no prejudice to influence his generalizations. He should not omit any linguistic facts because he himself considers there to be "inelegant" or

"substandard". Nor should he conceal facts that do not conform to his generalizations. His aim should be to present his analysis in such a way that every part of it can be tested and verified; not only by himself, but by anyone else who makes a description of different data based on the same set of principles. It is the insistence on these principles, particularly objectivity that gives linguistics the status of a science.

5) Point out three ways in which linguistics differs from traditional grammar.

Most linguistic analysis today is focused on speech rather than writing. Everything considered, speech is believed to be more representative of human language than writing. In spite of the common features they share, they differ because they are transmitted in different channels. This is one major difference between linguists today and the grammarians of the 19th century.

Modern linguistics is mostly descriptive while traditional grammar is hugely prescriptive. Many early grammars were based on "high" (literary, religious) written language. Grammarians often use logical and aesthetic criteria to judge the correctness of sentences and lay down rules for "correct" behavior. Linguists today, however, have made a special point of guarding against prescriptivism. They believe that whatever occurs in natural speech should be described in their analysis.

Another difference is the priority of synchronic descriptions over the traditional diachronic studies. Modern linguistics holds that unless the various states of a language are successfully studied it would be difficult to describe the changes that have taken place in its historical development.

6) What are the main differences between "competence" and "performance"?

This fundamental distinction is discussed by Chomsky in his *Aspects of the Theory of Syntax*. A language user's underlying knowledge about the system of rules is called linguistic competence. And performance refers to the actual use of language in concrete situations.

Competence enables a speaker to produce and understand an indefinite number of sentences and to recognize grammatical mistakes and ambiguities. A speaker's competence is stable but his performance is often influenced by psychological and social factors. For example, a speaker's competence is stable but on certain occasions he may not perform very well due to various factors such as pressure, distress, anxiety, or embarrassments. Slips of the tongue, false starts, unnecessary pauses, among other things, all belong to the imperfection of performance. A person may make grammatical mistakes in speech, but that does not mean that he does not know the rule. If he is given an ungrammatical sentence, he can recognize it as ungrammatical. The point is that a speaker's performance does not always match his competence.

Chomsky thinks that what linguists should study is the ideal speaker's competence, because the speaker's performance is too haphazard to be studied. The task of the linguists is to discover and specify the speaker's internalized rules.

Although Saussure's distinction and Chomsky's are very similar, they differ at least in that Saussure took a sociological view of language and his notion of langue is a matter of social conventions, while Chomsky looks at language from a psychological point of view and considers linguistic competence as a property of the mind of a speaker.

7) What is the major difference between Saussure's distinction of langue and parole and Chomsky's distinction of competence and performance? What should be studied in linguistics in your opinion and why?

The langue and parole distinction are not exactly the same as the competence and performance distinction. Saussure's langue is a social product; a set of conventions for a speech community. Chomsky regards competence as a property of the mind of each individual. Saussure looks at language more from a sociological point of view while Chomsky looks at it more from a psychological point of view.

Linguistics is the scientific study of language. Its ultimate goal is the discovery of the general principle which all languages are constructed and operated as systems of communication in societies in which they are used. Therefore, it is langue and competence that should be studied. Parole is a mass of confused facts and not suitable for systematic investigation. Instances of parole should be abstracted to discover the governing regularities. Similarly, competence, instead of performance, should be the object of investigation in linguistics. By definition linguistic competence is a set of rules, which can be applied over and over again to generate large numbers of sentences, including never before-heard sentences. The task of the linguists is to discover the roles underlying the speaker's performance and discover what an ideal speaker knows of his native language.

8) Explain "speech and writing", and cite two or more examples.

Speech is considered as the primary medium of language. The reasons for this are as follows. First, speech is prior to writing historically: speech existed long, long before writing systems came into being. Even today many well-developed languages do not have a writing system yet. Second, without exception, all written forms "cut in" at some point on the stream of spoken language. The written forms represent either the individual sounds, such as English and French, or syllables, such as Japanese, or the individual words like the Chinese writing system.

Writing is also important. Writing gives language new scope and uses that speech does not have. First, with writing, messages can be carried through space. Human voice is effective only within earshot. With the help of writing, we can send and receive messages across vast spaces. Second, with writing, messages can be carried through time. The spoken word "dies" immediately but a written message can be transmitted far beyond the moment of production often from generation to generation and from one culture to another. Third, oral messages are subject to distortion, either unintentional (when due to misunderstanding for example) or otherwise. Written messages, on the other hand, remain exactly the same whether read a thousand years later or ten thousand miles away.

Everything considered, speech is believed to be more representative of human language than writing. In spite of the common features they share, they differ because they are transmitted in different channels. Most linguistic analysis is focused on speech. This is one major difference between linguists today and the grammarians of the 19th century.

Chapters 3 & 4 Phonetics and Phonology

1. Define the Following Terms

1) minimal pair
2) sound assimilation
3) suprasegmental feature
4) free variation
5) rounded vowel
6) pitch
7) vowel glide
8) dentals
9) phonemes, phones and allophones
10) complementary distribution *vs* contrastive distribution
11) distinctive features
12) articulatory phonetics, acoustic phonetics and auditory phonetics
13) consonant
14) vowel
15) bilabials
16) cardinal vowels
17) glottals
18) diphthongs
19) triphthongs
20) lax vowels
21) place of articulation
22) manner of articulation
23) coarticulation
24) IPA
25) narrow transcription *vs* broad transcription
26) tone *vs* intonation
27) stress
28) palatals
29) alveolars
30) glides
31) juncture

2. Word Completion

Directions: Fill in the blanks with the most suitable words.

1) _____ phonetics studies the movement of the vocal organs of producing the sounds of speech.
2) Speech takes place when the organs of speech move to produce patterns of sound. These movements have an effect on the _____ coming from the lungs.
3) Consonant sounds can be either _____ or _____, while all vowel sounds are _____.
4) Consonant sounds can also be made when two organs of speech in the mouth are

brought close together so that the air is pushed out between them, causing _____.

5) The qualities of vowels depend upon the position of the _____ and the lips.

6) One element in the description of vowels is the part of the tongue which is at the highest point in the mouth. A second element is the _____ to which that part of the tongue is raised.

7) Consonants differ from vowels in that the latter are produced without _____.

8) In phonological analysis the words *fail* and *veil* are distinguishable simply because of the two phonemes /f/ and /v/. This is an example for illustrating _____.

9) In English there are a number of _____, which are produced by moving from one vowel position to another through intervening positions.

10) _____ refers to the phenomenon of sounds continually show the influence of their neighbors.

11) According to _____, when there is a choice as to where to place a consonant, it is put into the onset rather than the coda.

12) Phonetics has three sub-branches: _____ phonetics, _____ phonetics and _____ phonetics.

13) The vocal tract can be divided into two parts: the _____ and the _____.

14) A consonant is a speech sound in which the airstream from the lungs is either _____, or _____ or where the opening is so narrow that the air escapes with _____. A vowel is usually produced with _____ of the vocal cords.

■ 4. True or False Questions

Directions: Decide whether the following statements are true or false. Write "T" for true and "F" for false in the bracket before each of them.

1) (   ) Phonology is the study of speech sounds of all human languages.
2) (   ) Articulatory phonetics is concerned with how a sound is produced by the vocal organs.
3) (   ) All consonants are produced with vocal-cord vibration.
4) (   ) The spelling of words is not a reliable means of describing the English sounds.
5) (   ) There are 72 symbols for consonants and 25 for vowels in English.
6) (   ) Bilabials are different from alveolars in terms of manner of articulation.
7) (   ) When two articulators are brought together to form a complete closure which is followed by a sudden release, the sounds are called affricates.
8) (   ) The sound [z] is an oral voiced post-alveolar fricative.
9) (   ) In terms of tension of the muscles at pharynx, vowels are grouped into tense vowels and lax vowels.
10) (   ) All the back vowels are rounded vowels.

11) (   ) Triphthongs are produced by a glide from one vowel to another rapidly and continuously.
12) (   ) [e] may be marked with [−high], [+low], [+front], [−back], [−rounded] and [−tense].
13) (   ) Acoustic phonetics is concerned with how a sound is produced by the vocal organs.
14) (   ) Articulatory phonetics deals with how a sound is transmitted from the speaker's mouth to the listener's ears.
15) (   ) Auditory phonetics investigates how a sound is perceived by the listener.
16) (   ) According to the position of the velum, consonants are divided into oral consonants and nasal consonants.
17) (   ) The production of a stop consists of three stages: closure stage, hold stage and release stage.
18) (   ) The lowering of the soft palate causes the production of oral consonants while the rising of the soft palate brings about the production of nasal consonants.
19) (   ) In English, there are two nasal consonants. They are [m] and [n].
20) (   ) According to the presence or absence of vocal-cord vibration, the English consonants can be classified into two groups: voiceless consonants and voiced consonants.
21) (   ) In terms of lip rounding, vowels are classified into rounded vowels and unrounded vowels.
22) (   ) The space between the vocal cords is called glottis.
23) (   ) When the vocal cords are spread apart, the airstream is not blocked at the glottis and it passes freely into the vocal tract without vocal-cord vibration. The sounds produced in this way are called voiced consonants.
24) (   ) When the vocal cords are nearly touching each other but not completely closed, the airstream passing through the glottis has to cause vibration. The sounds made in this way are called voiceless consonants.
25) (   ) Stops can be divided into two types: plosives and nasals.
26) (   ) According to the state of the velum, vowels are divided into nasal vowels and oral vowels.
27) (   ) In English, nasal vowels occur only before nasal consonants, and oral vowels before oral consonants or at the end of words.
28) (   ) In English, all the back vowels except [ɑː] and [uː] are rounded vowels.
29) (   ) In terms of tongue position, vowels can be classified into front, central, back, high, mid and low vowels.

30) (   ) The sound [v] can be described as voiced, labiodental fricative.
31) (   ) Of the three phonetics branches, the longest established one, and until recently the most highly developed, is acoustic phonetics.
32) (   ) The sound [p] in the word *spit* is an unaspirated stop.
33) (   ) Suprasegmental phonology refers to the study of phonological properties of units larger than the segment-phoneme, such as a syllable, a word and a sentence.
34) (   ) The airstream provided by the lungs has to undergo a number of modifications to acquire the quality of a speech sound.
35) (   ) Two sounds are in free variation, when they occur in the same environment and do not contrast, namely, the substitution of one for the other does not produce a different word, but merely a different pronunciation.
36) (   ) The sound [p] is a voiced bilabial stop.
37) (   ) Acoustic phonetics is concerned with the perception of speech sounds.
38) (   ) When pure or monophthongs are pronounced, no vowel glides take place.
39) (   ) According to the tenseness or length of the pronunciation, vowels can be divided into tense *vs.* lax or long *vs.* short.
40) (   ) Received Pronunciation is the pronunciation accepted by most people.
41) (   ) The maximal onset principle states that when there is a choice as to where to place a consonant it is put into the coda rather than the onset.
42) (   ) The word "hour" contains a diphthong and a pure vowel.
43) (   ) The sound /p/ in the word "expensive" is pronounced as a voiceless consonant.
44) (   ) Broad transcription represents phonemes of a language whereas narrow transcription denotes its particular allophones.
45) (   ) The voiced dental fricative is /z/.
46) (   ) Allophones are described in phonetic terms.
47) (   ) /n/ is one of syllabic consonants.
48) (   ) The word "film" contains a syllabic consonant.
49) (   ) The hard roof of mouth is called hard palate.
50) (   ) A phoneme in one language or one dialect may be an allophone in another language or dialect.

■ 4. Multiple Choice

Directions: In each question there are four choices. Decide which one would be the best answer to the question or to complete the sentence best.

1) Pitch variation is known as _____ when its patterns are imposed on sentences.

A. intonation B. tone C. pronunciation D. voice

2) Conventionally a _____ is put in slashes.
   A. allophone B. phone C. phoneme D. morpheme

3) An aspirated [pʰ], an unaspirated [p] and an unreleased [p¬] are _____ of the phoneme /p/.
   A. analogues B. tagmemes C. morphemes D. allophones

4) The opening between the vocal cords is sometimes referred to as _____.
   A. glottis B. vocal cavity C. pharynx D. uvula

5) The diphthongs that are made with a movement of the tongue towards the center are known as _____ diphthongs.
   A. wide B. closing C. narrow D. centering

6) A phoneme is a group of similar sounds called _____.
   A. minimal pairs B. allomorphs
   C. phones D. allophones

7) Which branch of phonetics concerns the production of speech sounds?
   A. Acoustic phonetics. B. Articulatory phonetics.
   C. Auditory phonetics. D. Neither of them.

8) Which one is different from the others according to manners of articulation?
   A. [z] B. [w] C. [h] D. [v]

9) Which one is different from the others according to places of articulation?
   A. [n] B. [m] C. [b] D. [p]

10) Which vowel is different from the others according to the tongue position of vowels?
    A. [i] B. [u] C. [e] D. [ʌ]

11) What kind of sounds can we make when the vocal cords are vibrating?
    A. Voiceless. B. Voiced. C. Glottal stop. D. Consonant.

12) Which consonant represents the following description: voiceless labiodental fricative?
    A. [f] B. [t] C. [z] D. [s]

13) The _____ is the most flexible, and is responsible for more varieties of articulation than any other speech organ.
    A. lips B. nasal cavity C. tongue D. oral cavity

14) Liquids are classified in the light of _____.
    A. manner of articulation B. place of articulation
    C. place of tongue D. none of the above

15) In English, there is one glottal fricative. It is _____.
    A. [l] B. [h] C. [k] D. [f]

16) The phonetic symbol for "voiced bilabial glide" is _____.
    A. [v] B. [d] C. [f] D. [w]

17) The difference between [u] and [u:] is caused by _____.
   A. the openness of the mouth   B. the shape of the lips
   C. the length of the vowels   D. none of the above
18) What kind of tone is used when what is said is a straight-forward, matter-of-fact statement?
   A. The rising tone.   B. The falling tone.
   C. The fall-rise tone.   D. None of the above.
19) In a sentence, which of the following is usually not stressed?
   A. Nouns.   B. Demonstrative pronouns.
   C. Personal pronouns.   D. All of the above.
20) Which of the following is a typical tone language?
   A. English.   B. Chinese.
   C. French.   D. All of the above.
21) Two allophones of the same phoneme are said to be in _____.
   A. phonemic contrast   B. complimentary distribution
   C. minimal pair   D. None of the above
22) The sound [f] can be described as a _____.
   A. voiced labiodental fricative   B. voiceless labiodental affricate
   C. voiced alveolar fricative   D. None of the above
23) The sound [d] can be described as a _____.
   A. voiced labiodental fricative   B. voiceless labiodental affricate
   C. voiced alveolar plosive   D. None of the above
24) The sound [v] can be described as a _____.
   A. voiced labiodental fricative   B. voiceless labiodental affricate
   C. voiced alveolar fricative   D. None of the above
25) The sound [s] can be described as a _____.
   A. voiced bilabial stop   B. voiced alveolar fricative
   C. voiceless alveolar fricative   D. voiceless dental fricative

5. Answer the Following Questions

1) What are suprasegmental features? How do the major suprasegmental features of English function in conveying meaning?
2) Give the definitions of, with examples, the sequential rule, the assimilation rule, and the deletion rule.
3) Please use examples to explain the definitions of phones, phonemes and allophones.
4) What is free variation? Illustrate it with examples.
5) To what extent is phonology related to phonetics and how do they differ?
6) What are the contrastive and complementary distributions? Give examples.
7) Briefly explain what phonetics and phonology are concerned with and what kind of

relationships hold between the two.

8) How are consonants classified in terms of different criteria?

9) How are vowels classified in terms of different criteria?

Answers

1. Define the Following Terms

1) minimal pair

When two different phonetic forms are identical in every way except for one sound segment which occurs in the same place in the string, the two forms (i.e. words) are supposed to form a minimal pair, e.g. "pill" and "bill" are identical in form except for the initial.

2) sound assimilation

Speech sounds seldom occur in isolation. In connected speech, under the influence of their neighbours, some sounds are replaced by other sounds. Sometimes two neighbouring sounds influence each other and are replaced by a third sound, which is different from both the original sounds. This process is called sound assimilation.

3) suprasegmental feature

The distinctive (phonological) features which apply to groups larger than the single segment such as a syllable, a word, or a sentence, are known as suprasegmental features. The study of these features is known as prosody. The main suprasegmental features include stress, tone, juncture and intonation.

4) free variation

If two sounds occurring in the same environment do not contrast, i.e. the substitution of one for the other does not generate a new word but merely a different pronunciation of the same word, the two sounds are said to be in "free variation".

5) rounded vowel

One of the criteria used in the classification of vowels is the shape of the lips. If a vowel is pronounced with the lips rounded, then the vowel in question is a rounded vowel.

6) pitch

Pitch is a suprasegmental feature, whose domain of application is the syllable. Different rates of vibration produce what is known as different frequencies, and in auditory terms as different pitches. Pitch variations may be distinctive like phoneme, that is, when they may contribute to distinguish between different words. In this function, pitch variations are called tones.

7) vowel glide

When pure or monophthongs are pronounced, the quality remains constant throughout the articulation. In contrast, those where there is an audible change of quality are called vowel glides.

8) dentals

Consonants for which the flow of air is restricted by catching the tongue between the teeth. Dentals may be voiced or voiceless.

9) phonemes, phones and allophones

A phoneme is a phonological unit; it is a unit that is of distinctive value. A phone is a phonetic unit or segment. The speech sounds we hear and produce during linguistic communication are all phones. The different phones representing a phoneme in different phonetic environments are called its allophones.

10) complementary distribution *vs* contrastive distribution

If the phonetically similar sounds are two distinctive phonemes, e.g. /p/ and /b/ in "pit" and "bit", they are said to form a phonemic contrast, that is, the two sounds are in contrastive distribution. If they are allophones of the same phoneme, then they do not distinguish meaning, but complement each other in distribution, i.e. the clear [l] always occurs before a vowel while the dark [ɫ] always occurs between a vowel and a consonant or at the end of a word, so the allophones are said to be in complementary distribution.

11) distinctive features

A distinctive feature is a feature which distinguishes one phoneme from another. So distinctive features tell us how different phonemes are the same and how they differ from one another.

12) articulatory phonetics, acoustic phonetics and auditory phonetics

The study of the physical properties and of the transmission of speech sounds is called acoustic phonetics. The study of the way hearers perceive these sounds is called auditory phonetics. The study of how speech organs produce the sounds is called articulatory phonetics.

13) consonant

A consonant is a speech sound where the air from the lungs is either completely blocked, or partially blocked, or where the opening between the speech organs is so narrow that the air escapes with audible friction.

14) vowel

Vowels are a major type of speech sounds in terms of their articulatory characteristics. They are sound segments produced when the airstreams that come from the lungs meet with no obstruction of any kind in the throat, the nose, or the month, so no turbulence of a total stopping of the air can be perceived. Vowel sounds are differentiated by a number of factors: A. the position of the tongue, B. the openness of the mouth, C. the shape of the lips, and D. the length of the vowels. They are the nucleus of the syllable.

15) bilabials

Consonants for which the flow of air is stopped or restricted by the two lips. Bilabials may be voiced or voiceless. In present-day English, [p], [b], [m] and [w] as in *pat*, *bat*, *mail*, and *wave* are bilabials.

16) cardinal vowels

The idea of a system of "cardinal vowels" was first suggested by A. J. Ellis in 1844 and was taken up by A. M. Bell in his *Visible Speech*(1867). The most famous "cardinal vowels" system of all was put forward, by Daniel Jones in a number of writings from 1917 onwards, particularly in his *Outline of English Phonetics*(1962).

17) glottals

Sounds produced by bringing the vocal cords momentarily together to create the obstruction. The glottals in English include a glottal stop [?] and a glottal fricative [h].

18) diphthongs

In English, there are altogether eight diphthongs (also called complex vowels), which are produced by moving from one vowel position to another through intervening positions. The diphthongs can be further divided into two sub-groups: centering diphthongs (e.g. [iə], [ɛə], [uə]) and closing diphthongs (e.g. [ei], [ai], [ɔi], [əu] and [au]).

19) triphthongs

Triphthongs are those which are produced by moving from one vowel position to another and then rapidly and continuously to a third one. They include the following: [eiə], [aiə], [ɔiə], [əuə] and [auə].

20) lax vowels

Corresponding to the distinction of long and short vowels is the distinction of tense and lax vowels. All the long vowels are tense vowels but of the short vowels, [e] is a tense vowel as well, and the rest short vowels are lax vowels. When we pronounce a long vowel, the larynx is in a state of tension, and in the pronunciation of a short vowel (except [e]), the larynx is quite relaxed.

21) place of articulation

The place of articulation can be defined as the place in the mouth where the obstruction occurs. In terms of place of articulation, the English consonants can be classified into the following types: bilabials, labiodentals, dentals / interdentals, alveolars, post-alveolars, alveo-palatals, palatals velars, glottals, etc.

22) manner of articulation

Manner of articulation refers to the actual relationship between the articulators and thus the way in which the air passes through certain parts of the vocal tract. In terms of manner of articulation, the English consonants can be classified into the following types: stops, fricatives, affricates, liquids, glides, etc.

23) coarticulation

Coarticulation refers to the phenomenon of sounds continually show the influence of

their neighbours. For example, as in *lamb*, when "a" is followed by "m", the velum will begin to lower itself during the articulation of "a" so that it is ready for the following nasal. When such simultaneous or overlapping articulations are involved, we call the process coarticulation. If the sound becomes more like the following sound, it is known as anticipatory articulation. If the sound displays the influence of the preceding sound, it is preservative coarticulation.

24) IPA

The International Phonetic Alphabet was originally developed by British and French phoneticians under the auspices of the International Phonetic Association, established in Paris in 1886 (both the organization and the phonetic script are best known as IPA).

25) narrow transcription *vs* broad transcription

There are two ways to transcribe speech sounds. One is the "broad transcription", the transcription with letter-symbols only, and the other is "narrow transcription", the transcription with letter-symbols together with the diacritics which can help bring out the finer distinctions than the letters alone may possibly do. Broad Romic or transcription was intended to indicate only those sounds capable of distinguishing one word from another in a given language. So a broad transcription is phonemic while a narrow transcription is phonetic.

26) tone *vs* intonation

Tone refers to an identifiable movement or level of pitch that is used in a linguistically contrastive way. Tones are pitch variations caused by the differing rates of vibration of the vocal cords.

Intonation plays an important role in the conveyance of meaning in almost every language. English is an intonation language and, according to M. A. K. Halliday, has five basic types of tones: the falling tone (Tone 1), the rising tone (Tone 2), the level tone (Tone 3), the falling-rising tone (Tone 4) and the rising-falling tone (Tone 5). When spoken in different tones, the same sentence may have different meanings. Generally speaking, the falling pitch (Tone 1) conveys certainty; the rising pitch (Tone 2) indicates uncertainty; the level tone (Tone 3) means "not (yet) decided whether known or unknown"; the falling-rising tone (Tone 4) means "seems certain, but turns out not to be"; and the rising-falling tone (Tone 5) means "seems uncertain, but turns out to be certain".

27) stress

Stress refers to the degree of force used in producing a syllable.

28) palatals

Consonants made by bringing the back of the tongue to the hard palate. The palatals are [c], [ɟ], and [j].

29) alveolars

Consonants produced by bringing the tip of the tongue into contact with the upper teeth-ridge to create the obstruction. The alveolar sounds are [t], [d], [s], [z], [n], and [l].

 30) glides

 Glides are transition sounds, partly like consonants and partly like vowels. They are sometimes called semivowels.

 31) juncture

 Juncture is another suprasegmental feature which is frequently (but not necessarily) realized as a pause. It refers to the phonetic boundary features which may demarcate grammatical units such as morpheme, word or clause.

2. Word Completion:

 1) Articulatory   2) airstream
 3) voiced, voiceless, voiced   4) friction
 5) tongue   6) height
 7) obstruction   8) phonemes
 9) diphthongs   10) Coarticulation
 11) the maximal onset principle   12) acoustic, auditory, articulatory
 13) oral cavity, nasal cavity
 14) completely blocked, partially blocked, audible friction, vibration

3. True or False Questions

 1)—5) F T F T F   6)—10) F F F T F   11)—15) F F F F T
 16)—20) T T F F T   21)—25) T T F F T   26)—30) T T F T T
 31)—35) F T T T T   36)—40) F F T T F   41)—45) F F F T F
 46)—50) F T F T T

4. Multiple Choice

 1)—5) A C D A A   6)—10) D B B A B   11)—15) B A C A B
 16)—20) D C B C B   21)—25) B D C A C

5. Answer the Following Questions

 1) What are suprasegmental features? How do the major suprasegmental features of English function in conveying meaning?

 The distinctive features which have effect on more than one sound segment are called suprasegmental features. They may apply to a string of several sounds, such as a syllable, an entire word, or a sentence. The distinctive (phonological) features which apply to groups larger than the single segment such as a syllable, a word, or a sentence, are known as suprasegmental features. The study of these features is known as prosody. The main suprasegmental features include stress, tone, intonation and juncture.

2) Give the definitions of, with examples, the sequential rule, the assimilation rule, and the deletion rule.

Sequential rules state the possible combination of phonemes and the constraint over such a combination for a language. With this sort of linguistic knowledge which is stated in phonology as a phonological rule, a string of phonemes can be judged whether it is a word or a possible word for a language. For example, the native speaker of English can, without question, divide the following list into two groups: the group of English and the group of non-English words.

(a) creck   crick
(b) zbread   bread
(c) splash   zsplash
(d) block   blokc

An assimilation rule is a phonological rule that is to describe the effect of phonetic context or situation on a particular phone. The assimilation rule assimilates one segment to another by "copying" a feature of a sequential phoneme, thus making the two phones more similar. This rule accounts for the varying pronunciation of the nasal [n] that occurs within a word. The rule is that within a word the nasal consonant [n] assumes the same place of articulation as the following consonant. The negative prefix "in-" serves as a good example. It may be pronounced as [in], [iŋ] or [im] when occurring in different phonetic contexts, e.g. indiscrete [ˌindisˈkriːt] (alveolar), ink [iŋk] (velar), input [ˈimput] (bilabial).

(3) The deletion rule in phonology concerns the relation between letters and sounds within the phonetic condition. The deletion rule tells us when a sound is to be deleted although it is orthographically represented. While the letter "g" is mute in "sign", "design" and "paradigm", it is pronounced in their corresponding derivatives: "signature", "designation" and "paradigmatic". The rule then can be stated as: delete a [g] when it occurs before a final nasal consonant. This accounts for some of the seeming irregularities of the English spelling.

3) Please use examples to explain the definitions of phones, phonemes and allophones.

A phone is a phonetic unit or segment; the speech sounds we hear and produce during linguistic communication are all phones. When we hear the following words pronounced: [pit], [tip], [spit], etc., the similar phones we have heard are /p/ for one thing, and three different [p]'s, readily making possible the "narrow transcription or diacritics". Phones may and may not distinguish meaning. A phoneme is a phonological unit; it is a unit that is of distinctive value. As an abstract unit, a phoneme is not any particular sound, but rather it is represented or realized by a certain phone in a certain phonetic context. For example, the phoneme /p/ is represented differently in [pit], [tip] and [spit].

The phones representing a phoneme are called its allophones, i.e. the different members of a phoneme, sounds which are phonetically different but do not make one word so phonetically different as to create a new word or a new meaning thereof. So the different [p]'s in the above words are allophones of the same phoneme /p/. How a phoneme is represented by a phone, or which allophone is to be used, is determined by the phonetic context in which it occurs. But the choice of an allophone is not random. In most cases it is rule-governed; these rules are to be found out by a phonologist.

4) What is free variation? Illustrate it with examples.

If two sounds occurring in the same environment do not contrast, namely, if the substitution of one for the other does not generate a new word form but merely a different pronunciation of the same word, the two sounds then are said to be in free variation. The plosives, for example, may not be exploded when they occur before another plosive or a nasal. The minute distinctions may, if necessary, be transcribed in diacritics. These unexploded plosives are in free variation. Sounds in free variation should be assigned to the same phoneme.

5) To what extent is phonology related to phonetics and how do they differ?

Phonology is concerned with the linguistic patterning of sounds in human languages, with its primary aim being to discover the principles that govern the way sounds are organized in languages, and to explain the variations that occur. Phonetics is the study of all possible speech sounds while phonology studies the way in which speakers of a language systematically use a selection of these sounds in order to express meaning.

6) What are the contrastive and complementary distributions? Give examples.

Phonetically similar sounds might be related in two ways. If they are two distinctive phonemes, they are said to form a phonemic contrast, e.g. /p/ and /b/ in [pit] and [bit], [lip] and [lib]. /p/ and /b/ are then in contrastive distribution. When two sounds never occur in the same environment, they are in complementary distribution. For example, the aspirated English plosives never occur after [s], and the unsaturated ones never occur initially. Sounds in complementary distribution may be assigned to the same phoneme. The allophones of [l], for example, are also in complementary distribution. The clear [l] occurs only before a vowel, the voiceless equivalent of [l] occurs only after a voiceless consonant, such as in the words "please", "butler", "clear", etc., and the dark [ł] occurs only after a vowel or as a syllabic sound after a consonant, such as in the words "feel", "help", "middle", etc.

7) Briefly explain what phonetics and phonology are concerned with and what kind of relationships hold between the two.

Phonology is the study of sound systems—the invention of distinctive speech sounds that occur in a language and the patterns wherein they fall. Minimal pair, phonemes, allophones, free variation, complementary distribution, etc., are all to be investigated by a phonologist. Phonetics is the branch of linguistics studying the characteristics of speech sounds and provides methods for their description, classification and transcription. A phonetist is mainly interested in the physical properties of the speech sounds, whereas a phonologist studies what he believes are meaningful sounds related with their semantic, morphological features, and the way they are conceived and printed in the depth of the mind. Phonological knowledge permits a speaker to produce sounds, which form meaningful utterances, to recognize a foreign "accent", to make up new words, to add the appropriate phonetic segment, to form plurals and past tense and to know what is and what is not a sound in one's language.

8) How are consonants classified in terms of different criteria?

The consonants in English can be described in terms of four dimensions (or four criteria):

A. The position of the soft palate;
B. The presence or the absence of vocal-cord vibration;
C. The place of articulation;
D. The manner of articulation.

9) How are vowels classified in terms of different criteria?

Vowel sounds are differentiated by a number of factors:

A. the state of the velum;
B. the position of the tongue;
C. the openness of the mouth;
D. the shape of the lips;
E. the length of the vowels;
F. the tension of the muscles at pharynx.

Chapter 5 Morphology

1. Define the Following Terms

1) morpheme, allomorph and morph
2) free morpheme *vs* bound morpheme
3) affix
4) acronymy
5) abbreviation *vs* clipping
6) IC Analysis
7) stem, base and root
8) inflection
9) compounding
10) conversion
11) inflectional morpheme
12) morphology
13) backformation
14) blending
15) inflectional affix *vs* derivational affix

2. Multiple Choice

Directions: In each question there are four choices. Decide which one would be the best answer to the question or to complete the sentence best.

1) The word "hospitalize" is an example of _____.
   A. compound   B. derivation   C. inflection   D. blending
2) _____ refers to the study of the internal structure of words, and the rules by which words are formed.
   A. Morphology   B. Syntax   C. Semantics   D. Phonology
3) _____ doesn't belong to the most productive means of word-formation.
   A. Affixation   B. Compounding   C. Conversion   D. Blending
4) Nouns, verbs and adjectives can be classified as _____.
   A. lexical words   B. grammatical words
   C. function words   D. form words
5) Morphemes that represent tense, number, gender and case are called _____ morphemes.
   A. inflectional B. free   C. bound   D. derivational
6) There are _____ morphemes in the word *denationalization*.
   A. three   B. four   C. five   D. six

7) In English -ise and -tion are called _____.
   A. prefixes   B. suffixes   C. infixes   D. free morphemes
8) Morphology is generally divided into two fields: the study of word-formation and _____.
   A. affixation   B. etymology   C. inflection   D. root
9) The three subtypes of affixes are: prefix, suffix and _____.
   A. derivational affix   B. inflectional affix
   C. infix   D. backformation
10) _____ is a way in which new words may be formed from already existing words by subtracting an affix which is thought to be part of the word.
   A. Affixation   B. Backformation
   C. Insertion   D. Addition
11) The word *TB* is formed in the way of _____.
   A. acronymy   B. clipping   C. initialism   D. blending
12) There are different types of affixes or morphemes. The affix -ed in the word *learned* is known as a(n) _____.
   A. derivational morpheme   B. free morpheme
   C. inflectional morpheme   D. free form
13) The words like *comsat* and *sitcom* are formed by _____.
   A. blending   B. clipping   C. backformation   D. acronymy
14) The stem of *disagreements* is _____.
   A. agreement   B. agree   C. disagree   D. disagreement
15) All of the following are meaningful except _____.
   A. lexeme   B. phoneme   C. morpheme   D. allomorph
16) The word *boyish* contains two _____.
   A. phonemes   B. morphs   C. morphemes   D. allomorphs
17) Inflectional _____ studies inflections.
   A. phonetics   B. syntax   C. phonology   D. morphology
18) _____ morphemes are those that cannot be used independently but have to be combined with other morphemes, either free or bound, to form a word.
   A. Free   B. Bound   C. Root   D. Affixational
19) _____ modify the meaning of the stem, but usually do not change the part of speech of the original word.
   A. Prefixes   B. Suffixes   C. Roots   D. Affixes
20) There are rules that govern which affix can be added to what type of _____ to form a new word.
   A. root   B. affix   C. stem   D. word
21) Compound words consist of _____ morphemes.
   A. bound   B. free

C. both bound and free D. none of the above

22) *Radar* is a(n) _____.
A. acronym   B. blending   C. coinage   D. clipping

23) The words *take* and *table* are called _____ because they can occur unattached.
A. form words B. bound morphemes
C. free morphemes D. inflectional morphemes

24) A(n) _____ is any morpheme or combination of morphemes to which an inflectional affix can be added.
A. stem   B. root   C. allomorph   D. lexeme

25) _____ is made up from the first letters of the name of an organization, which has a heavily modified headword.
A. Blending   B. Acronymy   C. Abbreviation   D. Invention

26) The expansion of vocabulary in modern English depends chiefly on _____.
A. borrowing
B. word-formation
C. conversion
D. the number of the people speaking English

27) _____ is a grammatical category used for the analysis of word classes displaying such contrasts as masculine/feminine, animate/inanimate, etc.
A. Case   B. Gender   C. Number   D. Category

28) The relation between words *rose* and *flower* is that of _____.
A. synonymy   B. antonymy   C. homonymy   D. hyponymy

29) The adjective word *uniform* has _____ morphemes.
A. one   B. three   C. two   D. zero

30) Affixation is generally defined as the formation of words by adding word-forming or _____ to stems.
A. affixes B. suffixes
C. inflectional affixes D. derivational affixes

31) Prefixes do not generally change the _____ of the stem but only modify its meaning.
A. word-class   B. meaning   C. form   D. structure

32) The primary function of suffixes is to _____.
A. change the word-class of roots
B. change the meaning of stems
C. change the grammatical function of stems
D. change the structure of roots

33) Conversion is a method _____.
A. of turning words of one part of speech to those of a different part of speech

B. of converting words of one meaning into different meaning
C. of deriving words through grammatical means
D. of changing words in morphological structure

3. Word Completion

Directions: Fill in the blanks with the most suitable words.

1) Combining two parts of two already existing words is called _____ in word-formation.
2) *Take* is the _____ of *taking*, *taken* and *took*.
3) Bound morphemes are classified into two types: _____ and _____.
4) An _____ is pronounced letter by letter, while an _____ is pronounced as a word.
5) Lexicon, in most cases, is synonymous with _____.
6) Orthographically, compounds are written in three ways: _____, _____ and _____.
7) All words may be said to contain a root _____.
8) _____ is a reverse process of derivation, and therefore is a process of shortening.
9) _____ is extremely productive, because English had lost most of its inflectional endings by the end of Middle English period, which facilitated the use of words interchangeably as verbs or nouns, verbs or adjectives, and vice versa.
10) Words are divided into simple, compound and derived words on the _____ level.
11) A word formed by derivation is called a _____, and a word formed by compounding is called a _____.
12) *The poor* is an example of _____ conversion.
13) _____ is the smallest meaningful unit of language.
14) The affix *-es* conveys a _____ meaning.
15) _____ morphemes are independent units of meaning and can be used freely all by themselves.
16) _____ affixes manifest various grammatical relations or grammatical categories such as number, degree, and case.
17) The affixes occurring at the beginning of a word are called _____.
18) The combination of two or sometimes more than two words to create new words in called _____.
19) Semantically, the meaning of a _____ is often idiomatic, not always being the sum total of the meanings of its components.
20) _____ morphology studies word-formation.
21) _____ can never stand by itself although it bears clear, definite meaning.

22) _____ are added to the end of stems.

4. True or False Questions

Directions: Decide whether the following statements are true or false. Write "T" for true and "F" for false in the bracket before each of them.

1) (   ) Morphology studies the internal structure of words and the rules by which words are formed.
2) (   ) Inflectional morphology is one of the two sub-branches of morphology.
3) (   ) The structure of words is not governed by rules.
4) (   ) A morpheme is the basic unit in the study of morphology.
5) (   ) Free morphemes are the same as bound morphemes.
6) (   ) Sometimes bound morphemes can be used by themselves.
7) (   ) There is only one type of affixes in the English language.
8) (   ) Derivational affixes are added to an existing form to create a word.
9) (   ) Compounding is the addition of affixes to stems to form new words.
10) (   ) Phonetically, the stress of a compound always falls on the first element, while the second element receives secondary stress.
11) (   ) Morphemes are regarded as abstract constructs in the system.
12) (   ) We can always tell what it means by the words a compound contains because the meaning of a compound is always the sum of the meanings of its parts.
13) (   ) All roots are free and all affixes are bound.
14) (   ) Chinese language is heavily inflectional.
15) (   ) A morpheme is a minimal unit of meaning, which means that a morpheme has a lexical meaning.
16) (   ) *Fore* as in *foretell* is both a prefix and a bound morpheme.
17) (   ) Base refers to the part of word that remains when all inflectional affixes are removed.
18) (   ) In most cases, prefixes change the meaning of the base whereas suffixes change the word-class of the base.
19) (   ) Conversion from noun to verb is the most productive process of conversion.
20) (   ) Reduplicative compound is formed by repeating the same morpheme of a word.
21) (   ) The words *whimper*, *whisper* and *whistle* are formed in the way of onomatopoeia.
22) (   ) In most cases, the number of syllables of a word corresponds to the number of morphemes.
23) (   ) Backformation is a productive way of forming nouns in Modern English.

24) (   ) Inflection is a particular way of word-formations.

5. Tell the Root, Stem and Base of the Following Words

1) desirable   2) undesirable
3) undesirables   4) desired

6. Answer the Following Questions

1) What does morphology study?
2) What is a morpheme? Dissect the following words into morphemes:
   description   underdeveloped   photosynthetic
   anatomy   radiation   geography
   philharmonic   defrosted   refreshment
   demobilized   conducting   suppression
   circumspect   dialogue   deformed
   combination
3) Describe with examples various types of morpheme used in English.
4) What are the main inflectional affixes in English? What grammatical meaning do they convey?
5) Try to find out the meaning of the following roots in English and give two or three words that contain each of them:
   hydro   chron   demo   dur
   agr   kilo   nym   ped
   rupt   gress   poly   syn
6) State the morphological rules that govern the use of the given derivational affixes.
   Example: -er   The suffix -er is added to a verb to form a noun indicating the agent that carries out the action, e.g. write→writer
   -ant   -ment   sub-   -en
   en-   -ee   -ful   -some
   -wise   un-
7) What are the main features of the English compounds?
8) Explain the formation and meaning of the following compounds:
   Example: nightcap   Nightcap is a noun formed by combining two nouns, meaning a drink one takes before going to bed.
   tablecloth   green-eyed   green horn   update
   jet lag   bootleg   built-in   cockpit
   good-for-nothing

Answers

1. Define the Following Terms

1) morpheme, allomorph and morph

Morpheme is the smallest unit in terms of relationship between expressions and content, unit cannot be divided without destroying or drastically altering the meaning, whether it is lexical or grammatical. A morpheme is the minimal unit of meaning. It is not like the sound patterns or syllables, which can be further divided into segments. Words may consist of one morpheme or more than one morpheme.

Allomorph is any of the variant forms of a morpheme as conditioned by position or adjoining sounds. Allomorphs are the realizations of a particular morpheme. Morphemes are more abstract than their allomorphs.

Morphs are the realizations of morphemes in general and are the actual forms used to realize morphemes.

2) free morpheme vs bound morpheme

Morphemes can be classified into two types in terms of their capacity of occurring alone. Those which may occur alone, or which may constitute words by themselves, are free morphemes, such as *bee*, *tree*, *sing*, and *dance*. In contrast, those which may appear with at least one other morpheme and cannot stand by themselves are called bound morphemes, such as *-s* in *dogs*, *-al* in *national*, *dis-* in *disclose*, and so on.

3) affix

Affixes are morphemes that lexically depend on roots and do not convey the fundamental meaning of words. For example, the morpheme *-ful* in *careful* and *-less* in *careless* are two affixes. And the first part in each of the words *irregular*, *disappear* and *enrich* (i.e. *ir*, *dis* and *en*) is an affix. Affixes are a type of bound morphemes. They are limited in number in a language, and can be further classified in terms of either of the two criteria: position and function. Along the dimension of their position with reference to the root or stem of the word, affixes are generally classified into three types: prefixes, suffixes and infixes. Those which are added to the beginning of roots (i.e. occur before roots) are called prefixes, e.g. *dis-* in *dislike* and *re-* in *rebuild*. The affixes which follow roots (i.e. appear after roots) are called suffixes, e.g. *-ness* in *carelessness* and *-ful* in *careful*. The affixes which interrupt roots (i.e. appear within roots) are called infixes.

4) acronymy

Acronymy is the process of forming new words by joining the initial letters of several words together. Words created in this way are of two sorts: acronyms and initialisms. Acronyms are those which are pronounced as a single word rather than as a sequence of

letters. Initials are those which are pronounced as a series of letters (i. e. pronounced letter by letter).

5) abbreviation *vs* clipping

Abbreviation is sometimes used in the sense of acronymy. For example, the words like *USA*, *NATO*, *AIDS*, etc. are the results of the word formation of abbreviation. And sometimes, abbreviation equals to clipping. For instance, the words like *Prof.* (from *Professor*), *telly* (from *television*), etc. are considered as examples of abbreviation as well.

Clipping refers to the process of word-formation in which a word (usually a noun) is shortened by deleting one or more syllables without any change in the meaning or in the part of speech. However, clipping usually results in a stylistic change: from formal to informal style.

6) IC Analysis

Immediate Constituent Analysis (IC Analysis for short) is a method used to analyze the hierarchical order of morphemes. By IC Analysis, we mean that we divide the morphemes of a word (or the words of a sentence) into two groups, and then divide each of them into sub-groups, and so on, until we reach the irreducible constituents, i. e. the morphemes in the case of the analysis of a word, or the words in the case of the analysis of a sentence.

7) stem, base and root

A root is the basic part of a word that cannot be further analyzed without total loss of identity. In other words, a root is that part of the word left when all the affixes are removed. *Internationalism* is a four-morpheme derivative which keeps its free morphemes *nation* as its root when *inter-*, *-al* and *-ism* are taken away.

Different from the term root, both of the terms base and stem are used to talk about such a form to which an affix will be attached. If we are going to attach an derivational affix, we will call the form a base. But if we are going to attach an inflectional affix, we call the form a stem.

However, we have to see that the term base is a more general term. It can be a form that is a root and it can be a form that contains some affixes already. Just take *agree* and *disagree* for example. Either of them can be a base if we are going to attach a derivational affix *-ment* to it. Similarly, the term stem is also more covering. It can be a form that is a root or it can be a form that contains some affixes already. For example, either *open* or *reopen* can be a stem if we are going to attach an inflectional morpheme *-ed* to it. In fact, a stem can be any morpheme or combination of morphemes to which an inflectional affix can be added. It may be the same as, and in other cases, different from, a root. For example, in the word *friends*, *friend* is both the root and the stem, but in the word *friendships*, *friendship* is its stem, while *friend* is its root. Some words like compounds have more than one root, e.g. *mailman*, *girlfriend*, etc.

8) inflection

Inflection is the manifestation of grammatical relationships through the addition of inflectional affixes, such as number, person, finiteness, aspect and case, which do not change the grammatical class of the stems to which they are attached.

9) compounding

Compounding refers to a process of word-formation, in which two or more free morphemes are combined to form a new word, such as *forget-me-not*, *waterbed*, *sleepwalk*, etc. Words formed in this way are called compound words or compounds. Like derivation, compounding is also a very productive way to produce new words. There are three types of compounds: hyphenated compounds, solid compounds and open compounds.

10) conversion

Conversion is a term used in the study of word formation to refer to the derivational process whereby an item comes to belong to a new word class without the addition of an affixes. The conversion process is particularly productive in modern English, with new uses occurring frequently. Conversion is also known as functional shift or zero-derivation.

11) inflectional morpheme

Inflectional morphemes are also called inflectional affixes. They manifest various grammatical relations or grammatical categories such as number, tense, degree, and case. In English, all inflectional morphemes are suffixes, e.g. -(e)s (indicating plurality of nouns or third person singular present tense), -ing (indicating progressive aspect), -(e)d (indicating past tense for all three persons), -est (indicating superlative degree of adjectives and adverbs).

12) morphology

Morphology is the branch of grammar that studies the internal structure of words, and of the rules by which words are formed. Morphology is generally divided into two fields: the study of inflections (also called inflectional morphology), and of word-formation (often referred to as lexical or derivational morphology).

13) backformation

Backformation refers to an abnormal type of word-formation where a shorter word is derived by deleting an imagined affix from a longer form already in the language. Take *televise* for example, the word *television* predated the occurrence of the word *televise*. The first part of the word *television* was pulled out and analyzed as a root, even though no such root occurs elsewhere in the English language. Instead of taking out part of a word as a root, backformation allows us to take a word of a given category and form a new homophonous word of a different category.

14) blending

Blending is a relatively complex form of word compounding, in which two words are blended by joining the initial part of the first word and the final part of the second word, or by joining the initial parts of the two words. For example: transfer + resister→ transistor, smoke + fog→smog, boat + hotel→boatel.

15) inflectional affix *vs* derivational affix

If we classify affixes with reference to their function, we have the following two types: inflectional affixes and derivational affixes.

In all languages, there are many derivational affixes, but only a small number of inflectional affixes. Inflectional affixes serve to indicate grammatical relations, such as number, gender, tense, aspect, case and degree. For example, -s in *books*, -e in *fiancée*, -ed in (*he*) *studied*, -ing in (*he is*) *working*, -'s in *Gloria's*, and -er in *faster* are all inflectional affixes.

Inflectional affixes have different grammatical functions. However, when they are conjoined with other morphemes, they never produce new words. Nor do they cause any change in grammatical class. And, usually, no two inflectional affixes can coexist in the same word at the same time with the exception of the combination of plural number marker and possessive case marker (e.g. students' reading room, teachers' job). In contrast, derivational affixes can create new words. Derivational affixes often, but not always, change the grammatical classes of words.

2. Multiple Choice

1)—5) B A D A A　　6)—10) C B C B B　　11)—15) C C A D B
16)—20) C D B A C　　21)—25) B A C A B　　26)—30) B B D C D
31)—33) A C A

3. Word Completion

1) blending　　　　　　2) lexeme　　　　　　3) bound roots, affixes
4) initialism, acronym　　5) vocabulary　　　　6) solid, hyphenated, open
7) morpheme　　　　　8) Backformation　　　9) Conversion
10) morphemic　　　　11) derivative, compound
12) partial　　　　　　13) Morpheme　　　　14) grammatical
15) Free　　　　　　　16) Inflectional　　　　17) prefixes
18) compounding　　　19) compound　　　　20) Derivational
21) Root　　　　　　　22) Suffixes

4. True or False Question

1)—5) T T F T F　　6)—10) F F T F F　　11)—15) F F F T F
16)—20) T F T T F　　21)—24) T F F F

5. Tell the Root, Stem and Base of the Following Words

1) Desirable: desire is the root or base; but there is no stem for it.

2) Undesirable: desire is the root; desirable is the base; there is no stem for it.
3) Undesirables: desire is the root; undesirable is the stem or base.
4) Desired: desire is the root, stem or base.

6. Answer the Following Questions

1) What does morphology study?
   The internal structure of words and the rules that govern their formation.
2) What is a morpheme? Dissect the following words into morphemes:
   The smallest unit of meaning.

   de-scrip-tion   under-develop-ed   photo-synthe-tic
   ana-tomy   radia-tion   geo-graph-y
   phil-harmon-ic   de-frost-ed   re-fresh-ment
   de-mobil-iz-ed   con-duct-ing   sup-press-ion
   circum-spect   dia-logue   de-form-ed
   com-bina-tion

3) Describe with examples various types of morphemes used in English.
   Free morphemes: mate, sun, fame, like
   Bound morphemes: bound roots and affixes
   Roots: ter-, fin-, spect-, -cide, -wise
   Affixes: inflectional and derivational
   Inflectional affixes: -ing, -ed, -(e)s
   Derivational: prefix and suffix
   Prefixes: un-, dis-, de-, en-
   Suffixes: -ly, -less, -tion, -ize

4) What are the main inflectional affixes in English? What grammatical meaning do they convey?
   (-e)s: plural number
   (-e)s: third person singular present tense
   (-e)d: past tense
   -ing: progressive aspect
   -er: comparative degree
   -est: superlative degree
   -'s: possessive case

5) Try to find out the meaning of the following roots in English and give two or three words that contain each of them:
   hydro (water), e.g. hydraulic, dehydrate
   chro (time), e.g. chronological, chronicle
   demo (people), e.g. democracy, demography
   dur (lasting), e.g. during, durable

agr (farming), e.g. agriculture, agrarian
kilo (one thousand), e.g. kilometer, kilogram
nym (name), e.g. pseudonym, antonym
ped (foot), e.g. centipede, impede
rupt (breaking), e.g. rupture, abrupt
gress (movement), e.g. progress, digress
poly (various), e.g. polygon, polyglot
syn (identical), e.g. synchronic, synonym

6) -ant: suffix added to a verb to form a noun indicating the agent, e.g. assistant

-ment: suffix added to a verb to form its corresponding noun, e.g. development

sub-: prefix added to an adjective to form another adjective to indicate a lesser degree, e.g. substandard

-en: suffix added to an adjective to form a verb to indicate the acquisition of the quality denoted by the adjective, e.g. darken

en-: prefix added to an adjective to form a verb to indicate the acquisition of the quality denoted by the adjective, e.g. enrich

-ee: suffix added to a verb to form a noun indicating the recipient of the action denoted by the verb, e.g. employee

-ful: suffix added to a noun to form an adjective indicating the quality denoted by the noun, e.g. plentiful

-some: suffix added to a noun to form an adjective indicating the quality denoted by the noun, e.g. quarrelsome

-wise: suffix added to a noun to form an adverb meaning "with regard to the area indicating by the noun", e.g. careerwise

un-: prefix added to an adjective to indicate the absence of the quality indicated by the adjective, e.g. unemployed

7) Orthographically a compound can be written as one word, two separate words with or without a hyphen in between.

Syntactically, the part of speech of a compound is determined by the last element.

Semantically, the meaning of a compound is idiomatic, not calculable from the meanings of all its components.

Phonetically, the word stress of a compound usually falls on the first element.

8) tablecloth: A noun formed by combining two nouns, meaning a piece of cloth spread on a table to cover it.

green-eyed: An adjective formed by combining an adjective and an *-ed* form, meaning jealous.

green horn: A noun formed by combining an adjective and a noun, meaning a person not experienced for a job or occupation.

update: A verb formed by combining an adverb and a verb, meaning to bring something up to date.

jet lag: A noun formed by combining two nouns, meaning the feeling of fatigue caused by traveling in a jet plane crossing different time zones.

bootleg: A verb (also noun) formed by combining two nouns, meaning "to make, carry, or sell illicit goods".

built-in: An adjective formed by combining a past participle with a preposition, meaning "made as an integral part".

cockpit: A noun formed by joining two nouns, meaning the compartment in an aircraft where the pilot or the crew sit.

good-for-nothing: An adjective formed by joining an adjective, a preposition, and a pronoun, meaning irresponsible or worthless.

Chapter 6 Syntax

1. Define the Following Terms

1) syntax
2) hierarchical structure
3) grammatical relation
4) phrase structure rule
5) phrase markers
6) surface structure *vs* deep structure
7) constituency *vs* dependency
8) IC Analysis *vs* labeled IC Analysis
9) transformation rule
10) structural ambiguity
11) immediate constituent
12) syntagmatic relation *vs* paradigmatic relation
13) Transformational-Generative Grammar
14) theme *vs* rheme

2. Word Completion

Directions: Fill in the blanks with the most suitable words.

1) A _____ is a structurally independent unit that usually comprises a number of words to form a complete statement, question or command.

2) Syntactic movement is dictated by rules traditionally called _____ rules, whose operation may change the syntactic representation of a sentence.

3) Phrase structure rules can generate an infinite number of sentences and sentences with infinite length, due to their _____ properties.

4) The level of syntactic representation that exists before movement takes place is commonly termed _____ structure.

5) _____ construction refers to two or more words, phrases or clauses having equivalent syntactic status.

6) IC Analysis emphasizes the _____ structure of a sentence, seeing it as consisting

of word groups first.

7) _____ studies the sentence structure of language.

8) The system of internalized linguistic knowledge of a language speaker is known as linguistic _____.

9) Some transformational rules are obligatory and many are optional. The _____ T-rules have to be applied if we want to obtain well-formed sentences.

10) Technically speaking, a formalized T-rule consists of two parts: the structural _____ and the structural _____.

11) The _____ relations of a sentence concern the way each noun phrase in the sentence relates to the verb.

12) _____ structure rules allow us to better understand how words and phrases form sentences, and so on.

13) Phrase structure rules, with the insertion of the _____, generate sentences at the level of D-structure.

14) Transformational rules are used to _____ a sentence from the level of D-structure to that of S-structure.

15) According to the theory of Predication analysis, a proposition consists of two parts: _____ and _____.

16) Sentences can be studied in two ways: _____, we make structural descriptions of sentences to illustrate the parts of sentences and the relationships among them; _____, we examine the process by which sentences are generated by syntactic rules.

17) _____ is a science that is concerned with how words are combined to form phrases and how phrases are combined by rules to form sentences.

18) The _____ relation refers to the linear ordering of the words and the phrases within a sentence.

19) The _____ relation is a kind of relation between linguistic forms in a sentence and linguistic forms outside the sentence.

20) The linguistic forms that have _____ relations belong to the same _____.

21) The syntactic categories can be further divided into two groups: _____ category, such as noun and verb; _____ category, such as sentence, noun phrase and verb phrase.

22) The _____ relation shows us the inner layering of sentences.

23) In a hierarchical structure diagram of a sentence, there are three distinct levels or hierarchies: _____ which is the highest; _____ which is the lowest; _____ which is in between.

24) In a hierarchical structure diagram of a sentence, the forms at the word-level are _____ of the sentence; the forms at the word-level and the phrase-level are the _____ of the sentence; the constituents connected by the two lines that are

branching from the same point are called the _____ of the form above that point.

25) The same phrase or sentence may have two or more interpretations depending on the hierarchical arrangement of its constituents. Such a case is called _____.

26) Each branching point in a phrase marker is called a _____.

27) TG Grammar claims that the static study of sentences is only concerned with one level of structure, i. e. _____ structure, but the dynamic study of sentences deals with two levels of structure: both _____ structure and _____ structure.

28) TG Grammar has assumed that to generate sentences, we start with _____ structures and then transform them into _____ structures.

29) Deep structures are generated by _____ rules, and surface structures are derived from their deep structures by _____ rules.

30) A surface structure corresponds most closely to the _____ of words as they are pronounced.

31) A deep structure corresponds most closely to the _____ of words.

32) A surface structure is relatively concrete and gives the _____ of a sentence as it is used in communication.

33) A deep structure is abstract and gives the _____ of a sentence.

34) The constituent which is always present on the right side of the arrow in a PS rule is called a(n) _____ constituent.

35) In the deep structure, verbs always take the _____ form. That is to say, at the level of deep structure, the inflectional endings do not occur together with the verbs. They are separated from the verbs and are part of an _____ phrase.

36) The verbs in verb phrases are called _____ verbs; the other verbs are _____ verbs.

37) In TG Grammar, an auxiliary phrase consists of four components: _____, _____ verbs, the _____ aspect and the _____ aspect.

38) To generate the deep structure of an English sentence, we always start with the rule: _____.

3. Multiple Choice

Directions: In each question there are four choices. Decide which one would be the best answer to the question or to complete the sentence best.

1) Constituent sentences is the term used in _____.
   A. structural linguistics   B. functional analysis
   C. TG Grammar   D. traditional grammar

2) "When did you stop taking this medicine?" is an example of _____ in sense relationships.

A. entailment   B. presupposition   C. assumption   D. implicature

3) _____ refers to the relations holding between elements replaceable with each other at particular place in structure, or between one element present and the others absent.

A. Syntagmatic relation   B. Paradigmatic relation
C. Co-occurrence relation   D. Hierarchical relation

4) According to Standard Theory of Chomsky, _____ contain all the information necessary for the semantic interpretation of sentences.

A. deep structures   B. surface structures
C. transformational rules   D. PS-rules

5) In English, theme and rheme are often expressed by _____ and _____.

A. subject, object   B. subject, predicate
C. predicate, object   D. object, predicate

4. True or False Questions

Directions: Decide whether the following statements are true or false. Write "T" for true and "F" for false in the bracket before each of them.

1) (   ) "John participated in spreading rumors" entails "John engaged in spreading rumors".

2) (   ) I think their behavior was strange. This sentence presupposes that their behavior was strange.

3) (   ) Transformational-Generative linguists concentrate on finding elements and constructions that are available to all languages, whether or not they are employed.

4) (   ) The reason for giving theoretical recognition to the notion of constituent structure is that it helps to account for the ambiguity of certain constructions.

5) (   ) D-structure is the same as S-structure.

6) (   ) Grammatical sentences are formed following a set of syntactic rules.

7) (   ) Syntax consists of a set of abstract rules that allow words to be combined with other words to form grammatical sentences.

8) (   ) Some languages have ways of referring to some entity, some languages don't.

9) (   ) A simple sentence consists of a single clause which contains a subject and a predicate and stands alone as its own sentence.

10) (   ) One of the clauses in a coordinate sentence is subordinate to the other.

11) (   ) Language is only linearly structured.

12) (   ) Constituents that can be substituted for one another with loss of grammaticality belong to the same syntactic category.

13) (   ) Major lexical categories are open categories.

14) (   ) In English and many other languages, the subject usually follows the verb and the direct object usually precedes the verb.
15) (   ) Phrase structure rules are rewrite rules.
16) (   ) Phrase structure rules provide explanations on how syntactic categories are formed and sentences generated.
17) (   ) There is only one major type of syntactic movement, i. e. NP-movement.
18) (   ) WH movement is obligatory in English which changes a sentence from affirmative to interrogative.
19) (   ) Application of the transformational roles yields deep structure.
20) (   ) An endocentric construction is also known as a headed construction, it has just one head.
21) (   ) Move-a rule itself can rule out ungrammatical forms and result in grammatical strings.
22) (   ) Number and gender are categories of noun and pronoun.
23) (   ) Words in a paradigmatic relation are comparable in terms of syntax; they have the same syntactic features, so they are replaceable with each other semantically.
24) (   ) The relationship between an embedded clause and its matrix clause is one of a part to a whole.
25) (   ) A constituent which is not at the same time a construction is a morpheme, and a construction which is not at the same time a constituent is a sentence.
26) (   ) IC Analysis can be used to analyze all kinds of ambiguous structures.
27) (   ) Transformational rules do not change the basic meaning of sentences.
28) (   ) A sentence contains a point of departure and a goal of discourse. The goal of discourse presents the very information that is to be parted to the hearer. This is called the theme.
29) (   ) Syntactic category refers to all phrasal syntactic categories such as NP, VP, and PP, and word-level syntactic categories that serve as heads of phrasal syntactic categories such as N and V.
30) (   ) S-structure is a level of syntactic representation after the operation of necessary syntactic movement.

5. Answer the Following questions

1) What is the nature of Transformational-Generative Grammar? What are its main aspects? (about 200 words)
2) Explain and comment on the following pair of sentences:
   a. John is easy to please.

b. John is eager to please.

3) Examine each of the following sentences and indicate if it is a simple, coordinate, or complex sentence:
   A. Jane did it because she was asked to.
   B. The soldiers were warned to remain hidden and not to expose themselves.
   C. David was never there, but his brother was.
   D. She leads a tranquil life in the country.
   E. Unless I hear from her, I won't leave this town.

4) Use appropriate phrase structure rules to draw a phrase marker for the following sentence:
   A clever magician fooled the audience.

5) For each of the following two sentences, draw a tree diagram of its underlying structure that reveals the difference in the relationship between, *John*, *Mary* and the verb *see*:
   A. Mary advised John to see the dentist.
   B. Mary promised John to see the dentist.

6) The formation of many sentences involves the operation of syntactic movement. The following sentences are believed to have derived from their D-structure representations. Show the D-structure for each of these sentences:
   A. The leader of the majority party was severely criticized by the media.
   B. The man threw the rake away in the yard.
   C. Will the new shop owner hire her?
   D. What can the robot do for us?

7) Draw on your linguistic knowledge of English and paraphrase each of the following sentences in two different ways to show how syntactic rules account for the ambiguity of sentences:
   A. Smoking cigarettes can be nauseating.
   B. Tony is a dirty street fighter.
   C. After a two-day debate, they finally decided on the helicopter.
   D. The man is too heavy to move.
   E. The little girl saw the big man with the telescope.

Answers

1. Define the Following Terms

1) syntax

Syntax is a subfield of linguistics that studies the rules governing the way words are combined to form sentences in a language, or the study of the formation of sentences.

2) hierarchical structure

Hierarchical structure refers to the sentence structure that groups words into structural constituents and shows the syntactic category of each structural constituent, such as NP and VP.

3) grammatical relation

Grammatical relation refers to the structural and logical functional relations between every noun phrase and the verb in a sentence.

4) phrase structure rule

Phrase structure rule is a rewrite rule that allows for the possible combinations of words to form phrases and sentences.

5) phrase markers

The labeled IC Analysis does reveal the structural differences between the sentences. But such a method is too redundant and troublesome. And consequently, people give it further modification by removing all the linguistic forms at sentence level and those at phrase level. This new method used to analyze sentence structures can be defined as phrase markers. From the phrase markers, we can see that a phrase may sometimes be a single word. In this case, it must be labeled first as a phrase category, and then as a lexical category, because sentences are not directly made up of words, but of phrases, which, in turn, are composed of words.

6) surface structure *vs* deep structure

Surface structure is a level of syntactic representation after the operation of necessary syntactic movement. The surface structure is the final stage in the syntactic derivation of a construction, which closely corresponds to the structural organization of a construction people actually produce and receive. The deep structure is the abstract representation of the syntactic properties of a construction, i.e. the underlying level of structural relations between its different constituents.

7) constituency *vs* dependency

Sentences can be studied and analyzed in different ways. The type of syntactic analysis using the idea of constituency is called constituency analysis. According to the idea, a sentence can be analyzed into a series of constituents, such as subject + predicate, or NP + VP, etc. These units thus produced can, in turn, be analyzed into further constituents. And this constituent analysis process can be continued until no further subdivisions are possible. Constituent structure analysis is a hierarchical analysis showing the different constituents at different structural levels based on the distribution of linguistic forms.

Another type of syntactic analysis uses the concept of dependency. It is based on the function of linguistic forms. Dependency grammar is a type of formal grammar, which establishes types of dependencies between the elements of a construction as a means of explaining grammatical relationships. The main concern of dependency grammar is the description of dependency structures of sentences, that is, the structure of dependency relations between the elements of a sentence. It is assumed that in a syntactic connection between two elements one is the governing and the other the dependent element. When a governing element is dependent on another governing element, a complex hierarchical dependency order results.

8) IC Analysis *vs* labeled IC Analysis

The immediate constituent analysis may be defined as: the analysis of a sentence in terms of its immediate constituents—word groups (or phrases), which are in turn analyzed into the immediate constituents of their own, and the process goes on until the ultimate constituents are reached. In practice, however, for the sake of convenience, we usually stop at the level of word. The immediate constituent analysis of a sentence may be carried out with brackets or with a tree diagram. The criterion for the immediate constituent analysis is substitutability: whether a sequence of words can be substituted for a single word and the structure remains the same. Through IC Analysis, the internal structure of a sentence may be demonstrated clearly, and ambiguities, if any, will be revealed.

Sometimes, IC Analysis cannot reveal the differences between the sentences with the same or similar structue or with structural ambiguity. Some linguists tried to modify IC Analysis by labeling each constituent. And we refer to the revised method as labeled IC Analysis.

9) transformation rule

In Noam Chomsky's transformational grammar, transformational rules are those roles which change the deep structures generated by the phrase structure components into surface structures. A transformational rule consists of a sequence of symbols which is rewritten as another sequence according to certain convention.

10) structural ambiguity

Structural ambiguity refers to the ambiguity caused by ambiguous structures. For instance, John hit a person with a stone. The sentence is ambiguous because the structure "with a stone" can be understood as an adverbial to modify the whole sentence or as an attributive to modify the object, namely, "a person". It is generally accepted that structural ambiguity covers both surface structural ambiguity and underlying structural ambiguity.

11) ultimate constituent

The last level of constituents, i.e. morphemes, are known as ultimate constituents.

12) syntagmatic relation *vs* paradigmatic relation

The syntagmatic relation is a relation between one item and others in a sequence, or between elements which are all present. There are syntactic and semantic conditions the words in a syntagmatic relation must meet.

The paradigmatic (or associative) relation is a relation holding between elements

replaceable with each other at a particular place in a structure, or between one element present and the others absent. They can substitute for each other without violating syntactic rules. Words in a paradigmatic relation are comparable only in terms of syntax. Semantic factors are not taken into consideration here. These words have the same syntactic features. But they are not replaceable with each other semantically.

The syntagmatic and paradigmatic relations together, like the two axes of a coordinate, determine the identity of a linguistic sign. The syntagmatic relation is also referred to as the horizontal relation, or chain relation. And the paradigmatic relation is also known as the vertical relation, or choice relation.

13) Transformational-Generative Grammar

In the 1950s the school of linguistic thought known as Transformational-Generative Grammar received wide acclaim through the works of Noam Chomsky. Chomsky postulated a syntactic base of language (called deep structure), which consists of a series of phrase-structure rewrite rules, i.e. a series of (possibly universal) rules that generates the underlying phrase-structure of a sentence, and a series of rules (called transformations) that act upon the phrase-structure to form more complex sentences. The end result of a Transformational-Generative Grammar is a surface structure that, after the addition of words and pronunciations, is identical to an actual sentence of a language. All languages have the same deep structure, but they differ from each other in surface structure because of the application of different rules for transformations, pronunciation, and word insertion. Another important distinction made in Transformational-Generative Grammar is the difference between language competence (the subconscious control of a linguistic system) and language performance (the speaker's actual use of language). Although the first work done in Transformational-Generative Grammar was syntactic, later studies have applied the theory, to the phonological and semantic components of language.

14) theme *vs* rheme

A sentence may be analyzed from the functional side as well as the grammatical side. Apart from the analysis of a sentence in terms of subject and predicate, there may also be a functional analysis in terms of theme and rheme. Theme is "that which is known or at least obvious in the given situation and from which the speaker proceeds". Rheme is "what the speaker states about, or in regard to the starting point of the utterance".

2. Word Completion

1) sentence 2) transformational 3) recursive
4) deep 5) Coordinate 6) hierarchical
7) Syntax 8) competence 9) obligatory
10) description, change 11) grammatical 12) Phrase
13) lexicon 14) transform 15) predicate, argument
16) statically, dynamically 17) Syntax 18) sequential / syntagmatic

19) substitutional / paradigmatic
20) substitutional / paradigmatic, syntactic
21) lexical, non-lexical   22) hierarchical
23) sentence level, word level, phrase level
24) ultimate constituents, constituents, immediate constituents
25) structural ambiguity   26) node   27) surface, surface, deep
28) deep, surface   29) PS rules, T-   30) linear arrangement
31) meaningful grouping   32) form   33) meaning
34) compulsory   35) base, auxiliary   36) main, helping
37) tense, modal, perfect, progressive
38) S→NP AUX VP

3. Multiple Choice

1)—5) A B B A B

4. True or False Questions

1)—5) F F T T F   6)—10) T T F T F   11)—15) F F T F T
16)—20) T F T F F   21)—25) F T F T T   26)—30) F T F F T

5. Answer the Following Questions

1) What is the nature of Transformational-Generative Grammar? What are its main aspects? (about 200 words)

Transformational-generative grammar linguistic theory is associated with Noam Chomsky, particularly with his *Syntactic Structures* (1957). Generative grammar attempts to define rules that can generate the infinite number of grammatical (well-formed) sentences possible in a language. It starts not from a behaviorist analysis of minimal sounds but from a rationalist assumption that a deep structure underlies a language, and that a similar deep structure underlies all languages. Transformational grammar seeks to identify rules (transformations) that govern relations between parts of a sentence, on the assumption that beneath such aspects as word order a fundamental structure exists. Transformational and Generative Grammar together were the starting point for the tremendous growth in linguistic studies since the 1950s. TG Grammar has the following features. First, it sees language as a set of rules or principles. Second, the aim of linguistics is to produce a generative grammar which captures the linguistic competence of the native speaker. This concerns the question of learning theory and the question of linguistic universals. Third, grammarians are interested in any data that can reveal the native speaker's knowledge instead of what native speakers actually say; they rely on their own intuition. Fourth, the methodology used is hypothesis-deductive, which operates at two levels: A. the linguist formulates a hypothesis about language structure—a general linguistic theory; this is tested by grammars of particular languages, and B. each such grammar is a hypothesis on the general linguistic theory. Finally, the researchers follow rationalism in philosophy and mentalism in psychology.

2) Explain and comment on the following pair of sentences:
   a. John is easy to please.
   b. John is eager to please.

The two sentences have similar surface structure. But in spite of this surface similarity the grammar of the two is quite different. *John* has a different logical relationship to *please* in the two sentences. In the first sentence, though it is not apparent, from the surface word order, *John* functions as the direct object of the verb to please; the sentence means: it is easy for someone to please John. Whereas in the second sentence *John* functions as the subject of the verb *to please*; the sentence means: John is eager that he pleases someone. It cannot be paraphrased as " * It is eager to please John" or as " * pleasing John is eager". Deep structure specifies these relationships: A. (Someone pleases John) is easy; B. John is eager (John pleases someone).

3) Examine each of the following sentences and indicate if it is a simple, coordinate, or complex sentence:
   A. complex
   B. simple
   C. coordinate
   D. simple
   E. complex

4) Use appropriate phrase structure rules to draw a phrase marker for the following sentence:

A clever magician fooled the audience.

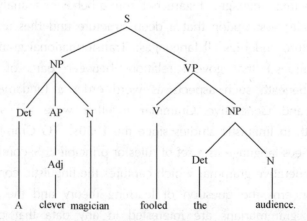

5) For each of the following two sentences, draw a tree diagram of its underlying structure that reveals the difference in the relationship between *John*, *Mary* and the verb *see*:

A. Mary advised John to see the dentist.

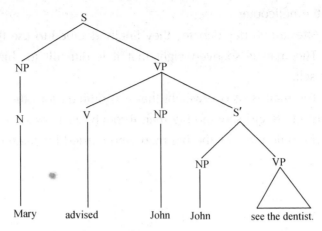

B. Mary promised John to see the dentist.

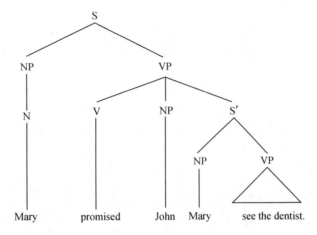

6) The formation of many sentences involves the operation of syntactic movement. The following sentences are believed to have derived from their D-structure representations. Show the D-structure for each of these sentences:
   A. the media severely criticized the leader of the majority party
   B. the man threw away the rake in the yard
   C. the new shop owner will hire her
   D. the robot can do what for us.

7) Draw on your linguistic knowledge of English and paraphrase each of the following sentences in two different ways to show how syntactic rules account for the ambiguity of sentences:
   A. a. Putting tobacco in rolled-up paper and then smoking it can make one feel sick.
   b. A cigarette which gives out smoke can make one feel sick.
   B. a. Tony is a bad guy who likes to fight in the street.
   b. Tony is a sanitation worker who cleans dirty streets.

C. a. After a two-day debate, they reached a final decision while they were on the helicopter.

   b. After a two-day debate, they finally decided to use the helicopter.

D. a. The man is so overweight that it is difficult for him to move around by himself.

   b. The man is so overweight that it is difficult for others to remove him.

E. a. The little girl saw the big man through her telescope.

   b. The little girl saw the big man who carried his telescope.

Chapter 7 Semantics

1. Define the Following Terms

1) referent
2) polysemy
3) hyponymy
4) sense
5) proposition
6) reference
7) contextualism
8) componential analysis
9) complementarity
10) gradable antonyms
11) entailment *vs* presupposition
12) denotation *vs* connotation
13) semantic field theory
14) semantic field
15) predication analysis
16) predicate, argument
17) relational opposites
18) lexical relation *vs* sense relation
19) synonymy
20) lexical semantics
21) absolute homonyms
22) homonymy
23) homophones
24) homographs
25) extension *vs* intension

2. Multiple Choice

Directions: In each question there are four choices. Decide which one would be the best answer to the question or to complete the sentence best.

1) Cold and hot are a pair of _____ antonyms.
 A. gradable   B. complementary   C. reversal   D. converse

2) Idioms are _____.
 A. sentences   B. naming units
 C. phrases   D. communication units

3) _____ describes whether a proposition is true or false.
 A. Truth   B. Truth value
 C. Truth condition   D. Falsehood

4) "John hit Peter" and "Peter was hit by John" are the same _____.
 A. proposition   B. sentence   C. utterance   D. truth

5) Man: [+ HUMAN] [+ MALE] [+ ADULT] [− FEMALE] is an example

of _____.
   A. componential analysis B. predication analysis
   C. IC Analysis D. selection restriction
6) The semantic triangle holds that the meaning of a word _____.
   A. is interpreted through the mediation of concept
   B. is related to the thing it refers to
   C. is the idea associated with that word in the minds of speakers
   D. is the image it is represented in the mind
7) When the truth of sentence A guarantees the truth of sentence B, and the falsity of sentence B guarantees the falsity of sentence A, we can say that _____.
   A. sentence A presupposes sentence B
   B. sentence A entails sentence B
   C. sentence A is inconsistent with sentence B
   D. sentence A contradicts sentence B
8) "Socrates is a philosopher" is a case of _____.
   A. two-place predicate B. one-place predicate
   C. two-place argument D. one-place argument
9) "John killed Bill but Bill didn't die" is a(n) _____.
   A. entailment B. presupposition
   C. anomaly D. contradiction
10) The particular words or constructions that produce presuppositions is called _____.
    A. presupposition condition B. truth condition
    C. presupposition trigger D. truth value
11) Lexical ambiguity arises from polysemy or _____ which can not be determined by the context.
    A. homonymy B. antonymy C. meronymy D. synonymy
12) The sense relationship between "John plays the violin" and "John plays a musical instrument" is _____.
    A. hyponymy B. antonymy C. entailment D. presupposition
13) "Semantics is the scientific study of meaning" is a _____.
    A. synonymy B. polysemy C. antonymy D. tautology
14) Conceptual meaning is _____.
    A. denotative B. connotative C. associative D. affective
15) When the word *root* means "part of plant that keeps it firmly in the soil and absorbs water and food from the soil", the meaning is _____ meaning.
    A. connotative B. conceptual C. reflected D. associative
16) *Lorry* and *truck* are _____.
    A. dialectal synonyms

B. stylistic synonyms
C. synonyms that differ in their emotive meaning
D. none of the above

17) Which pair is the emotive synonyms—_____?
    A. dad, father   B. flat, apartment
    C. mean, frugal   D. charge, accuse

18) In the collocational synonyms, *rebuke* is collocated by _____.
    A. with   B. for   C. of   D. against

19) The noun *tear* and the verb *tear* are _____.
    A. homophones   B. homographs
    C. complete homonyms   D. none of the above

20) The sentence "John likes ice-cream" contains _____ arguments.
    A. one   B. two   C. none   D. three

21) The classic semantic triangle reflects _____.
    A. the naming theory   B. the conceptual view
    C. the contextualist view   D. the behaviorist view

22) _____ concerns with the inherent meaning of the linguistic form; it's abstract and de-contextualized.
    A. Reference   B. Semantic
    C. Sense   D. none of the above

23) The same word may have more than one meaning, which is called _____.
    A. synonymy   B. homonymy   C. hyponymy   D. polysemy

24) _____ analysis is a way to analyze sentence meaning.
    A. Componential   B. Predication
    C. Syntactic   D. none of the above

25) Whether a sentence is semantically meaningful is governed by rules called _____.
    A. selectional restrictions   B. grammatical rules
    C. phrase structure rules   D. all of the above

26) Semantics can be defined as the study of _____.
    A. naming   B. meaning   C. communication   D. context

27) In the study of meaning, the _____ are interested in understanding the relations between linguistic expressions and what they refer to in the real world.
    A. linguists   B. philosophers   C. psychologists   D. phoneticians

28) The linguistic _____ is sometimes known as co-text.
    A. context   B. situation
    C. contextualization   D. situation of context

29) Bloomfield drew on _____ psychology when trying to define the meaning of linguistic forms.

A. contextual   B. conceptualist   C. behaviorist   D. naming

30) Sense and reference are two related _____ different aspects of meaning.
A. but   B. and   C. or   D. as well as

31) _____ means what a linguistic form refers to in the real, physical world.
A. Sense   B. Reference   C. Meaning   D. Semantics

32) Dialectal synonyms are synonyms used in different _____ dialects.
A. personal   B. regional   C. social   D. professional

33) Hyponyms of the same _____ are co-hyponyms.
A. word   B. lexical item   C. superordinate   D. hyponymy

34) Words that are opposite in meaning are _____.
A. synonyms   B. hyponyms   C. antonyms   D. homophones

35) A(n) _____ is a logical participant in a predication.
A. argument   B. predicate   C. predication   D. agent

3. Word Completion

1) In semantic analysis, _____ is the abstraction of the meaning of a sentence.
2) _____ restrictions are constraints on what lexical items can go with what others.
3) _____ analysis is based upon the belief that the meaning of a word can be divided into meaning components.
4) _____ is a relation of inclusion.
5) For _____ antonyms, it is a matter of either one or the other.
6) There are often intermediate forms between the two members of a pair of _____ antonyms.
7) The various meanings of a _____ word are related to some degree.
8) Synonyms which differ in the words they go together with are called _____ synonyms.
9) Linguistic forms having the same sense may have different _____ in different situations.
10) _____ is concerned with the inherent meaning of the linguistic form.
11) _____ is based on the presumption that one can derive meaning from observable contexts.
12) There is no direct link between a linguistic form and what it refers to according to the _____ view.
13) According to Wittgenstein, for a large class of cases, the meaning of a word is its _____ in the language.
14) In the study of meaning, _____ focus their interest on understanding the human mind through language.
15) According to the _____ theory of meaning, the words in a language are taken to be labels of the objects they stand for.

16) *Autumn* and *fall* are two _____.
17) The words of English are classified into _____ words and _____ words.
18) Hyponymy, also referred to as subordination, is a relationship which obtains between _____ and _____.
19) *Father* and *son* are _____.
20) In the sentences of entailment, if X is true, Y is _____.
21) _____ means what a linguistic form refers to in the real, physical world.
22) The same one word may have more than one meaning, this is what we called _____, and such a word is called _____ word.
23) _____ refers to the sense relation between a more general, more inclusive word and a more specific word.
24) In semantic analysis of a sentence, the basic unit is called _____.
25) Name five of the associative meaning categorized by Leech: _____ _____ _____ _____ _____.
26) Predication analysis is to break down predications into their constituents: _____ and _____.
27) The sense relation between "A lent a book to B" and "B borrowed a book from A" is _____.
28) Antonyms like *husband* and *wife* are _____ antonyms.
29) Terms like *desk* and *stool* are _____ of the term *furniture*.
30) According to Leech, _____ meaning refers to logic, cognitive, or denotative content.
31) We use the term _____ to refer to the relation between the following two sentences:
    A. Jack's bike needs repairing.
    B. Jack has a bike.
32) Semantic ambiguity can be divided into two types: _____ ambiguity and _____ ambiguity.
33) Inspired by the medieval grammarians, Ogden and Richard (1923) presented the classic "semantic triangle" in their book _____.
34) *Alive* and *dead* are _____ antonyms, while *borrow* and *lend*, *over* and *under* are _____ opposites.
35) _____ is the fact that would have to obtain in reality to make a proposition true or false.
36) *Charge* and *accuse* are said to be _____ synonyms.
37) Sentence meaning is the combination of the meanings of the component words and _____.
38) _____ opposites may be seen in terms of degrees of quality involved.
39) _____ sentences express judgment.

40) The ambiguity of a sentence may arise from _____ and _____.
41) *Mean* and *frugal* are said to be _____ synonyms.
42) We call the relation between *animal* and *cow* as _____.
43) The hyponyms under the same superordinate are called _____.
44) "Words are names of labels for things." This view is called _____ theory in semantic studies.
45) *Wide* and *narrow* is an example of _____.
46) *Moon* is a _____ of *satellite*.

■ 4. True or False Questions

1) (   ) The conceptualist view holds that there is no direct link between a linguistic form and what it refers to (i. e. between language and the real world) rather in the interpretation of meaning they are linked through the meditation of concepts in the mind.

2) (   ) Sense and reference are two terms often encountered in the study of meaning.

3) (   ) There are words with more or less the same meaning based in different regional dialects.

4) (   ) Componential analysis is based upon the belief that the meaning of a word can not be dissected into meaning components, called semantic features.

5) (   ) One advantage of componential analysis is that by specifying the semantic features of certain words, it will be possible to show how these words are related in meaning.

6) (   ) Among the approaches to the study of meaning, the naming theory is better than others.

7) (   ) *Kid* and *child* are stylistic synonyms.

8) (   ) *Furniture* is the superordinate of *bed*.

9) (   ) Antonyms contrast each other only on a single dimension, such as *live* and *die*.

10) (   ) *Cold* and *hot* are complementary antonyms.

11) (   ) In English, there is no argument in some sentences.

12) (   ) The sentence "Tom, smoke!" and "Tom smokes" have the same semantic predication.

13) (   ) The sentences that contain the same words are the same in meaning.

14) (   ) The meaning of a word is the combination of all its elements, and so is the sentence.

15) (   ) The meaning of the word we often used is the primary meaning.

16) (   ) Meaning is central to the study of communication.

17) (   ) The naming theory of meaning was proposed by the ancient Greek

scholar Plato.

18) (   ) In the classic semantic triangle, the symbol is directly related to the referent.
19) (   ) Sense and reference are the same.
20) (   ) Complete synonyms are rare in language.
21) (   ) Stylistic synonyms differ in style because they come from different regions.
22) (   ) Polysemy is the same as homonymy.
23) (   ) Homophones are words which are identical in sound.
24) (   ) The superordinate term is more general in meaning than its hyponyms.
25) (   ) In a pair of gradable antonyms, the denial of one member of the pair implies the assertion of the other.
26) (   ) In componential analysis, the plus sign is used to indicate that a certain semantic feature is present.
27) (   ) The grammatical meaning of a sentence refers to its grammaticality.
28) (   ) All the grammatically well-formed sentences are semantically well-formed.
29) (   ) A predicate is something said about on argument.
30) (   ) There is only one argument in the sentence "Kids like apples".
31) (   ) The meaning relationship between *man* and *grown-up* is hyponymous because the semantic features of *man* are included in those of *grown-up*.
32) (   ) Semantically, *beef* is excluded in *meat*.
33) (   ) *Kids* and *children* are synonyms despite their stylistic difference.
34) (   ) In the following pair of sentences, sentence B presupposes sentence A: John managed to finish in time. B John tried to finish in time.
35) (   ) In the semantic triangle, there is no direct relationship between symbol and referent.
36) (   ) If a word has sense, it must have reference.
37) (   ) Predication of a sentence is identical to the proposition of the sentence.
38) (   ) After comparing "They stopped at the end of the corridor" with "At the end of the corridor, they stopped", you may find some difference in meaning, and the difference can be interpreted in terms of collocative meaning.
39) (   ) *Tulip*, *rose* and *violet* are all included in the notion of *flower*, therefore they are superordinates of *flower*.
40) (   ) The theory of meaning which relates the meaning of a word to the thing it refers to, or stands for, is known as the referential theory.
41) (   ) Conceptualists maintain that there is no direct link between linguistic form and what it refers to. This view can be seen by the semantic triangle.

42) (   ) The relationship between *human body* and *face/nose* is hyponymy.

43) (   ) Hyponymy is a matter of class membership, so it is the same as meronymy.

44) (   ) Two sentences using the same words may mean quite differently.

45) (   ) The linguistic context considers the probability of one word's co-occurrence or collocation with another, which forms part of the meaning, and an important factor in communication.

46) (   ) Linguistic forms having the same sense may have different references in different situations while linguistic forms with the same reference always have the same sense.

47) (   ) An important difference between presupposition and entailment is that presupposition, unlike entailment, is not vulnerable to negation. That is to say, if a sentence is negated, the original presupposition is still true.

5. Answer the Following Questions

1) What is a semantic field? Can you illustrate it?
2) What are the possible colours of Chinese "青" in English? And what does this reflect in semantics?
3) Please give two examples of two-place predicates.
4) Analyze hyponymy and incompatibility by using componential analysis.
5) Illustrate the difference between sense and reference from the following four aspects:
   A. A word having reference must have sense;
   B. A word having sense might not have reference;
   C. A certain sense can be realized by more than one reference;
   D. A certain reference can be expressed by more than one sense.

Answers

1. Define the Following Terms

1) referent

By referent, we mean the object or state of affairs in extra-linguistic reality or a linguistic element to which the speaker or writer is referring by using a linguistic sign.

2) polysemy

Polysemy refers to the semantic phenomenon that a word may have more than one meaning. For example, *negative* means a statement saying or meaning "no", a refusal or denial, one of the following words and expressions: no, not, nothing, never, not at all, etc. But sometimes we can hardly tell whether it is a form with several meanings or a different word taking the same form; hence the difference between polysemy and homonymy.

3) hyponymy

Hyponymy refers to the sense relations between a more general, inclusive word and a more specific word. The word that is more general in meaning is called superordinate, and the more specific words are called its hyponyms. Hyponyms of the same superordinate are co-hyponyms to each other. Hyponymy is a relation of inclusion; in terms of meaning, the superordinate includes all its hyponyms.

4) sense

Sense is concerned with the inherent meaning of the linguistic form. It is the collection of all the features of the linguistic form; it is abstract and de-contextualized. It is the aspect of meaning dictionary compilers are interested in. For example, the word *dog* is given the definition of "a domesticated canine mammal, occurring in many breeds that show a great variety, in size and form. This does not refer to any particular dog that exists in the real world, but applies to any animal that meets the factors described in the definition. So this is the sense of the word *dog*.

5) proposition

Proposition is what is talked about in an utterance, or that part of the speech act which has to do with reference. Propositions can be a way of capturing part of the meaning of sentences. They are more abstract than sentences because the same proposition can be represented by several different statements. More over in non-statements like questions, orders, etc. they cannot be the complete meaning since such sentences include an indication of the speaker's attitude to the proposition.

6) reference

Reference means what a linguistic form refers to in the real, physical world; it deals with the relationship between the linguistic element and the non-linguistic world of experience. If we say "The dog is barking", we must be talking about a certain dog existing in the situation; the word *dog* refers to a dog known to both the speaker and the hearer. This is the reference of the word *dog* in this particular situation.

7) contextualism

Contextualism is based on the presumption that one can derive meaning from, or reduce it to, observable context: the "situational context" and the "linguistic context". Every utterance occurs in a particular spatio-temporal situation, as the following factors are related to the situational context: A. the speaker and the hearer; B. the actions they are performing at the time; C. various external objects and events; D. deictic features. The "linguistic context" is another aspect of contextualism. It considers the probability of one word's co-occurrence or collocation with another, which forms part of the meaning, and an important factor in communication.

8) componential analysis

Componential analysis is a way proposed by the structural semanticists to analyze word meaning. The approach is based upon the belief that the meaning of a word can be dissected into meaning components, called semantic features. This is parallel to the way a phoneme is analyzed into smaller components called distinctive features. Plus and minus signs are used to indicate whether a certain semantic feature is present or absent in the meaning of a word, and these feature symbols are usually written in capitalized letters. For example, the word *man* is analyzed as comprising the features of +HUMAN, +ADULT, +MALE. One advantage of componential analysis is that by specifying the semantic features of certain words, it will be possible to show how these words are related in meaning. For example, the two words *man* and *woman* share the features of HUMAN and ADULT, but differ in the feature of MALE. And the words *man* and *boy* share the features of HUMAN and MALE, but differ in the feature of ADULT.

Componential analysis provides an insight into the meaning of words and a way to study the relationships between words that are related in meaning.

9) Complementarity may be regarded as special case of incompatibility holding over two-term sets. It is characteristic of such pairs of lexical items that the approval of one implies the denial of the other. In other words, it is not a matter of degree between two extremes, but a matter of either one or the other. For example, a person can be either "alive", or "dead", either "male" or "female"; there is no third possibility.

10) gradable antonyms

The term antonymy is used for oppositeness of meaning; words that are opposite in meaning are antonyms. Words do not contrast each other only on a single dimension; in fact, oppositeness can be found on different dimensions and different kinds of antonyms have been recognized.

Gradable antonyms are antonyms that are gradable because there are often intermediate forms between the two members of a pair. For example, *old* and *young* are immediately recognized as antonyms, but they stand for two extremes, between which there exist intermediate forms representing differing degrees of being old or young, such as *middle-aged*, *mature*, *elderly*.

11) entailment *vs* presupposition

Entailment can be illustrated by the following two sentences, with Sentence A entailing Sentence B:

A: He married a blonde heiress.

B: He married a blonde.

In terms of truth value, the following relationships exist between these two sentences: a. when A is true, B is necessarily true; b. when B is false, A is false too; c. when A is false, B may be true or false; d. when B is true, A may be true or false. Entailment is basically a semantic relation or logical implication, but we have to assume co-reference of

He in sentence A and sentence B, before we have A entail B.

12) denotation *vs* connotation

The term denotation is from the Latin word *denotare*, which means "to mark, to indicate, to mean". The denotative meaning of a linguistic form is the person, object, abstract notion, event, or state which the word or sentence denotes. Bussmann defines denotation as "the constant, abstract, and basic meaning of a linguistic expression independent of context and situation, as opposed to the connotative, i.e. subjectively variable, emotive components of meaning".

Connotation refers to "the emotive or affective component of a linguistic expression (such as style, idiolect, dialect, and emotional charge), which is superimposed upon its basic meaning and which—in contrast to the static conceptual meaning—is difficult to describe generally and context-independently".

13) semantic field theory

Semantic field theory (also lexical field theory) is a theory of the German structuralist school which developed in the 1930s. According to this theory, "the vocabulary of a language is not simply a listing of independent items (as the head words in a dictionary would suggest), but is organized into areas, or fields, within which words interrelate and define each other in various ways".

14) semantic field

It is an organizational principle that the lexicon and groups of words in the lexicon can be semantically related, rather than a listing of words as in a published dictionary. On a very general and intuitive level, we can say that the words in a semantic field, though not synonymous, are all used to talk about the same general phenomenon, and there is a meaning inclusion relation between the items in the field and the field category itself. Classical examples of semantic fields include color terms (*red, green, blue, yellow*), kinship terms (*mother, father, sister, brother*), and cooking terms (*boil, fry, broil, steam*) as semantic fields.

15) predication analysis

Predication analysis is an important step in the analysis of sentential meaning. The predication is the common category shared by propositions, questions, commands, etc. Predication analysis is to break down predications into their constituents: arguments (logical participants) and a predicate (a relational element). Between them, the predicate is the major element that governs the arguments. We may distinguish between a two-place predicate which governs two arguments, a one-place predicate which governs one argument, and a no-place predicate which has no argument at all.

16) predicate, argument

Bussmann (2000) defines the two terms as follows: in formal logic, the term predicate is a linguistic expression which, together with the expressions for the arguments, forms a proposition. In most cases, predicates are verbs, but they are likely to be adjectives, prepositions or nouns as well. And the term argument denotes the empty slot of a predicate. Depending on how many arguments a predicate requires, it is called a one-, two-, or three-place predicate. One-place predicates indicate characteristics or properties of their arguments; in this case the argument / predicate relation corresponds to the subject/ predicate distinction in traditional grammar.

17) relational opposites

If two words exhibit the reversal of a relationship between each other, they are called relational opposites. For example, if A is the employer of B, then B is the employee of A. Therefore, employer and employee are a pair of relational opposites.

18) lexical relation *vs* sense relation

Lexical relations are classified into three broad groups: form relation, sense relations and object relations.

Sense relations (also semantic relations) are of two kinds: syntagmatic and paradigmatic, which, in the terms of John Lyons (2000: 124), are called substitutional and combinatorial respectively.

19) synonymy

Synonymy is used to mean sameness or dose similarity of meaning. Dictionary makers (lexicographers) rely on the existence of synonymy for their definitions. Some semanticians maintain, however, that there are no real synonyms, because two or more words named synonyms are expected without exception to differ from one another in one of the following aspects.

A. In shades of meaning (e.g. *finish, complete, close, conclude, terminate, finalize, end*, etc.);

B. in stylistic meaning;

C. in emotive (or affective) meaning;

D. in range of use (or collocative meaning);

E. in British and American English usages (e.g. *autumn* [BrE], *fall* [AmE]).

Simeon Potter said, "Language is like dress. We vary our dress to suit the occasion. We do not appear at a friend's silver-wedding anniversary in gardening clothes, nor do we go fishing on the river in a dinner-jacket." This means the learning of synonyms is important to anyone that wishes to use his language freely and well.

20) lexical semantics

Lexical semantics, as the name suggests, is concerned with the meaning of lexical items, i.e. words.

21) absolute homonyms

Absolute homonyms are the words which are identical both phonologically and orthographically but different semantically.

22) homonymy

Homonymy is a type of lexical ambiguity involving two or more different words.

When two or more lexical items have the same form but differ in meaning, they are said to be homonymous. Homonymous words often have distinct etymological origins. They can be divided into three kinds: absolute (or perfect) homonyms, homophones, and homographs.

23) homophones

Homophones are the words which are identical phonologically but different orthographically and semantically. The following are examples of homophones:

ad (colloquial word for advertisement) and *add* (join as increase or supplement)

blue (colored like clear sky) and *blew* (past of *blow*)

24) homograghs

Homographs are the words which are identical orthographically but different phonologically and semantically. Examples of homographs are given below:

bass (/bæs/ common perch) and *bass* (/beis/ lowest adult male voice)

25) extension *vs* intension

Both extension and intension are terms in philosophy and logic, and are now used as part of a theoretical framework for linguistic semantics. The former refers to the class of entities to which a linguistic expression is correctly applied, whereas the latter, to the set of defining properties which determines the applicability of a linguistic expression.

2. Multiple Choice

1)—5) A B B A A   6)—10) A B B D C   11)—15) A C D A B
16)—20) A C B B B   21)—25) B C D B A   26)—30) B B A C A
31)—35) B B C C A

3. Word Completion

1) predication   2) Selectional   3) Componential
4) Entailment   5) complementary   6) gradable
7) polysemic   8) collocational   9) references
10) Sense   11) Contextualization   12) conceptualist
13) use   14) psychologists   15) naming
16) dialectal synonyms 17) native, loan
18) hyponyms, hyperonyms 19) relational opposites
20) true   21) Reference   22) polysemy, polysemic
23) Hyponymy   24) predication
25) connotative meaning, social meaning, affective meaning, reflected meaning, collocative meaning
26) argument, predicate 27) synonym   28) converse/relational
29) co-hyponyms   30) conceptual   31) presupposition
32) lexical, structural 33) *The Meaning of Meaning*

34) complementary, relational   35) Truth condition
36) collocational   37) the meaning of its structure
38) Gradable   39) Declarative
40) lexical ambiguity, structural ambiguity
41) emotive   42) hyponymy   43) co-hyponyms
44) naming   45) gradable opposites   46) hyponym

4. True or False Questions

1)—5) T T T F T   6)—10) F F T F F   11)—15) T T F F F
16)—20) T T F F T   21)—25) F F T T F   26)—30) T T F T F
31)—35) T F T T T   36)—40) F T F F T   41)—45) T F F T T
46)—47) F T

5. Answer the Fallowing Questions

1) What is a semantic field? Can you illustrate it?

It is an organizational principle that the lexicon and groups of words in the lexicon can be semantically related, rather than a listing of words as in a published dictionary. On a very general and intuitive level, we can say that the words in a semantic field, though not synonymous, are all used to talk about the same general phenomenon, and there is a meaning inclusion relation between the items in the field and the field category itself. Classical examples of semantic fields include color terms (*red*, *green*, *blue*, *yellow*), kinship terms (*mother*, *father*, *sister*, *brother*), and cooking terms (*boil*, *fry*, *broil*, *steam*) as semantic fields.

2) What are the possible colours of Chinese "青" in English? And what does this reflect in semantics.

The Chinese word "青" can be three colours: blue, as in "青,取之于蓝而青于蓝" or "青箬笠,绿蓑衣"; black, as in "青牛白马"; and dark green, as in "两岸青山相对出". This example reflects that the same word may have a set of different meanings, that is, the polysemy of a word.

3) Please give two examples of two-place predicates.

A. The building is next to the library.

B. John likes ice cream.

4) Analyze hyponymy and incompatibility by using componential analysis.

Like distinctive features in phonology, componential analysis attempts to define word meaning as complexes made up of meaning components which are semantic primitives. With componential analysis we can formally define not only word meaning but also the basic semantic relations such as hyponymy and incompatibility.

The analysis of hyponymy by using componential analysis can be illustrated in the following example:

A. Man: [+HUMAN][+ADULT][+MALE]
B. Woman: [+HUMAN][+ADULT][-MALE]
C. Boy: [+HUMAN][-ADULT][+MALE]
D. Gift: [+HUMAN][-ADULT][-MALE]

The analysis of incompatibility:

E. Alive: -DEAD (or +LIVE)→Alive: [-DEAD] or [+LIVE]
F. Dead: +DEAD (or -LIVE)→Dead: [+DEAD] or [-LIVE]

5) Illustrate the difference between sense and reference from the following four aspects:

A. A word having reference must have sense;
B. A word having sense might not have reference;
C. A certain sense can be realized by more than one reference;
D. A certain reference can be expressed by more than one sense.

The distinction between "sense" and "reference" is comparable to that between "connotation" and "denotation". The former refers to some abstract properties, while the latter refers to some concrete entities. To some extent, we can say every word has a sense, i.e. some conceptual content, otherwise we will not be able to use it or understand it. But not every word has a reference. There are linguistic expressions which can never be used to refer, for example, the words *so*, *very*, *maybe*, *if*, *not*, and *all*. These words do of course contribute meaning to the sentences they occur in and thus help sentences denote, but they do not themselves identify entities in the world. They are intrinsically non-referring items. And words like *God*, *ghost*, and *dragon* refer to imaginary things, which do not exist in reality. Some expressions will have the same referent across a range of utterances, e.g. *the Eiffel Tower* or *the Pacific Ocean*, such expressions are sometimes described as having constant reference. Others have their reference totally dependent on context, expressions like *I*, *you*, *she*, etc. are said to have variable reference. There are cases when a reference can be expressed by more than one sense. *Evening star* and *morning star* nearly always refers to *Venus*, but each of them presents a particular emotional temperament and a particular sense of values, meaning, ideals and appreciation.

Chapter 8 Pragmatics

1. Define the Following Terms

1) constative *vs* performative
2) cooperative principle
3) illocutionary act *vs* perlocutionary act
4) conversational implicature
5) speech act theory

2. Glossary Translation

1) commissive
2) illocutionary act
3) performative
4) discourse markers
5) relevant theory
6) 取效行为
7) 描述句
8) 话语意义
9) 预设触发语
10) 合适条件
11) adjacency pair
12) preferred second parts
13) deixis
14) indirect speech act
15) extralinguistic context

3. Multiple Choice

Directions: In each question there are four choices. Decide which one would be the best answer to the question or to complete the sentence best.

1) According to Searle, those illocutionary acts whose point is to commit the speaker to some future course of action are called _____.
   A. commissives   B. directives   C. expressives   D. declaratives

2) An illocutionary act is identical with _____.
   A. sentence meaning   B. the speaker's intention
   C. language understanding   D. the speaker's competence

3) The Indirect Speech Act was developed by _____.
   A. John Austin   B. Levinson   C. John Lyons   D. John Searle

4) _____ is a branch of linguistics which is the study of meaning in the context of

use.

　　A. Morphology　　B. Syntax　　C. Pragmatics　　D. Semantics

5) Tautologies like boys are boys and war is war are extreme examples in which the maxim of _____ is violated.

　　A. quality　　B. quantity　　C. relevance　　D. manner

6) _____ is the study of how speakers of a language use sentences to effect successful communication.

　　A. Semantics　　B. Pragmatics　　C. Sociolinguistics　　D. Psycholinguistics

7) _____ found that natural language had its own logic and conclude cooperative principle.

　　A. John Austin　　B. John Firth　　C. Paul Grice　　D. William Jones

8) The branch of linguistics that studies how context influences the way speakers interpret sentences is called _____.

　　A. semantics　　B. pragmatics　　C. sociolinguistics　　D. psycholinguistics

9) _____ proposed that speech act can fall into five general categories.

　　A. Austin　　B. Searle　　C. Sapir　　D. Chomsky

10) Promising, undertaking, vowing are the most typical of the _____.

　　A. declarations　　B. directives　　C. commissives　　D. expressives

11) The illocutionary point of the _____ is to express the psychological state specified in the utterance.

　　A. declarations　　B. expressives　　C. commissives　　D. directives

12) Y's utterance in the following conversation exchange violates the maxim of _____.

　　X: Who was that you were with last night?
　　Y: Did you know that you were wearing odd socks?

　　A. quality　　B. quantity　　C. relation　　D. manner

13) The violation of one or more of the conversational _____ (of the CP) can, when the listener fully understands the speaker, create conversational implicatures, and humor sometimes.

　　A. standards　　B. principles　　C. levels　　D. maxim

14) Most of the violations of the maxims of the CP give rise to _____.

　　A. breakdown of conversation
　　B. confusion of one's intention
　　C. hostility between speakers and the listeners
　　D. conversational implicatures

15) Speech act theory was proposed by _____ in 1962.

　　A. Saussure　　B. Austin　　C. Chomsky　　D. Grimm

16) The maxim of quantity requires: _____.

　　A. make your contribution as informative as required

B. do not make contribution more informative than required
C. do not say that for which you lack adequate evidence
D. Both A and B

17) Once the notion of _____ was taken into consideration, semantics split into pragmatics.
A. meaning   B. context   C. form   D. content

18) If a sentence is regarded as what people actually utter in the course of communication, it becomes _____.
A. a sentence   B. an act   C. a unit   D. an utterance

19) A _____ analysis of an utterance will reveal what the speaker intends to do with it.
A. semantic   B. syntactic   C. pragmatic   D. grammatical

20) _____ act theory is an important theory in the pragmatic study of language.
A. Speaking   B. Speech   C. Sound   D. Spoken

21) _____ act is the act performed by or resulting from saying something.
A. A Locutionary   B. An illocutionary
C. A perlocutionary   D. A speech

22) One of the contributions Searle has made is his classification of _____ acts.
A. locutionary   B. illocutionary
C. perlocutionary   D. speech

23) The illocutionary point of _____ is to express the psychological state specified in the utterance.
A. directives   B. commissives
C. expressives   D. declarations

24) Linguistics found that it would be impossible to give an adequate description of meaning if the _____ of language use was left unconsidered.
A. brevity   B. context
C. accuracy   D. none of the above

25) Of the three speech acts, linguistics are most interested in the _____.
A. locutionary act   B. perlocutionary act
C. illocutionary act   D. none of the above

4. True or False Questions

Directions: Decide whether the following statements are true or false. Write "T" for true and "F" for false in the bracket before each of them.

1) (   ) "He didn't stop smoking" presupposes that he had been smoking.
2) (   ) A locutionary act is the act of expressing the speaker's intention.
3) (   ) When performing an illocutionary act of representative, the speaker is making a statement or giving a description which he himself believes to be

true.

4) (　　) The utterance meaning of the sentence varies with the context in which it is uttered.

5) (　　) While conversation participants nearly always observe the CP, they do not always observe these maxims strictly.

6) (　　) Inviting, suggesting, warning, ordering are instances of commissives.

7) (　　) Only when a maxim under Cooperative Principle is blatantly violated and the hearer knows that it is being violated do conversational implicatures arise.

8) (　　) Of the three speech acts, linguists are most interested in the illocutionary act because this kind of speech is identical with the speaker's intention.

9) (　　) Of the views concerning the study of semantics, the contextual view, which places the study of meaning in the context in which language is used, is often considered as the initial effort to study meaning in a pragmatic sense.

10) (　　) Pragmatics covers the study of language use in relation to context, and in particular the study of linguistic communication.

11) (　　) As the process of communication is essentially a process of conveying meaning in a certain context, pragmatics can also be considered as a kind of meaning study.

12) (　　) Utterance is based on sentence meaning; it is the realization of the abstract meaning of a sentence in a real situation of communication or simply in a context.

13) (　　) A sentence is a grammatical unit and an utterance is a pragmatic notion.

14) (　　) "John has been to Asia" entails "John has been to Japan".

15) (　　) Without the shared knowledge both by the speaker and the hearer, linguistic communication would not be possible, and without considering such knowledge, linguistic communication cannot be satisfactorily accounted for in a semantic sense.

16) (　　) The contextual view is often considered as the initial effort to study meaning in a pragmatic sense.

17) (　　) Pragmatics is related to and also different from semantics.

18) (　　) The notion of context is not important to the pragmatic study of language

19) (　　) All utterances take the form of sentences.

20) (　　) Speech act theory was proposed by the British philosopher John Austin in 1962.

21) (　　) Grice made a distinction between what he called "constatives" and "performatives".

22) (　　) A locutionary act is the act of conveying literal meaning by means of

syntax, lexicon, and phonology.

23) (   ) In their study of language communication. linguists are only interested in how a speaker expresses his intention and pay no attention to how his intention is recognized by the hearer.

24) (   ) Directives are attempts by the speaker to get the hearer to do something.

25) (   ) The cooperative principle was proposed by John Searle.

26) (   ) There are four maxims under the cooperative principle.

27) (   ) The violations of the maxims make our language indirect.

28) (   ) Austin thought that stating was also a kind of act, and that we can perform with language.

29) (   ) According to the speech act theory, when we are speaking a language, we are doing something, or in other words performing acts; and the process of linguistic communication consists of a sequence of acts.

30) (   ) All the acts that belong to the same category of illocutionary act share the same purpose or the same illocutionary act, and they are the same in their strength or force.

31) (   ) All the utterances that can be made to serve the same purpose may vary in the syntactic form.

32) (   ) Conversation participants nearly always observe the CP and the maxims of the CP.

33) (   ) A sentence is a grammatical concept, and the meaning of a sentence, is often studied as the abstract intrinsic property of the sentence itself in terms of a predication.

34) (   ) Performatives, on the other hand, were sentences that stated a fact or described a state, and were verifiable.

35) (   ) Gradually linguists found that it would be impossible to give an adequate description of meaning if the context of language use was left considered.

36) (   ) What essentially distinguishes semantics and pragmatics is whether in the study of meaning the context of use is considered.

37) (   ) "His wife was a worker" presupposes that "He has been married".

■ 5. Answer the Following Questions

1) Which of the conversational maxims is being violated in the following dialogue?
   A: Is Mr. Smith a good teacher?
   B: He is a very handsome man.

2) What are the five general types of illocutionary speech acts John Searle has specified? Give one example to each of them.

3) Illustrate the difference between constative and performative utterance.

4) Explain the relationship between cooperative principle and conversational

implicature.

5) How do you explain the following example with the cooperative principle?
   A: Can you answer the telephone?
   B: I'm in the bathroom.

Answers

1. Define the Following Terms

1) constative *vs* performative

Constatives are statements that either state or describe, asserting something that is either true or false and are thus verifiable, bearing the truth value. Performatives are sentences that do not state a fact or describe a state and are not verifiable, in other words, performatives are utterances that perform an act—"do things".

2) cooperative principle

The cooperative principle is proposed by the philosopher and logician Herbert Paul Grice to explain the course of natural conversation, in which implicated messages are frequently involved.

His idea is that in making a conversation, the participants must first of all be willing to cooperate; otherwise, it would not be possible for them to carry on the talk. This general principle is called the Cooperative Principle, abbreviated as CP. It goes as follows: Make your conversational contribution such as required, at the stage at which it occurs, by the accepted purpose or direction of the talk exchange in which you are engaged. To be more specific, there are four maxims under this general principle.

The maxim of quantity:

A. Make your contribution as informative as required (for the current purpose of the exchange).

B. Do not make your contribution more informative than is required.

The maxim of quality:

A. Do not say what you believe to be false.

B. Do not say that for which you lack adequate evidence.

The maxim of relation: Be relevant.

The maxim of manner:

A. Avoid obscurity of expression.

B. Avoid ambiguity.

C. Be brief (avoid unnecessary prolixity).

D. Be orderly.

3) illocutionary act *vs* perlocutionary act

J. L. Austin suggests three basic senses in which in saying someone is doing something. They are locutionary acts, illocutionary acts, and perlocutionary acts. An illocutionary act is the act of expressing the speaker's intention; it is the act performed in saying something. A perlocutionary act is the act performed by or resulting from saying something; it is the consequence of, or the change brought about by the utterance. Take the sentence "You have left the door wide open" for example. The illocutionary act performed by the speaker is that by making such an utterance he has expressed his intention of speaking, i. e. asking someone to close the door, or making a complaint, depending on the context. The perlocutionary act refers to the effect of the utterance. If the hearer gets the speaker's message and sees that the speaker means to tell him to close the door, the speaker has successfully brought about the change in the real world he has intended to; then the perlocutionary act is successfully performed.

4) conversational implicature

Conversational implicature is a type of implicated meaning, which is deduced on the basis of the conversational meaning of words together with the context, under the guidance of the CP and its maxims. Implicature is comparable to illocutionary force in speech act theory in that they are both concerned with the contextual side of meaning. The two theories differ only in the mechanisms they offer for explaining the generation of contextual meaning.

5) speech act theory

According to Austin, a speaker might be performing three acts simultaneously when speaking. A locutionary act is the uttering of words, phrases and clauses, which conveys meaning by giving out meaningful sounds. An illocutionary act is the act of expressing the speaker's intention; it is the act performed in saying something. A perlocutionary act is the effect of the utterance. Linguists are most interested in the illocutionary act because it is identical with the speaker's intention. So the speech act theory is in fact the illocutionary act theory.

2. Glossary Translation

1) commissive: 承诺类
2) illocutionary act: 行事行为
3) performative: 施为句
4) discourse markers: 话语标记语
5) relevant theory: 关联理论
6) 取效行为: perlocutionary act
7) 描述句: constative
8) 话语意义: utterance meaning
9) 预设触发语: presupposition trigger
10) 合适条件: felicity condition

11）adjacency pair：比邻对

12）preferred second parts：优先应答

13）deixis：指示语

14）indirect speech act：间接言语行为

15）extralinguistic context：语言外语境

3. Multiple Choice

1）—5）A B D C A   6）—10）B C B B C   11）—15）B C D D B

16）—20）D B D C B   21）—25）C B C B C

4. True or False Questions

1）—5）T F T T T   6）—10）F T T T F   11）—15）T T T F F

16）—20）T T F F T   21）—25）F T F T F   26）—30）T T T T F

31）—35）T F T F F   36）—37）T T

5. Answer the Following Questions

1）Which of the conversational maxims is being violated in the following dialogue?

A：Is Mr. Smith a good teacher?

B：He is a very handsome man.

In the above exchange, B violates the maxim of relation because his answer is irrelevant to A's question. By doing so, B is likely to derive the implicature that "He is not a good teacher".

2）What are the five general types of illocutionary speech acts John Searle has specified? Give one example to each of them.

The five general types of illocutionary speech acts are：

A. assertives：sentences that commit the speaker to the truth of something. Typical cases are "I think the film is moving" and "I'm certain that he had got it".

B. directives：sentences by which the speaker tries to get the hearer to do something. "I beg you to give me some advice", for example, is an attempt to get something done by the hearer.

C. commissives：sentences that commit the speaker to some future action. Promises, offers, and warnings are characteristic of this group, e. g. "If you do that again I'll beat you to death".

D. expressives：sentences that express the speaker's psychological state about something, e. g. "Thanks a lot".

E. declarations：sentences that bring about immediate change in the existing state of affairs. As soon as an employer says to an employee "You are fired", the employee loses his job.

3）Illustrate the difference between constative and performative utterance.

The distinction between constative and performative utterance is made by J. L. Austin. Constatives refer to statements that either state or describe, and are verifiable; performatives, on the other hand, are sentences that do not state a fact or describe a situation, and are not verifiable. When a person who is authorized to name a ship smashes a bottle of champagne against the stem of an unnamed ship, he is required by the convention, and says "I name this ship Elizabeth", this ship is named. So this sentence, which is used to perform the act of naming, is a performative utterance. In contrast, the utterance "I pour some liquid into the tube" said by a chemistry teacher in a demonstration of an experiment is not a performative. It is a description of what the speaker is doing at the time of speaking. The speaker cannot pour any liquid into a tube by simply uttering these words. He must accompany his words with the actual pouring. Otherwise one can accuse him of making a false statement. Sentences of this type are constatives.

4) Explain the relationship between cooperative principle and conversational implicature.

In daily conversations people do not usually say things directly but tend to imply them. The word "implicature" is used to refer to the extra meaning that is not explicitly expressed in the utterance.

In making a conversation, the participants must first of all be willing to cooperate; otherwise, it would not be possible for them to carry on the talk. This general principle is called the cooperative principle. It goes as follows: Make your conversational contribution such as required, at the stage at which it occurs, by the accepted purpose or direction of the talk exchange in which you are engaged. To be more specific, there are four maxims under this general principle: the maxim of quantity, the maxim of quality, the maxim of relation, and the maxim of manner.

While conversation participants nearly always observe the CP, they do not always observe these maxims. These maxims can be violated for various reasons, but when they are "flouted", to use Grice's term, does "conversational implicature" occur. Flouting a maxim means violating it blatantly, i.e. both the speaker and the hearer are aware of the violation. When a speaker flouts a maxim, his language becomes indirect.

5) How do you explain the following example with the cooperative principle?

A: Can you answer the telephone?

B: I'm in the bathroom.

In reply to A's request, B violates the maxim of relation since his/her response seems irrelevant to the point. But A would assume that B is cooperative in the conversation, and would try to explore the link between the seemingly irrelevant response to something relevant. Thus, A would interpret B's utterance as a refusal to comply with the request and as a request of A to answer the phone instead. This seemingly unconnected conversation is very coherent on a speech act level, and that in saying things people are in fact "doing" things.

Chapter 9 Discourse Analysis

1. Define the Following Terms

1) discourse analysis
2) texture
3) coherence
4) cohesion
5) critical discourse analysis
6) positive discourse analysis
7) pre-sequence
8) turn-taking

2. Glossary Translation

1) pre-sequence
2) turn-taking
3) text
4) reiteration
5) preferred second parts
6) collocation
7) dispreferred second parts
8) reference
9) 批评话语分析
10) 积极话语分析

3. True or False Questions

Directions: Decide whether the following statements are true or false. Write "T" for true and "F" for false in the bracket before each of them.

1) (   ) A text is best regarded as a semantic unit, a unit not of form but of meaning.
2) (   ) Cohesion and coherence is identical with each other in essence.
3) (   ) If a text has no cohesive words, we say the text is not coherent.
4) (   ) Coherence is a logical, orderly and aesthetical relationship between parts, in speech, writing, or argument.
5) (   ) Coherence is an important principle we should abide by in academic writing.
6) (   ) Discourse marking is also one of the cohesive devices in a discourse.

4. Answer the Following Questions

1) What is the difference between cohesion and coherence?
2) What do you know about critical discourse analysis?

Answers

1. Define the Following Terms

1) discourse analysis

It is generally recognized that the term discourse analysis was first used by Z. Harris in the essay *Discourse Analysis*. It may deal with how the choices of the articles, pronouns and cases affect the structure of discourse; or deal with the relationship between utterances or sentences in discourse, and the linguistic, social, cultural or the psychological links; or deal with the moves made by the speaker to introduce a new topic, or change the topic to assert a higher role relationship to the other participants. Thus, discourse analysis is mainly concerned with the study of relationship between language and context in which language is used.

2) texture

The concept texture is appropriate to express the property of being a text. A discourse has texture, which distinguishes it from anything that is not a text. It derives this texture from the fact that it functions as a unity with respect to its background. If a passage of English containing more than one sentence is perceived as a text, there will be certain linguistic features presented in that passage that can be identified as contributing to its total unity and giving it texture, such as cohesion, coherence, linearization in structure and so on.

3) coherence

Coherence generally means natural or reasonable connection. In language communication, it refers to a logical, orderly and aesthetical relationship between parts, in speech, writing, or argument. Coherence is an important principle which we should abide by in academic writing.

4) cohesion

Cohesion is a term from the work on textual structure by Halliday and Hasan, given to the logical linkage between textual units, as indicated by overt formal markers of the relations between texts.

5) critical discourse analysis

Critical discourse analysis was generally considered to be first illustrated by Fowler, Hodge, Kress and Trew in *Language and Control* (1979). The purpose of CDA is to disclose the ideology hidden in any public discourse and its influence on discourse as well as the counteractive influence the discourse exerts on ideology.

6) positive discourse analysis

Positive discourse analysis is a term or a sub-branch which newly appears in discourse analysis. It is said to be first advanced by linguists of functional school who are represented

by Martin, J. R. Linguists of this school claim that some theories of functional grammar such as the evaluative theory can be used not only for critical discourse analysis (CDA) but also for positive discourse analysis. In the July of 2005, in Sydney, they held the 29th International Functional Linguistic Conference with the aim to advocate more hopeful discourses: peace, reconciliation, learning and alteration, the purport of which is to make the critical thinking develop more in the direction of positive discourse analysis. That is, the initiators hope that linguistic researchers will exert themselves to study how they will avail themselves of the corresponding researches to make our world more beautiful and how scholars of functional school linguistics can make some contributions to this project.

7) pre-sequence

Pre-sequence refers to the kind of sequences that are used to set up some specific potential actions.

8) turn-taking

According to Harvey Sacks, the founder of the conversation analytic method, the basic unit of the conversation is the "turn", that is, a shift in the direction of the speaking "flow" which is characteristic of normal conversation. Furthermore, according to Mey (1993/2001: 139), in normal civilized, Western-type conversation, conversationalists do not speak all at the same time, they wait for their "turn", also in this sense of the word. Yielding the right to speak, or the "floor", to the next speaker constitutes a turn. But how do people go about allocating turns to each other or themselves? This is where the so-called "turn-taking mechanism" come into the picture.

2. Glossary Translation

1) pre-sequence: 前置序列
2) turn-taking: 话轮转换
3) text: 文本或语篇
4) reiteration: 复现
5) preferred second parts: 优先应答
6) collocation: 搭配
7) dispreferred second parts: 次要应答
8) reference: 照应
9) 批评话语分析: critical discourse analysis
10) 积极话语分析: positive discourse analysis

3. True or False Questions

1)—6) T F F T T T

4. Answer the Following Questions

1) What is the difference between cohesion and coherence?

Cohesion and coherence may seem almost interchangeable. But there is an important difference between them. Cohesion refers to the linguistics devices by which the speaker can signal the experiential and interpersonal coherence of the text, and is thus a textual phenomenon: we can point to features of the text which serve a cohesive function. Coherence, on the other hand, is in the mind of the writer and reader: it is a mental phenomenon and cannot be identified or quantified in the same way as cohesion. The two are in most cases linked, in that a text which exploits the cohesive resources of the language effectively should normally be perceived as coherent. However, all language users are generally predisposed to construct coherence even from language with few recognizable cohesive signals, if they have reason to believe that it is intended to be coherent. The following pair of sentences, has only one cohesive link (Hugo = He), but they make sense together, that is, they are coherent (although you might like to consider what cultural knowledge the reader needs in order to reconstruct the coherence): Hugo spent all of his legacy laying down wine. He was ensuring a happy middle age. Nevertheless, cohesion is a crucial linguistic resource in the expression of coherent meanings; and the analyst may gain equally important insights into how it works from cases where a lack of cohesive devices in a text does not lead to the interactants perceiving it as incoherent.

2) What do you know about critical discourse analysis?

Critical discourse analysis was generally considered to be first illustrated by Fowler, Hodge, Kress and Trew in *Language and Control* (1979). The purpose of CDA is to disclose the ideology hidden in any public discourse and its influence on discourse as well as the counteractive influence the discourse exerts on ideology.

Ruth Wodak, writing in *Language, Power and Ideology*, defines her field, which she calls "critical linguistics", as "an interdisciplinary approach to language study with a critical point of view" for the purpose of studying "language behavior in natural speech situations of social relevance". Wodak also stresses the importance of "diverse theoretical and methodological concepts" and suggests that these can also be used for "analyzing issues of social relevance", while attempting to expose "inequality and injustice". Wodak underscores and encourages "the use of multiple methods" in language research while emphasizing the importance of recognizing the "historical and social aspects".

Chapter 10 Sociolinguistics

1. Define the Following Terms

1) diglossia
2) ideolect
3) bilingualism
4) register
5) pidgin
6) slang
7) communicative competence
8) lingua franca
9) sociolect
10) sociolinguistics
11) speech community
12) speech variety

2. Word Completion

Directions: In each question there are four choices. Decide which one would be the best answer to the question or to complete the sentence best.

1) A speech _____ is a group of people who share the same language or a particular variety of language.
2) The _____ language is a superposed, socially prestigious dialect of language.
3) A _____ language is originally a pidgin that has become established as a native language in some speech community.
4) A linguistic _____ refers to a word or expression that is prohibited by the "polite" society from general use.
5) Taboo and _____ are two faces of the same communication coin.
6) Whorf proposed that all higher levels of thinking are dependent on _____.
7) Language itself is not sexist, but its use may reflect the _____ attitude connoted in the language that is sexist.
8) An ethnic dialect is spoken mainly by a less privileged population that has experienced some sort of social isolation, such as _____ discrimination.
9) In terms of sociolinguistics, _____ is sometimes used to refer to the whole of a person's language.
10) _____ may take place in a conversation when one speaker uses one language and the other speaker answers in a different language.
11) _____ refers to a linguistic situation in which two standard languages are used

either by an individual or by a group of speakers.

3. Multiple Choice

Directions: In each question there are four choices. Decide which one would be the best answer to the question or to complete the sentence best.

1) Speech variety may be used instead of _____.
   A. vernacular language, dialect, pidgin, creole
   B. standard language
   C. both A and B
   D. none of the above

2) In sociolinguistics, _____ refers to a group of institutionalized social situations typically constrained by a common set of behavioral rules.
   A. domain   B. situation   C. society   D. community

3) _____ is defined as any regionally or socially definable human group identified by shared linguistic system.
   A. A speech community   B. A race
   C. A society   D. A country

4) _____ variation of language is the most discernible and definable in speech variation.
   A. Regional   B. Social   C. Stylistic   D. Idiolectal

5) _____ is not a typical example of official bilingualism.
   A. Canada   B. Finland   C. Belgium   D. Germany

6) _____ refers to a marginal language of few lexical items and straight forward grammatical rules, used as a medium of communication.
   A. Lingua franca   B. Creole
   C. Pidgin   D. Standard language

7) The most recognizable differences between American English and British English are in _____ and vocabulary.
   A. diglossia   B. bilingualism   C. pidginization   D. blending

8) _____ is a causal use of language that consists of expressive but nonstandard vocabulary, typically of arbitrary, flashy and often ephemeral coinages and figures of speech.
   A. Language taboo   B. Slang
   C. Address terms   D. Register variety

9) _____ variety refers to speech variation according to the particular area where a speaker comes from.
   A. Regional   B. Social   C. Stylistic   D. Idiolectal

10) In a speech community people have something in common _____—a language or a particular variety of language and rules for using it.

A. socially B. linguistically C. culturally D. pragmatically

11) The situation in which two or more languages are used side by side is referred to as _____.
A. diglossia B. bilingualism C. pidginization D. blending

12) When a pidgin comes to be adopted by a population as its primary language, and children learn it as their first language, then the pidgin language is called a _____.
A. creole B. pidgin
C. lingua franca D. standard language

13) A _____ is a variety of language that serves as a medium of communication among groups of people for diverse linguistic backgrounds.
A. pidgin B. lingua franca C. creole D. national language

14) Linguistic taboo reflects _____.
A. social taboo B. social convention
C. habit D. law

15) A _____ is a mild, indirect or less offensive word or expression substituted when a speaker or writer fears more direct wording might be harsh, unpleasantly direct, or offensive.
A. linguistic taboo B. euphemism
C. address term D. pidgin

16) The use of sexist language reflects a(n) _____ attitude.
A. social B. linguistic C. traditional D. all of the above

17) Black English has a number of distinctive features in its phonological, morphological and syntactic systems which are _____.
A. rule-governed B. systematic
C. arbitrary D. both A and B

18) It is _____ for individuals to be a perfect user of two languages in a full range of situations.
A. common B. rare
C. impossible D. none of the above

19) _____ in a person's speech, or writing, usually ranges on a continuum from casual to formal according to the type of communicative situation.
A. Stylistic variation B. Idiolectal variation
C. Social variation D. Regional variation

20) _____ are language varieties appropriate for use in particular speech situations.
A. Slang B. Address terms
C. Registers D. Education varieties

Answers

1. Define the Following Terms

1) diglossia

When two languages or language varieties exist side by side in a community and each one is used for different purposes, this is called diglossia. Usually, one is a more standard variety called the High variety or H-variety, which is used in government, the media, education, and for religious services. The other one is usually a non-prestige variety called the Low-variety or L-variety, which is used in the family, with friends, when shopping, etc.

2) idiolect

Idiolect is a personal dialect of an individual speaker that combines aspects of all the elements regarding regional, social, and stylistic variation, in one form or another.

3) bilingualism

Bilingualism refers to a linguistic situation in which two standard languages are used either by an individual or by a group of speakers.

4) register

It is a speech variety used by a particular group of people, usually sharing the same occupation (e.g. doctors, lawyers) or the same interests (e.g. stamp collectors, baseball fans).

A particular register often distinguishes itself from other registers by having a number of distinctive words, by using words or phrases in a particular way (e.g. in tennis: deuce, love, tramlines), and sometimes by special grammatical constructions (e.g. legal language).

5) pidgin

It is a language which develops as a contact language when groups of people who speak different languages try to communicate with one another on a regular basis. For example, this might occur where foreign traders have to communicate with the local population or groups of workers from different language backgrounds on plantations or in factories. A pidgin usually has a limited vocabulary and a reduced grammatical structure which may expand when a pidgin is used over a long period and for many purposes.

6) slang

It refers to casual, very informal speech, using expressive but informal words and expressions.

For some people, slang is equivalent to colloquial speech but for others, it means "undesirable speech". Usually, "colloquial speech" refers to a speech variety used in

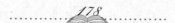

informal situations with colleagues, friends or relatives, and "slang" is used for a very informal speech variety which often serves as an "in-group" language for a particular set of people such as teenagers, army recruits, pop-groups, etc. Most slang is rather unstable as its words and expressions can change quite rapidly, for example, "Beat it!", "Scram!", and "Rack off!" for "leave".

7) communicative competence

It is the ability not only to apply the grammatical rules of a language in order to form grammatically correct sentences but also to know when and where to use these sentences and to whom.

8) lingua franca

The term lingua franca refers to an auxiliary language which is used to enable routine communication to take place between groups of people who speak different native languages or different language varieties. English, which has become a world language, is the world's most common lingua franca, followed by French. In east Africa, Swahili is the lingua franca. Mandarin can be said to be the lingua franca among speakers of 56 different nationalities, even among speakers of different dialects of Chinese.

9) sociolect

Social dialect, or sociolect, is a variety of a language (a dialect) used by people belonging to a particular social class. The speakers of a sociolect usually share a similar socioeconomic and/or educational background. Sociolects may be classed as high (in status) or low (in status).

The study of social dialects concerns a variety of social parameters such as education, age and gender. It also examines register or style variety, forms of address, choice of slang, taboo, and euphemism.

10) sociolinguistics

It is the field that studies the relation ship between language and society, between the uses of language and the social structures in which the users of language live.

11) speech community

It is a group of people who form a community, e.g. a village, a region, a nation, and who have at least one speech variety in common as well as similar linguistic norms.

In bilingual and multilingual communities, people would usually have more than one speech variety in common.

12) speech variety

It is a term sometimes used instead of language, dialect, sociolect, pidgin, creole, etc., because it is considered more neutral than such terms. It may also be used for different varieties of one language, e.g. American English, Australian English, Indian English.

2. Word Completion

1) community
2) standard
3) creole
4) taboo
5) euphemism
6) language
7) social
8) racial
9) idiolect
10) Code-switching
11) Bilingualism

3. Multiple Choice

1)—5) C A A A D
6)—10) C C B A B
11)—15) B A B B B
16)—20) A D B A C

Chapter 11 Psycholinguistics

1. Define the Following Terms

1) psycholinguistics
2) Sapir-Whorf hypothesis
3) interlanguage
4) language acquisition
5) error analysis

2. True or False Questions

Directions: Decide whether the following statements are true or false. Write "T" for true and "F" for false in the bracket before each of them.

1) (　　) Although the age at which children will pass through a given stage can vary significantly from child to child, the particular sequence of stages seems to be the same for all children acquiring a given language.

2) (　　) It's normally assumed that, by the age of five, with an operating vocabulary of more 2,000 words, children have completed the greater part of the language acquisition process.

3) (　　) It has been recognized that in ideal acquisition situations, many adults can reach native-like proficiency in all aspects of a second language.

4) (　　) If language learners are provided with sufficient and the right kind of language exposure and opportunities to interact with language input, they will acquire native-like competence in the target language.

5) (　　) The optimum age for SLA always accords with the maxim of "the younger the better".

6) (　　) In general, language acquisition refers to children's development of their first language, that is, the native language of the community in which a child has been brought up.

7) (　　) Children first acquire the sounds found in all languages of the world, no matter what language they are exposed to and in later stages acquire the more difficult sounds.

8) (　　) Language acquisition is in accordance with language learning on the assumption that there are different processes.

9) (   ) SLA is primarily the study of how learners acquire or learn an additional language after they acquired their first language.

10) (   ) A weak version of the Sapir-Whorf hypothesis states that the presence of linguistic categories influences the ease with which various cognitive operations are performed.

11) (   ) Although it is found that formal instruction hardly affects the natural route of SLA, it does enable the classroom learner to perform a wider range of linguistic tasks than the naturalistic learner and thereby accelerates the rate of acquisition.

12) (   ) Children acquire a language simply as internalizing individual expressions of language.

13) (   ) Children acquiring their first language beyond the critical age are hardly successful, such as the case of "Genie".

14) (   ) At the multiword stage, simple prepositions, especially those that indicate positions such as "in", "on" and "up", begin to turn up in children's speech.

15) (   ) Like one-word expression, two-word expressions are absent of syntactic or morphological markers.

16) (   ) There is a three-word sentence stage in first language acquisition.

17) (   ) Utterances at the multiword stage are often referred to as telegraphic speech.

18) (   ) The emergence of articulatory skills begins around the age when children start to produce babbling sounds.

19) (   ) When children's language develops towards the early multiword stage, negative words occur between the subject and the predicate.

20) (   ) Overgeneralization only occur in children's acquisition of syntax and morphology.

3. Multiple Choice

Directions: In each question there are four choices. Decide which one would be the best answer to the question or to complete the sentence best.

1) _____ deals with how language is acquired, understood and produced.
   A. Sociolinguistics   B. Psycholinguistics
   C. Pragmatics   D. Morphology

2) At the age of four, children _____.
   A. can master the essentials of their mother tongue
   B. can only babble several sounds
   C. can name the things around them only
   D. can write out the grammatical rules of their language

3) _____ refers to the gradual and subconscious development of ability in the first language by using it naturally in daily communicative situations.
   A. Learning   B. Competence
   C. Performance   D. Acquisition
4) Whorf believed that speakers of different languages perceive and experience the world differently, that is, relative to their linguistic backgrounds, hence the notion of _____.
   A. linguistic determinism   B. linguistic relativism
   C. linguistic nativism   D. linguistic behaviorism
5) In first language acquistion children usually _____ grammatical rules from the linguistic information they hear.
   A. use   B. accept   C. generalize   D. reconstruct
6) By the time children are going beyond the _____ stage, they begin to incorporate some of the inflectional morphemes.
   A. telegraphic   B. multiword   C. two-word   D. one-word
7) _____ is defined as a conscious process of accumulating knowledge of a second language usually obtained in school settings.
   A. Acquisition   B. Learning   C. Studying   D. Acquirement
8) _____ transfer is a process that is more commonly known as interference.
   A. Intentional   B. Positive   C. Negative   D. Interrogative
9) In general, the two-word stage begins roughly in the _____ half of the child's second year.
   A. early   B. late   C. first   D. second
10) By the age of _____, children have completed the greater part of the language acquisition process.
    A. three   B. four   C. five   D. six
11) At the _____ stage negation is simply expressed by single words with negative meaning.
    A. prelinguistic B. multiword C. two-word   D. one-word
12) The optimum age for SLA is _____.
    A. childhood   B. early teens C. teens   D. adulthood
13) Which of the following isn't a factor that may influence SLA?
    A. Age.   B. Motivation. C. Personality.   D. Sex.
14) In general, _____ language acquisition refers to children's development of their language of the community in which a child has been brought up.
    A. first   B. second   C. third   D. fourth
15) Children follow a similar _____ schedule of predictable stages along the route of language development across cultures.
    A. learning   B. studying   C. acquisition   D. acquiring

16) The development of linguistic skills involves the acquisition of _____ rules rather than the mere memorization of words and sentences.
   A. morphological   B. grammatical
   C. linguistic   D. syntactic

17) By the age of _____, children's vocabulary increases by about twenty words each day.
   A. two and a half years   B. three
   C. five   D. six

18) _____ are a crucial period for first language acquisition.
   A. The pre-school years   B. School years
   C. Teenage period   D. Adulthood

19) _____ was believed to be the major source of difficulties experienced and errors made by L2 learners.
   A. Transfer   B. Positive transfer
   C. Negative transfer   D. Overgeneralization

20) _____ approach shows that there are striking similarities in the ways in which different L2 learners acquire a new language.
   A. Transfer   B. Interference
   C. Contrastive analysis   D. Error analysis

21) During the process of SLA, a learner constructs a series of internal representations that comprises the learner's interior knowledge of the target language, this is _____.
   A. interlanguage   B. first language
   C. second language   D. foreign language

22) Which stage does the child belong to according to the stage of first language acquisition when we heard his saying like "Baby chair", "Mummy sock" or "Me going", etc.?
   A. Babbling stage.   B. One-word stage.
   C. Two-word stage.   D. Multi word stage.

23) Which stage does the child belong to according to the development of the grammatical system when we heard his saying like "No heavy", "No eat", "He no bite you", etc.?
   A. The development of phonology.
   B. The development of syntax.
   C. The development of morphology.
   D. The development of vocabulary and semantics.

24) Language acquisition is primarily the acquisition of the _____ system of language.
   A. phonological   B. semantic   C. grammatical   D. communicative

25) Which of the following terms doesn't belong to the same category?
   A. Caretaker speech.　　　　　　B. Babytalk.
   C. Mother tongue.　　　　　　　D. Motherese.
26) Which of the stages doesn't belong to the recognizable stage of language?
   A. The prelinguistic stage.　　　　B. The one-word stage.
   C. The two-word stage.　　　　　D. The multiword stage.
27) In general, the two-word stage begins roughly _____.
   A. in the late part of the first year
   B. in the early part of the second year
   C. during the second year
   D. between two and three years old
28) Children's language begins to reflect the distinction between sentence-types at _____ stage.
   A. the prelinguistic　　　　　　　B. the one-word
   C. the two-word　　　　　　　　D. the multiword
29) What's the salient feature of the utterances at the multiword stage?
   A. The number of words.　　　　B. The sequence of words.
   C. The intonation.　　　　　　　D. The gender of words.

■ 4. Word Completion

1) In learning a second language, a learner will subconsciously use his L1 knowledge. This process is called language _____.
2) The development of a first or native language is called first language _____.
3) Within the framework of _____ analysis, second language learning was believed to be a matter of overcoming the differences between L1 and L2 systems.
4) For the vast majority of children, language development occurs spontaneously and requires little conscious _____ on the part of adults.
5) The pre-school years are a _____ period for first language acquisition.

■ 5. Answer the Following Questions

1) What are the two parts of the Sapir-Whorf hypothesis? And can you distinguish between the strong and weak versions of the linguistic determinism view?
2) What are the major individual factors for SLA?
3) What is language acquisition and what is L2 acquisition? What is learner language and what is target language?

Answers

1. Define the Following Terms

1) psycholinguistics

It is the study of language in relation to the mind, with focus on the processes of language comprehension, production and acquisition. It takes upon itself the job of exploring the biological basis of human language, critical periods for child language acquisition, and the relationship between the language and thought.

2) Sapir-Whorf hypothesis

It is a theory put forward by the American anthropological linguist Sapir and his student Whorf (and also a belief held by some scholars) which states that the way people view the world is determined wholly or partly by the structure of their native language. Their theory has two thrusts: linguistic determinism and linguistic relativity.

3) interlanguage

Interlanguage is a term coined by Selinker to refer to the systematic knowledge of an L2 that is independent of both the target language and the learner's L1.

4) language acquisition

Language acquisition: It is a general term used to refer to the development of a person's first, second, or foreign language.

5) error analysis

It is an approach to the study and analysis of the errors made by second language learners, which suggests that many learner errors are not due to the learner's mother tongue interference but reflect universal learning strategies such as overgeneralization and simplification of roles.

2. True or False Questions

1)—5) T T F F F　　6)—10) T T F T T　　11—15) T F T T F
16—20) F F T F F

3. Multiple Choice

1)—5) B A D B C　　6)—10) A B C D C　　11—15) D B D A C
16—20) B C A D D　　21—25) A C B C C　　26—29) A C C B

4. Word Completion

1) transfer　2) acquisition　3) contrastive　4) instruction　5) crucial

5. Answer the Following Questions

1) What are the two parts of the Sapir-Whorf hypothesis? And can you distinguish between the strong and weak versions of the linguistic determinism view?

The Sapir-Whorf hypothesis consists of two parts: linguistic determinism and linguistic relativity. Linguistic determinism refers to the notion that a language determines certain nonlinguistic cognitive processes. That is, learning a language changes the way a person thinks. Linguistic relativity refers to the claim that the cognitive processes that are determined are different for different languages. Thus, speakers of different languages are said to think in different ways.

The linguistic determinism hypothesis can be interpreted in at least two different ways. The strong version states that language determines cognition: the presence of linguistic categories creates cognitive categories. Alternatively, a weak version of the hypothesis states that the presence of linguistic categories influences the ease with which various cognitive operations are performed.

2) What are the major individual factors for SLA?

The acquisition of a second language is dependent on a combination of factors. The rate and ultimate success in SLA are affected not only by learners' experience with optimal input and instruction, but also by individual learner factors. There is no uniform way in which learners acquire the knowledge of a second language. A number of factors that pertain to the learner potentially influence the way in which a second language is acquired.

A. The optimum age occurs during the early years of one's life before puberty.

B. They must have strong motivation, instrumental or integrative.

C. The extent to which learners differ in the process of adapting to the new culture of the L2 community, that is acculturation.

D. Learners' personality.

3) What is language acquisition and what is L2 acquisition? What is learner language and what is target language?

Language acquisition is a general term used to refer to the development of a person's first, second, or foreign language. L2 acquisition refers to the way in which people learn a language other than their mother tongue, inside or outside a classroom.

Learner language refers to the language that learners produce in speech and writing during the course of language acquisition. Target language refers to the language that learner is trying to learn.

Chapter 12 Linguistic Theories and FLT

■ 1. Define the Following Terms

1) language acquisition *vs* language learning
2) interlanguage
3) error analysis
4) negative transfer
5) applied linguistics

■ 2. True or False Questions

Directions: Decide whether the following statements are true or false. Write "T" for true and "F" for false in the bracket before each of them.

1) (　) *Wife* and *husband* are converse opposites while *cold* and *hot* are complementary opposites.
2) (　) Morphology is the branch of linguistics that studies the ways in which words are combined to form sentences in a language.
3) (　) Both the word *threatened* and *description* contain two morphemes.
4) (　) "Tom hit Mary and Mary hit Tom" is an exocentric construction while "men and women" is an endocentric construction.
5) (　) All roots are free morphemes while not all free morpheme are roots.

■ 3. Answer the Following Question

What contribution has linguistics made to the Teaching of English as a Foreign Language?

Answers

1. Define the Following Terms

1) language acquisition *vs* language learning

Language acquisition contrasted with language learning on the assumption that these are different processes. According to Stephen Krashen, the American SLS scholar, acquisition refers to the gradual and subconscious development of ability in the first language by using it naturally in daily communicative situations. Learning, however, is defined as a conscious process of accumulating knowledge of a second language usually obtained in school settings. It is recognized that children acquire their native language without explicit learning. A second language is more commonly learned but to some degree may also be acquired, depending on the environmental setting and the input received by the L2 learner. A rule can be learned before it is acquired, but having learned a rule does not necessarily preclude having to acquire it later.

2) interlanguage

The type of language constructed by second or foreign language learners who are still in the process of learning a language is often referred to as interlanguage. As the name signals, interlanguage is a language system between the target language and the learner's native language. It is imperfect compared with the target language, but it is not mere translation from the learner's native language.

3) error analysis

Error analysis is the study and analysis of error and is confined to the language learner. Here, "error" refers generally to the learner's misuse or misunderstanding of the target language, may it be grammatical or pragmatic.

4) negative transfer

In learning a second language learners will subconsciously use their mother tongue knowledge. This is known as language transfer. When the structures of the two languages are different, negative transfer or interference occurs and results in errors.

5) applied linguistics

Applied linguistics is the study of language and linguistics in relation to language-related problems, such as lexicography, translation, etc. Applied linguistics uses information from linguistics in order to develop its own theoretical model of areas, such as syllabus design, speech therapy, language planning, stylistics, etc. In its narrow sense, here, applied linguistics refers to the study of second and foreign language learning and teaching, i.e. the study of language and linguistics in relation to language teaching and learning.

2. True or False Questions:

1)—5) F F F F F

3. Answer the Following Question

What contribution has linguistics made to the Teaching of English as a Foreign Language?

Language is viewed as a system of forms in linguistics, but it is regarded as a set of skills in the field of language teaching. Linguistic research is concerned with the establishment of theories which explains the phenomena of language, whereas language teaching aims at the learner's mastery of language.

Applied linguistics is the study of language and linguistics in relation to language-related problems, such as lexicography, translation, etc. Applied linguistics uses information from linguistics in order to develop its own theoretical model of areas, such as syllabus design, speech therapy, language planning, stylistics, etc. In its narrow sense, here, applied linguistics refers to the study of second and foreign language learning and teaching, i.e. the study of language and linguistics in relation to language teaching and learning.

To bridge the gap between the theories of linguistics and the practice of foreign language teaching, applied linguistics serves as a mediating area which interprets the results of linguistic theories and makes them user-friendly to the language teacher and learner. Applied linguistics is conducive to foreign language teaching in two major aspects (Hu Zhuanglin, 2001: 352 – 353):

Firstly, applied linguistics extends theoretical linguistics in the direction of language learning and teaching, so that the teacher is enabled to make better decisions on the goal and content of the teaching. When faced with the task of designing a syllabus, the teacher has a number of choices. Should he set out to teach the language used in literary works, or that used in daily communication? Should he teach the general system of the language, or a part of this system? What are the principles of compiling or choosing textbooks? What kind of exercises is the most suitable? To answer these questions, the teacher is consciously or unconsciously using his understanding of the nature of language learning. Applied linguistics provides the teacher with a formal knowledge of the nature of language and language system, and thus increases his understanding of the nature of language learning. As a result, the teacher can make more informed decisions on what approach to take, hence what to teach.

Secondly, applied linguistics states the insights and implications that linguistic theories have on the language teaching methodology. Once the goal and content of the teaching are settled, the teacher has to consider questions of how to teach. Should the teaching-learning process be teacher-centered, textbook-centered, or learner-centered? How should the learners' errors be treated? What techniques should be adopted in the classroom? Since applied linguistics defines the nature of language learning in connection with various linguistic theories, it helps the teacher to choose teaching methods and techniques

Chapter 13 Schools of Modern Linguistics

1. Define the Following Terms

1) structural linguistics
2) ideational function
3) the Prague School
4) the London School
5) American Structuralism
6) Transformational-Generative (TG) Grammar

2. Word Completion

1) The Prague School practiced a special style of _____ linguistics.
2) The Prague School is best known and remembered for its contribution to phonology and the distinction between _____ and phonology.
3) The man who turned linguistics proper into a recognized distinct academic subject in Britain was _____.
4) Halliday's Systemic Grammar contains a functional component, and the theory behind his Functional Grammar is _____.
5) Systemic-Functional Grammar is a(n) _____ oriented functional linguistic approach.
6) Structuralism is based on the assumption that grammatical categories should be defined not in terms of meaning but in terms of _____.
7) In the history of American linguistics, the period between 1933 and 1950 is also known as the _____ Age.
8) _____ in language theories is characteristic of America.
9) The starting point of Chomsky's TG Grammar is his _____ hypothesis.
10) Chomsky argues that LAD probably consists of three elements, that is a _____, linguistic universal, and an evaluation procedure.
11) Systemic-Functional Grammar takes the actual uses of language as the object of study, while Chomsky's TG Grammar takes the ideal speaker's linguistic _____ as the object of study.
12) The specific method of Relational Grammar in describing language structure is the

multi-level analysis of _____ relations.

13) For Bloomfield, linguistics is a branch of psychology, and specifically of the positivistic brand of psychology known as _____.

14) The Prague School can be traced back to its first meeting under the leadership of _____.

15) The distinction between the ideal language user's knowledge of the rules of the language, which is called _____, and the actual realization of this knowledge in utterance, which is called _____, is made by American linguist Noam Chomsky.

16) The context of situation of a text has been theorized by Halliday in terms of the contextual variables of _____, _____ and _____.

17) According to Halliday, language and social context are complementary and he interprets context as including two communication planes: _____ (context of situation) and _____ (context of culture).

18) The London School can be classified into two stages of development: the establishment and development period represented by _____ and _____; the prime period represented by _____.

3. Multiple Choice

1) Discovering procedures are practiced by _____.
   A. descriptive grammar   B. TG Grammar
   C. traditional grammar   D. functional grammar

2) In which of the following stage did Chomsky add the semantic component to his TG Grammar for the first time?
   A. The Classic Theory.   B. The Standard Theory.
   C. The Extended Standard Theory.   D. The Minimalist Program.

3) According to Halliday, the three metafunctions of language are _____.
   A. ideational, interpersonal and textual
   B. ideational, informative and textual
   C. metalinguistic, interpersonal and textual
   D. ideational, interpersonal and referential

4) The person who is often described as "father of modern linguistics" is _____.
   A. Firth   B. Saussure   C. Halliday   D. Chomsky

5) The most important contribution of the Prague School to linguistics is that it sees language in terms of _____.
   A. function   B. meaning   C. signs   D. system

6) The principal representative of American descriptive linguistics is _____.
   A. Boas   B. Sapir   C. Bloomfield   D. Harris

7) The theory of _____ considers that all sentences are generated from a semantic

structure.

A. Case Grammar B. Stratificational Grammar
C. Relational Grammar D. Generative Semantics

8) _____ grammar is the most widespread and the best understood method of discussing Indo-European languages.

A. Traditional B. Structural
C. Functional D. Generative

9) Hjelmslev is a Danish linguist and the central figure of the _____.

A. Prague School B. Copenhagen School
C. London School D. Generative Semantics

10) In Halliday's view, the _____ function is the function that the child uses to know about his surroundings.

A. personal B. heuristic C. imaginative D. informative

11) The theme in the sentence "On it stood Jane" is _____.

A. On it B. stood C. On it stood D. Jane

12) Chomsky follows _____ in philosophy and mentalism in psychology.

A. empiricism B. behaviourism C. rationalism D. mentalism

13) TG Grammar has seen _____ stages of development.

A. three B. four C. five D. six

4. True or False Questions

1) In the Classical theory, Chomsky's aim is to make linguistics a science. This theory is characterized by three features: emphasis on prescription of language, introduction of transformational rules, and grammatical description regardless of language formation.

2) Generative grammar is a system of rules that in some explicit and well-defined way assigns structural descriptions to sentences.

3) Following Saussure's distinction between langue and parole, Trubetzkoy argued that phonetics belonged to langue whereas phonology belonged to parole.

4) The subject-predicate distinction is the same as the theme and rheme contrast.

5) The London School is also known as systemic linguistics and functional linguistics.

6) According to Firth, a system is a set of mutually exclusive options that come into play at some point in a linguistic structure.

7) American structuralism is a branch of diachronic linguistics that emerged independently in the United States at the beginning of the twentieth century.

8) The Standard Theory focuses discussion on language universals and universal grammar.

9) American descriptive linguistics is empiricist and focuses on diversities of languages.

10) Chomsky's concept of linguistic performance is similar to Saussure's concept of parole, while his use of linguistic competence is somewhat different from Saussure's langue.

11) If two sentences have exactly the same ideational and interpersonal functions, they would be the same in terms of textual coherence.

12) The structuralists follow behaviorism in philosophy and empiricism in psychology.

5. Answer the Following Questions

1) When is the beginning of modern linguistics?
2) Why is Saussure considered as the father of modern linguistics?
3) How many stages of development has American structuralism undergone?
4) What is behaviorism? What is the relationship between linguistics and behaviorism according to Bloomfield?
5) How many stages of development has Chomsky's TG Grammar undergone?
6) What is transformational grammar? What is generative grammar?
7) What is characteristic of TG Grammar?
8) What is Functional Sentence Perspective?
9) Can you make a brief introduction to the Copenhagen School?
10) How many stages of development has the London School undergone?
11) What did Firth inherit from Malinowski's and Saussure's views?
12) Can you state briefly about Halliday's seven functions in children's model of language?
13) Can you state briefly about Halliday's three metafunctions in adults' language?

Answers

1. Define the Following Terms

1) structural linguistics

Structural linguistics is a principally American phenomenon of the mid-20th century, typified by the work of Leonard Bloomfield, who drew on ideas of the behaviorist school of psychology. The structuralists are primarily concerned with phonology, morphology, and syntax. They focus on the physical features of utterances with little regard for meaning or lexicon. Structural linguistics describes linguistic features in terms of structures and systems. Dissatisfied with traditional grammar, structuralist grammar sets out to describe the current spoken language which people use in communication. For the first time, structuralist grammar provides description of phonological systems which aids the systematic teaching of pronunciation. However, like traditional grammar, the focus of structuralist grammar is still on the grammatical structures of a language.

2) ideational function

The ideational function is to convey new information, to communicate a content that is unknown to the hearer, present in all language uses, the ideational function is a potential, because whatever specific use one is making of language he has to refer to categories of his experience of the world. The ideational function mainly consists of "transitivity" and "voice". The whole of the transitivity system is part of the ideational component, this function, therefore, not only specifies the available options in meaning but also determines the nature of their structural realizations.

3) the Prague School

The Prague School practices a special style of synchronic linguistics, and its most important contribution to linguistics is that it sees language in terms of function and its contribution to phonology and the distinction between phonetics and phonology. Three most important points of its ideas are the emphasis on the synchronic study of language, the systemic character of language and the function of language.

4) the London School

The London School refers to the kind of linguistic scholar ship in England. J. R. Firth turned linguistics proper into a recognized distinct academic subject in Britain. Firth, under the influence of the anthropologist B. Malinowski, influenced his student, M. A. K. Halliday. They all stressed the importance of context of situation and the system aspect of language. Thus, the London School is also known as systemic linguistics and functional linguistics. Halliday's Systemic-Functional Grammar has two inseparable components: Systemic Grammar and Functional Grammar. There are six major characteristics of Systemic Grammar. A. It attaches great importance to the sociological aspects of language. B. It views language as a form of doing rather than a form of knowing. It distinguishes linguistic behavior potential from actual linguistic behavior. C. It gives a relatively high priority to description of the characteristics of particular languages and particular varieties of languages. D. It explains a number of aspects of language in terms of clines. E. It seeks verification of its hypotheses by means of observation from texts and of statistical techniques. F. It has as its central category the category of the system. The Functional Grammar puts forward three metafunctions: ideational, interpersonal and textual function.

5) American Structuralism

The school includes Boas and Sapir's theory in the beginning and Bloomfield's theory later. From the behaviorists' point of view, it holds that children learn language through a chain of stimulus-response reinforcement, and the adult's use of language is also a process of stimulus-response. Its famous formula is S→r ...... s→R. Here S stands for practical stimulus, r stands for the substitute reaction of speech, s stands for the substitute stimulus, and R stands for external practical reaction. Post-Bloomfieldian linguistics focused on direct observation, is characterized by a strict empiricism. Its goal is to devise explicit discovery procedures to enable the computer to process raw data about any language and form a complete grammar without intervention by the human linguists.

6) Transformational-Generative (TG) Grammar

The publication of Chomsky's *Syntactic Structures* in 1957 marked the beginning of the TG Grammar. Contrary to Bloomfield's data-oriented discovery procedure, Chomsky insists on the hypothesis-deduction method and his research is called evaluation process. TG Grammar has seen five stages of development: the classical theory, the standard theory, the extended standard theory, the revised extended standard theory and the minimalist program. Generative Grammar means "a system of rules that in some explicit and well-defined way assigns structural descriptions to sentences". Chomsky believes that every speaker of a language has mastered and internalised a generative grammar that expresses his knowledge of his language. TG Grammar tries to reveal the unity of particular grammars and universal grammars, to explore the universal rules with the hope of revealing the human cognitive system and the essential nature of human beings. The Innate Hypothesis states that linguistic ability is innate and that children are born with an innate faculty for language in general—LAD. Children are born with some basic knowledge on grammar, which is general and universal.

2. Word Completion

1) synchronic
2) phonetics
3) J. R. Firth
4) systemic
5) sociologically
6) distribution
7) Bloomfieldian
8) Descriptivism
9) innateness
10) hypothesis-maker
11) competence
12) grammatical
13) behaviorism
14) Vilem Mathesius
15) linguistic competence, performance
16) field, tenor, mode
17) register, genre
18) Malinowski, Firth, Halliday

3. Multiple Choice

1)—5) A B A B A   6)—10) C D A B B   11)—13) D C C

4. True or False Questions

1)—5) F T F F T   6)—10) T F F T T   11)—12) F F

5. Answer the Following Questions

1) When is the beginning of modern linguistics?

We date modern linguistics from the early twentieth century when scholars worked out detailed scientific methods for establishing relationships among languages. This is marked by the publication of Ferdinand de Saussure's book *Course in General Linguistics* (1916).

During the years from 1907 to 1911, Saussure (1857 – 1913) lectured on general linguistics in the University of Geneva. After he died in 1913, his colleagues and students thought that his ideas concerning linguistic questions were original and insightful and should be preserved.

Two of his students, C. Bally and A. Sechehaye, collected lecture notes from students and put them together to produce the great work, *Course in General Linguistics*, in 1916. This book became the most important source of Saussure's ideas and of his influence upon succeeding generations of linguists.

2) Why is Saussure considered as the father of modern linguistics?

Saussure occupies such an important place in the history of linguistics that he is often described as "father of modern linguistics":

The book *Course in General Linguistics* (1916), which is the most important source of Saussure's ideas, marked the beginning of modern linguistics.

Saussure was the first to notice the complexities of language. He believed that language is a system of signs, called conventions. He held that the sign is the union of the signifier and the signified.

By providing answers to questions concerning many aspects of language, Saussure made clear the object of study for linguistics as a science. His ideas on the arbitrary nature of sign, on the relational nature of linguistic units, on the distinction of langue and parole and of synchronic and diachronic linguistics, etc. pushed linguistics into a brand new stage.

3) How many stages of development has American structuralism undergone?

The development of American structuralism can be roughly classified into three stages:

A. Boas and Sapir Period (1911 – 1932);

B. Bloomfieldian Period (1933 – 1950);

C. Post-Bloomfieldian Period (1952 – 1956).

Debates in a true sense started only in the 1950s, when structuralism was opposed by Chomsky's Transformational-Generative Grammar.

4) What is behaviorism? What is the relationship between linguistics and behaviorism according to Bloomfield?

Behaviorism is a principle of scientific method, based on the belief that human beings cannot know anything they have not experienced. Behaviorism in linguistics holds that children learn language through a chain of "stimulus-response reinforcement", and the adult's use of language is also a process of "stimulus-response".

For Bloomfield, linguistics is a branch of the positivistic brand of psychology known as "behaviorism". When the behaviorist methodology entered linguistics via Bloomfield's writings, the popular practice in linguistic studies was to accept what a native speaker says in his language and to discern what he says about it. This is because of the belief that a linguistic description was reliable when based on observation of unstudied utterances by speakers; it was unreliable if the analyst had resorted to asking speakers questions such as "Can you say ... in your language?".

5) How many stages of development has Chomsky's TG Grammar undergone?

From its birth to the present day, TG Grammar has seen five stages of development:

A. The Classical Theory(1955 – 1965). It aims to make linguistics a science.

B. The Standard Theory(1965 – 1970). It deals with how semantics should be studied in a linguistic theory.

C. The Extended Standard Theory(1970 – 1980). It focuses discussion on language universals and universal grammar.

D. The Revised Extended Standard Theory(1980 – 1992). It focuses discussion on government and binding. It is also called Government and Binding(GB) Theory.

E. The Minimalist Program (starting from 1992). It is a further revision of the previous theory.

6) What is transformational grammar? What is generative grammar?

Transformational grammar is a theory of language structure initiated by the US linguist Noam Chomsky, which proposes that below the actual phrases and sentences of a language (its surface structure) there lies a more basic layer (its deep structure), which is processed by various transformational rules when we speak and write.

Generative grammar is a general term for the system of language analysis originated by Noam Chomsky in the 1950s to bring scientific rigor to the field of linguistics. It is a linguistic theory that attempts to describe a native speaker's tacit grammatical knowledge with a system of roles that in an explicit and well-defined way specify all of the well-formed, or grammatical sentences of a language while excluding all ungrammatical, or impossible sentences.

2) What is characteristic of TG Grammar?

Chomsky's TG Grammar has the following features. First, Chomsky defines language as a set of rules or principles. Secondly, Chomsky believes that the aim of linguistics is to produce a generative grammar which captures the tacit knowledge of the native speaker of his language. This concerns the question of learning theory and the question of linguistic universals. Thirdly, Chomsky and his followers are interested in any data that can reveal the native speaker's tacit knowledge. They seldom use what native speakers say; they rely on their own intuition. Fourthly, Chomsky's methodology is hypothesis-deductive, which operates at two levels: the linguist formulates a hypothesis about language structure—a general linguistic theory; this is tested by grammars for particular languages, and each such grammar is a hypothesis on the general linguistic theory. Finally, Chomsky follows rationalism in philosophy and mentalism in psychology.

Structural grammar and TG Grammar have different views on the nature of language. First, Bloomfield discern language as a set of utterances and a set of "lexical and grammatical habits", while Chomsky defined language as a set of rules and principles, Secondly, the two grammars have different aims in linguistics. For structural grammar, the aim of linguistics is to describe one or a set of languages; such a description is often evaluated in terms of the use to which it is going to be put. For Chomsky, the aim of linguistics is to produce a generative grammar which captures the tacit knowledge of the native speaker of his language. This concerns the question of learning theory and the question of linguistic universals. Thirdly, the two grammars make use of different types of data in their analysis. The structuralists only make use of naturally occurring utterances, observable and observed. Chomsky and his followers are interested in any data that can reveal the native speaker's tacit knowledge. Fourthly, the two grammars employ different methods. The structuralist methodology is essentially inductive, whereas Chomsky's is hypothesis-deductive. Finally, the two grammars view language learning differently. The structuralist follow empiricism in philosophy and behaviorisrn in psychology. Chomsky follows rationalism in philosophy and mentalism in psychology.

8) What is Functional Sentence Perspective?

Functional Sentence Perspective (FSP) is a theory of linguistic analysis which refers to an analysis of utterances (or texts) in terms of the information they contain. It deals particularly with the effect of the distribution of known (or given) information and new information in discourse. The known information refers to information that is not new to the reader or hearer, and the new information is what to be transmitted to the reader or hearer. Besides, the subject-predicate distinction is not always the same as the theme and rheme contrast. For example,

A. Sally	stands on the table	B. On the table stands	Sally
Subject	Predicate	Predicate	Subject
Theme	Rheme	Theme	Rheme

Sally is the grammatical subject in both sentences, but the theme in A and the rheme in B.

9) Can you make a brief introduction to the Copenhagen School?

The Copenhagen School is a structuralist and formalist group of linguists founded by the Danish linguists Louis Hjelmslev (1899-1966) and Viggo Brondal (1887-1953). Roman Jakobson (1896-1982) was associated with this group from 1939 to 1949. Influenced by Saussure, its most distinctive contribution was a concern with "gloss-matics".

Glossmatics emphasizes the name and status of linguistic theory and its relation to description. It has also developed a distinction between system and process. One of the principal features of glossmatics is the emphasis of the study of relations and not of things.

10) How many stages of development has the London School undergone?

Briefly, the London School can be classified into two stages of development:

A. The establishment and development period represented by Malinowski and Firth;

B. The prime period represented by Halliday.

11) What did Firth inherit from Malinowski's and Saussure's views?

Influenced by Malinowski, Firth regarded language as a social process, as a means of social life, rather than simply as a set of agreed-upon semiotics and signals. He held that in order to live, human beings have to learn, and learning language is a means of participation in social activities. Language is a means of doing things and of making others do things. It is a means of acting and living.

Following Saussure, Firth held that language consists of two elements: system and structure. While structure is the syntagmatic ordering of elements, system is a set of paradigmatic units, each of which can be substituted by others in certain places. Thus, structure is horizontal and system is longitudinal.

However, Firth did not fully agree with Saussure on the distinction of langue and parole, nor did Firth agree to the statement that the object of linguistic study is langue. Besides, Firth did not see language as something wholly inborn or totally acquired. He seemed to adopt a riding-on-the-wall attitude, seeing language as something both inborn and acquired.

12) Can you state briefly about Halliday's seven functions in children's model of language?

Halliday views language development in children as "the mastery of linguistic functions", and "learning a language is learning how to mean". So he proposes seven functions in children's model of language:

A. The instrumental function: the function that the child uses to meet his material needs, getting goods and services. For example, "I want it."

B. The regulatory function: the function that the child uses to control others' behavior. For example, "Give me some milk."

C. The interactional function: the function that the child uses to communicate with other people. For example, "How do you do?"

D. The personal function: the function that the child uses to express his own feelings, interests, likes and dislikes, etc. For example, "I don't like it."

E. The heuristic function: the function that the child uses to know about his surroundings and the world. For example, "What's this?"

F. The imaginative function: the function that the child uses to create his own su-rroundings. For example, "Is he going to leave me alone?"

F. The informative function: the function that the child, over eighteen months old, uses to provide information to others. For example, "Mama is out."

13) Can you state briefly about Halliday's three metafunctions in adults' language?

Since the adult's language is more complex and has to serve many functions, the original functional range of the child's language is gradually reduced to a set of highly coded and abstract functions, which are metafunctions, that is, the ideational, the

interpersonal, and the textual functions:

A. The ideational function is to convey new information to communicate a content that is unknown to the hearer.

B. The interpersonal function embodies all uses of language to express social and personal relations.

C. The textual function refers to the fact that language has mechanisms to make any stretch of spoken or written discourse into a coherent and unified text and make a living message different from a random list of sentences.

第三部分

综合模拟练习

语言学概论试卷(一)

I. **Choose from the given choices the correct one and write the corresponding letter in the brackets. (15 points in all, 1 point for each)**

1. Auditory phonetics is concerned with _____. ( )
   A. how a sound is acquired by second language learners
   B. how a sound is transmitted from the speaker's mouth to the listener's ears
   C. how a sound is perceived by the listener
   D. how a sound is produced by the vocal organs

2. Velars are sounds _____. ( )
   A. formed by bringing the tip of the tongue to the rear part of the alveolar ridge
   B. made by bringing the front of the tongue to the hard palate
   C. articulated by raising the back of the tongue to the soft palate
   D. articulated by raising the tip or the blade of the tongue to the alveolar ridge

3. Morphs are defined as _____. ( )
   A. the realizations of morphemes in general
   B. the realizations of a particular morpheme
   C. the realizations of phonemes in general
   D. the realizations of a specific phoneme

4. If two sounds can never occur in the same environment, then they are said to be in _____. ( )
   A. contrastive distribution   B. free distribution
   C. free variation   D. complementary distribution

5. _____ are never found alone as words, but are always joined with other morphemes. ( )
   A. Root morphemes   B. Bound morphemes
   C. Free morphemes   D. Affixational morphemes

6. If two sounds are always in free variation, they are said to be _____. ( )
   A. allophones of the same phoneme B. phones in general
   C. separate phonemes   D. different phones

7. Compounding refers to the process in which _____. ( )
   A. a compound is made by blending parts of two words
   B. new words are created simply by changing their parts of speech

  C. a new word is formed by putting an affix to the base

  D. two or more separate words are conjoined to produce a form which is used as a single word

8. In a hierarchical structure diagram of a word, all the forms except the one at the top are called _____ of the word.   ( )

  A. ultimate constituents   B. constituents

  C. compulsory constituents   D. immediate constituents

9. The sound _____ is a voiceless palatal plosive.   ( )

  A. [k]   B. [c]   C. [t]   D. [p]

10. According to Chomsky's TG Grammar, _____.   ( )

  A. to generate sentences, we start with deep structures and then transform them into surface structures

  B. to generate sentences, we start with surface structures and then transform them into deep structures

  C. deep structures are generated by transformational rules

  D. surface structures are derived from their deep structures by phrase structure rules

11. The sound [r] is _____.   ( )

  A. a voiced velar fricative   B. a voiceless dental plosive

  C. a central liquid   D. a bilabial glide

12. The high vowels are different from the low vowels in terms of _____. ( )

  A. the shape of the lips

  B. the tongue position

  C. the state of the soft palate

  D. the tension of the muscles of pharynx

13. The sound [iː] is _____ vowel.   ( )

  A. an oral low back rounded tense

  B. a nasal mid back rounded tense

  C. a nasal high back rounded lax

  D. an oral front high unrounded tense

14. Semantics _____.   ( )

  A. is the study of speech sounds of all human languages

  B. is the science that deals with the sound system of a language

  C. is concerned with how words are combined to form phrases and how phrases are combined by rules to form sentences

  D. is the study of the meaning of words and sentences

15. Plosives are sounds _____.   ( )

  A. that are produced by bringing two articulators very close without a complete closure so that the air-stream moves between them with audible friction

B. produced when two articulators are brought together to form a complete closure, which is followed by a sudden release

C. produced with some obstruction of the air-stream in the mouth but not enough to cause friction

D. produced when two articulators are close to each other, but not close to such an extent that a turbulent air-stream is created

Ⅱ. **Fill in each of the following blanks with a word or an expression. (10 points in all, 1 point for each blank)**

16. _____ linguistics attempts to establish a model that describes the rules of one particular language.
17. In syntax, the linguistic forms which have paradigmatic relations are said to belong to the same _____.
18. The speech organs, which are also called articulators, above the larynx, form the _____.
19. There are three types of distribution: _____ distribution, complementary distribution and free variation.
20. In English, nasal vowels occur only before _____, and oral vowels before oral consonants or at the end of words.
21. In terms of position, we may divide affixes into _____, suffixes and infixes.
22. In a hierarchical structure diagram of a sentence, the forms at the word-level are _____ of the sentence; the forms at the word-level and the phrase-level are the constituents of the sentence; the constituents connected by the two lines that are branching from the same point are called the immediate constituents of the form above that point.
23. TG Grammar has assumed that to generate sentences, we start with _____ structures.
24. All transformational rules perform three kinds of operations: _____ the sentence elements; adding a new element to the phrase marker; deleting an element from the phrase marker.
25. Semantics has two sub-branches: lexical semantics and _____ semantics.

Ⅲ. **Judge whether each of the following statements is true or false. Write "T" for true or "F" for false in the blank offered after each statement. (10 points in all, 1 point for each)**

26. Productivity is a feature of all languages that novel utterances are continually being created. _____
27. Inflectional affixes serve to indicate grammatical relations, such as number,

gender, tense, aspect, case and degree. _____

28. All consonants are produced with vocal-cord vibration. _____
29. Deep structures are generated by transformational rules while surface structures are derived from their deep structures by phrase structure rules. _____
30. English is an intonation language. _____
31. When a new word is formed by putting an affix to the base, the process involved is called affixation. Here the term base refers to the root. _____
32. In the following two sentences, S1 presupposes S2:
    S1: The victim was dead.
    S2: The victim was alive. _____
33. The dynamic study of sentences deals with two levels of structure: both surface structure and deep structure. _____
34. T-Agent-deletion must be applied immediately after T-Passive. _____
35. All the basic features of an antonymous pair of words contrast with each other. _____

Ⅳ. Translate the following terms from English into Chinese. (15 points in all, 1 points for each)

36. discreteness _____
37. microlinguistics _____
38. bilabials _____
39. suprasegmental feature _____
40. inflectional affixes _____
41. hierarchical relation _____
42. associative meaning _____
43. synonym _____
44. register _____
45. LAD _____
46. functional sentence perspective _____
47. relational opposites _____
48. surface structure _____
49. denizen _____
50. free variation _____

Ⅴ. Answer the following questions. (20 points in all)

51. Use examples to explain the three types of distribution. (6%)
52. What are the essential factors for determining sentence meaning? (6%)
53. Explain the term Labeled IC Analysis. (8%)

Ⅵ. **Practical work.（30 points in all）**

54. Describe the vowels using the table below：（10%）

vowels	front, central or back	rounded or unrounded
[iː]		
[u]		
[ɔ]		
[ɑː]		
[ə]		

55. Change the following phonemic transcriptions into phonetic transcriptions：（4%）

   1）/wiːk/ _____
   2）/ˈkɔkteil/ _____
   3）/milt/ _____
   4）/ˈkʌmfətəbl/ _____

56. Divide the following words into separate morphemes by placing a "＋" between each morpheme and the next：（6%）

   Example： bookshelf＝book＋shelf
   1）endearment＝_____
   2）basically＝_____
   3）phoneme＝_____
   4）unhappily＝_____
   5）television＝_____
   6）sputnik＝_____

57. Draw the deep structure phrase markers for the following two sentences：（10%）

   1）Has Tom finished the work?
   2）Are they playing football?

答　案

Ⅰ. 1-5　C C A D B　　6-10　A D B B A　　11-15　C B D D B

Ⅱ. 本项拼写错误、大小写错误、单复数错误均不得分！

   16. Descriptive　　　　　　　17. syntactic category
   18. vocal tract　　　　　　　 19. contrastive
   20. nasal consonants　　　　　21. prefixes
   22. ultimate constituents　　 23. deep
   24. rearranging　　　　　　　 25. sentence

Ⅲ. 26-30 T T F F T   31-35 F F T T F

Ⅳ. 36. 离散性   37. 微观语言学
     38. 双唇音   39. 超切分特征
     40. 屈折词缀   41. 等级关系
     42. 联想意义   43. 同义词
     44. 语域   45. 语言习得机制
     46. 句法功能观   47. 关系反义词
     48. 表层结构   49. 同化词
     50. 自由变异

Ⅴ. 51. 三种类型,各2分,共6分。1) **Contrastive distribution**: If two or more sounds can occur in the same environment and the substitution of one sound for another brings about a change of meaning, they are said to be in **contrastive distribution.** Obviously, the different sounds involved in a minimal pair, such as [m] in met and [n] in net are in contrastive distribution because substituting [m] for [n] will result in a change of meaning. 2) **Complementary distribution**: If two or more sounds never appear in the same environment, that is, each sound only appears in the environments where the other sound never occurs, then they are said to be in **complementary distribution.** For example, the aspirated plosive [pʰ] and the unaspirated plosive [p] are in complementary distribution because the former occurs either initially in a word or initially in a stressed syllable while the latter never occurs in such environments. 3) **Free variation**: When two sounds can appear in the same environment and the substitution of one for the other does not cause any change in meaning, then they are said to be in **free variation.** In this case, the substitution only causes a change in pronunciation of the same word. For example, in English, the word *direct* may be pronounced in two ways: /diˈrekt/ and /daiˈrekt/, and the two different sounds /i/ and /ai/ can be said to be in free variation.

52. 6点,各1分。We can summarize six essential factors for determining sentence meaning: i) the meanings of individual words which make up a sentence; ii) grammaticality of a sentence; iii) the linear ordering of the linguistic forms in a sentence; iv) the phonological features like stress and intonation; v) the hierarchical order of a sentence; and vi) the semantic roles of the nouns in relation to the verb in a sentence. All these aspects contribute to deciding the meaning of a sentence.

53. 共8分。By IC Analysis, we mean that we divide the morphemes of a word or the words of a sentence into two groups and then divide each group into subgroups, and so on, until we reach single morphemes of the word or single words of the sentence. (4分) Some linguists have modified IC Analysis by labeling each constituent with a syntactic category. The revised method is called Labeled IC

Analysis. (4分)

VI. 54.

vowels	front, central or back	rounded or unrounded
[iː]	front	unrounded
[u]	back	rounded
[ɔ]	back	rounded
[ɑː]	back	unrounded
[ə]	central	unrounded

55. 1) [wiːc] or [wiːc̚] 2) [ˈkʰɔk̚ teiɫ]
    3) [miɫt] or [miɫt̚] 4) [ˈcʰʌ̃ɱfətəbɫ]

56. 1) endearment = en + dear + ment
    2) basically = bas + ic + al + ly
    3) phoneme = phon + eme
    4) unhappily = un + happi + ly
    5) television = tele + vis + ion
    6) sputnik = sputnik

57. 1)

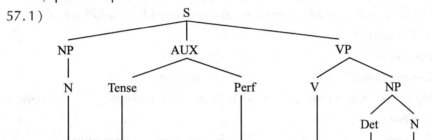

2)

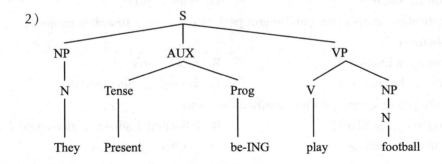

语言学概论试卷（二）

I. **Choose from the given choices the correct one and write the corresponding letter in the brackets.** (10 points in all, 1 point for each)

1. A _____ relation is a relation between a linguistic element in an utterance and linguistic elements outside that utterance, but belonging to the same sub-system of the language. ( )
   A. syntagmatic   B. sequential
   C. hierarchical   D. paradigmatic

2. By saying language is _____ we mean that every language contains an infinite number of sentences, which, however, are generated by a small set of rules and a finite set of words. ( )
   A. changeable   B. creative
   C. double-structured   D. arbitrary

3. According to the state of the velum, vowels are divided into _____ vowels and _____ vowels. ( )
   A. lax ... tense   B. rounded ... unrounded
   C. oral ... nasal   D. high ... low

4. Semantically, morphemes can be grouped into _____ morphemes and _____ morphemes. ( )
   A. root ... affixational   B. root ... free
   C. free ... bound   D. bound ... affixational

5. According to function, we can classify affixes into _____ and _____. ( )
   A. prefixes ... suffixes   B. inflectional affixes ... derivational affixes
   C. suffixes ... infixes   D. prefixes ... infixes

6. The _____ meaning of a linguistic form is the person, object, abstract notion, event, or state which the word or sentence denotes. ( )
   A. denotative   B. grammatical
   C. connotative   D. stylistic

7. The words that sound different but have the same or nearly the same meaning are called _____. ( )
   A. antonyms   B. homonyms
   C. hyponyms   D. synonyms

8. Of the sub-branches of linguistics, _____ is concerned with how words are combined into phrases and how phrases are combined into sentences.　　(　　)
   A. phonetics　　　　　　　　　B. phonology
   C. morphology　　　　　　　　D. syntax
9. If two or more separate words are conjoined to produce a form which is used as a single word, the combining process is known as _____.　　(　　)
   A. blending　　　　　　　　　B. conversion
   C. compounding　　　　　　　D. clipping
10. In the deep structure, the ordering of the four components contained in an auxiliary phrase is _____.　　(　　)
    A. Tense Modal Perf Prog　　　B. Tense Modal Prog Perf
    C. Modal Tense Perf Prog　　　D. Tense Perf Modal Prog

Ⅱ. **Fill in each of the following blanks with a word or an expression. (10 points in all, 1 point for each)**

11. Of the sub-branches of linguistics, _____ examines word formation and the internal structure of words.
12. According to Chomsky, _____ is "the speaker-hearer's knowledge of his language", while performance is "the actual use of language in concrete situations".
13. In English, nasal vowels occur only before nasal consonants, and oral vowels occur before _____ or at the end of words.
14. The distinctive features that can affect more than one sound segment and can also contrast meaning are called _____ features.
15. If two or more sounds can occur in the same environment and the substitution of one sound for another brings about a change of meaning, they are in _____.
16. The morphemes which can stand by themselves as individual words are called _____ morphemes.
17. Morphs are related to morphemes in general, while _____ are always related to a specific morpheme.
18. Inflectional affixes serve to indicate _____ relations, such as number, gender, tense, aspect, case and degree.
19. Sentences can be studied in two ways: _____, we make structural descriptions of sentences to illustrate the parts of sentences and the relationships among them; dynamically, we examine the process by which sentences are generated by syntactic rules.
20. In a hierarchical structure diagram of a sentence, the forms at the word-level are _____ of the sentence.

III. Judge whether each of the following statements is true or false. Write "T" for true (of the ten statements, only ONE is true) or "F" for false in the blank offered after each statement. Give a correct version for each of the false statements. (20 points in all, 2 points for each)

21. Linguistic symbols are a kind of visual symbols, which include vocal symbols.

22. All the sounds produced by human speech organs are linguistic symbols.

23. Competence is more concrete than performance.

24. Descriptive linguistics studies one specific language.

25. All consonants are produced with vocal-cord vibration.

26. All the back vowels are rounded vowels.

27. Allophones are the realizations of phonemes in general.

28. If two sounds can occur in the same environment and the substitution of one sound for the other does not cause a change of meaning, then they are said to be in complementary distribution.

29. All roots are free morphemes.

30. A complementary pair of antonyms is characterized by relativity.

IV. Translate the following terms from English into Chinese. (10 points in all, 1 point for each)

31. discreteness
32. microlinguistics
33. articulatory phonetics
34. tone languages
35. inflectional affixes
36. syntactic category
37. rheme
38. homographs
39. presupposition

40. Innateness Hypothesis　　　　　　　　　　_____

V. Answer the following questions. (20 points in all)

41. What are the differences between competence and performance? (6%)

42. How are surface structures different from deep structures? (6%)

43. What is the relationship between roots, affixes, free morphemes and bound morphemes? (8%)

VI. Practical work. (30 points in all)

44. Fill in the following table with "+" or "-": (8%)

	[r]	[h]
consonantal		
vocalic		
anterior		
continuant		

45. Read the following carefully and make your choices: (4%)
    1) Choose the words that begin with a bilabial consonant:
       sat, mat, pat, cat, fat　　　　　_____
    2) Choose the words that begin with a velar consonant:
       knot, lot, got, hot, cot　　　　　_____
    3) Choose the words that end with a fricative:
       ray, reach, rough, real, breathe　_____
    4) Choose the words that contain a rounded vowel:
       him, but, horse, who, us _____

46. After each basic word write two words made by the addition of prefixes or suffixes: (8%)
    1) act _____ _____
    2) appear _____ _____
    3) friend _____ _____
    4) direct _____ _____

47. Draw the deep structure phrase markers for the following two sentences: (10%)
    1) Gloria was typing a letter.
    2) They may have arrived in Nanjing.

答 案

Ⅰ. 1-5　DBCAB　　　　　6-10　ADDCA

Ⅱ. 本项拼写错误、大小写错误、单复数错误均不得分！

　　11. morphology　　　　　　　　12. competence
　　13. oral consonants　　　　　　14. suprasegmental
　　15. contrastive distribution　　　16. free
　　17. allomorphs　　　　　　　　18. grammatical
　　19. statically　　　　　　　　　20. ultimate constituents

Ⅲ. 21. F：Linguistic symbols are vocal symbols, which are part of auditory symbols.
　　22. F：Not all the sounds produced by human speech organs are linguistic symbols.
　　23. F：Competence is more abstract than performance. / Performance is more concrete than competence.
　　24. T
　　25. F：Not all consonants are produced with vocal-cord vibration. / All consonants are not produced with vocal-cord vibration. / Some consonants are produced with vocal-cord vibration but some are not.
　　26. F：All the back vowels are rounded vowels except [ɑː].
　　27. F：Allophones are the realizations of a particular phoneme. / Phones are the realizations of phonemes in general.
　　28. F：If two sounds can occur in the same environment and the substitution of one sound for the other does not cause a change of meaning, then they are said to be in free variation.
　　29. F：All roots are not free morphemes. / Not all roots are free morphemes. / Roots are not necessarily free morphemes.
　　30. F：A gradable pair of antonyms is characterized by relativity.

Ⅳ. 31. 离散性　　　　　　　　　　32. 微观语言学
　　33. 发音语音学　　　　　　　　34. 声调语言
　　35. 屈折词缀　　　　　　　　　36. 句法范畴
　　37. 述位　　　　　　　　　　　38. 同形异义词
　　39. 预设　　　　　　　　　　　40. 先天主义假说

Ⅴ. 41. According to Chomsky, competence refers to a native speaker's knowledge about his mother tongue while performance refers to the actual speech in concrete situations. Competence is more abstract and cannot be directly observed, but performance is more concrete and can be observed directly.
　　42. They are different from each other in the following four aspects：
　　　　1）Surface structures correspond to the linear arrangements of words while deep

structures correspond to the meaningful grouping of words.

2) Surface structures are more concrete while deep structures are more abstract.

3) Surface structures give the forms of sentences while deep structures give the meanings of sentences.

4) Surface structures are pronounceable while deep structures are not. (四点区别答出三点即可)

43. All free morphemes are roots, but not all roots are free morphemes. (4 分) All affixes are bound morphemes, but not all bound morphemes are affixes. (4 分)

Ⅵ. 44.

	[r]	[h]
consonantal	+	+
vocalic	+	−
anterior	−	−
continuant	+	+

45. 1) mat, pat 2) got, cot
    3) rough, breathe 4) horse, who

46. 1) act   action   active
    2) appear   disappear   appearance
    3) friend   friendly   friendship
    4) direct   direction   indirect

47. 1)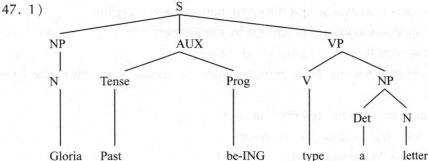

2)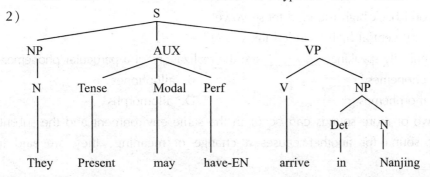

语言学概论试卷(三)

I. **Choose from the given choices the correct one and write the corresponding letter in the brackets. (10 points in all, 1 point for each)**

1. Of the design features of human language, _____ is one of the defining properties of human language, which refers to the fact that human language can be used to talk about things that are present or not present, real or not real, and about matters in the past, present or future, or in far-away places.　(　)
   A. displacement　　　　　　　　B. productivity
   C. discreteness　　　　　　　　D. arbitrariness

2. A _____ study of a language is concerned with the historical development of the language over a long period of time.　(　)
   A. synchronic　　　　　　　　　B. diachronic
   C. syntagmatic　　　　　　　　D. paradigmatic

3. Acoustic phonetics deals with _____.　(　)
   A. how speech sounds are produced by human speech organs
   B. how speech sounds are perceived by the listener
   C. how speech sounds are taught and learned
   D. how speech sounds are transmitted from the speaker's mouth to the listener's ears

4. The sound [uː] can be described as a(n) _____.　(　)
   A. oral front high rounded tense vowel
   B. nasal back low unrounded tense vowel
   C. oral back high rounded tense vowel
   D. oral central high rounded lax vowel

5. Technically speaking, _____ are the realizations of a particular phoneme.　(　)
   A. phonemes　　　　　　　　　　B. allophones
   C. morphemes　　　　　　　　　D. allomorphs

6. If two or more sounds can occur in the same environment and the substitution of one sound for another causes a change of meaning, they are said to be in _____.　(　)
   A. free variation　　　　　　　B. complementary distribution
   C. contrastive distribution　　D. overlapping distribution

7. In IC analysis, the forms at the bottom of a tree-branch diagram are called
   _____.   (   )
   A. immediate constituents   B. constituents
   C. optional constituents   D. ultimate constituents
8. The inner layering of a sentence constitutes its _____ structure.   (   )
   A. syntagmatic   B. substitutional
   C. paradigmatic   D. hierarchical
9. By _____, we mean the object or state of affairs in extra-linguistic reality or a linguistic element to which the speaker or writer is referring by using a linguistic sign.   (   )
   A. referent   B. reference   C. sense   D. concept
10. The _____ is the doer of an action and the patient is the target (animate or inanimate) on which the action has influence.   (   )
    A. agent   B. instrument   C. cause   D. locative

Ⅱ. **Fill in each of the following blanks with a word or an expression. (10 points in all, 1 point for each)**

11. Two types of symbols may be identified: _____ symbols and auditory symbols.
12. According to Chomsky, _____ is "the speaker-hearer's knowledge of his language".
13. A native speaker has several different types of knowledge about his mother tongue. _____ knowledge is a native speaker's intuition about how a word is formed.
14. The space between the vocal cords is called _____.
15. When the vocal cords are spread apart, the air-stream is not blocked at the glottis and it passes freely into the vocal tract without vocal-cord vibration. The sounds produced in this way are called _____.
16. Distinctive features are used to describe phonemes, while _____ features are used to describe their allophones.
17. Tone languages are languages that use pitch to contrast meaning at word level, whereas _____ languages are languages that use pitch to distinguish different meanings at phrase level or sentence level.
18. When a new word is formed by putting an affix to the base, the process involved is called _____.
19. The _____ relation refers to the linear ordering of the words and the phrases within a sentence.
20. The meaning of _____ pairs of antonyms is characterized by relativity.

III.
Judge whether each of the following statements is true or false. Write "T" for true (of the ten statements, only ONE is true) or "F" for false in the blank offered after each statement. Give a correct version for each of the false statements. (20 points in all, 2 points for each)

21. In theory, the length of sentences is limited.

22. General linguistics aims at developing a theory that describes the rules of a particular language.

23. Language is arbitrary, which means that any individual speaker has the freedom to determine the pronunciation of a word.

24. Bilabials are different from alveolars in terms of manner of articulation.

25. English is a tone language.

26. The sound [e] may be marked with [−high], [+low], [+front], [−back], [−rounded] and [−tense].

27. Some synonyms have the same denotative meaning but show differences in connotative meaning.

28. The sounds that are in free variation are allophones of the same phoneme.

29. A morpheme is a minimal distinctive unit in the grammatical system of a language.

30. A deep structure gives the form of a sentence.

IV.
Translate the following terms from English into Chinese. (10 points in all, 1 point for each)

31. imaginative function
32. non-verbal communication
33. International Phonetic Alphabet
34. tone languages
35. inflectional affixes

36. lexical ambiguity
37. homophones
38. entailment
39. The Prague School
40. behaviorism

V. Answer the following questions. (20 points in all)

41. What are the differences between general linguistics and descriptive linguistics? And what's the relationship between them? (6%)

42. What are the differences between English phonetics and English phonology? (6%)

43. How many theories of meaning do you know? List at least four of them and explain them briefly. (8%)

VI. Practical work. (30 points in all)

44. Combine the following individual rules in each group into one: (4%)

  1) NP→N
   NP→Det N
   NP→AP N
   NP→Det AP N

  2) X→A B
   X→A C
   X→A
   X→A B C

  3) T→L M N
   T→L N
   T→N
   T→M N

  4) R→A B
   R→B
   R→C
   R→C D
   R→E F

45. Describe the consonants using the following table: (8%)

	the position of the velum	the presence or the absence of vocal-cord vibration	the place of articulation	the manner of articulation
[b]				
[r]				
[n]				
[k]				

46. Match the names of linguistic figures in column A with the descriptions in column B: (8%)

         A   B

1) Halliday ( )   a. the distinctive feature theory
2) Chomsky ( )   b. The London School
3) Saussure ( )   c. American Structuralism
4) Jakobson ( )   d. Stratificational Grammar
5) Hjelmslev ( )   e. SF Grammar
6) Bloomfield ( )   f. The Standard Theory
7) Firth ( )   g. the father of modern linguistics
8) Lamb ( )   h. The Copenhagen School

47. Draw the deep structure phrase markers for the following two sentences: (10%)

1) They had solved the problem.

2) He might be waiting for us.

答　案

I. 1–5　ABDCB　　　　6–10　CDDAA

II. 本项拼写错误、大小写错误、单复数错误均不得分!

11. visual　　　　12. competence　　　　13. Morphological
14. glottis　　　　15. voiceless consonants / voiceless sounds
16. phonetic　　　17. intonation　　　　18. affixation / derivation
19. syntagmatic　　20. gradable

III.

21. F: In theory, the length of sentences has no limit.

22. F: General linguistics aims at developing a theory that describes the rules of the whole human language. / General linguistics aims at developing a theory that describes the rules of the language in general. / Descriptive linguistics aims at

developing a theory that describes the rules of a particular language.

23. F: Language is arbitrary, which doesn't mean that any individual speaker has the freedom to determine the pronunciation of a word.
24. F: Bilabials are different from alveolars in terms of place of articulation.
25. F: English is an intonation language. / Chinese is a tone language.
26. F: The sound [e] may be marked with [−high], [−low], [+front], [−back], [−rounded] and [+tense].
27. T
28. F: The sounds that are always in free variation are allophones of the same phoneme.
29. F: A morpheme is a minimal meaningful unit in the grammatical system of a language.
30. F: A deep structure gives the meaning of a sentence. / A surface structure gives the form of a sentence.

Ⅳ. 31. 想象功能　　　　32. 非言语交际　　　　33. 国际音标
　　34. 声调语言　　　　35. 屈折词缀　　　　　36. 词汇歧义
　　37. 同音异义词　　　38. 蕴涵　　　　　　　39. 布拉格学派
　　40. 行为主义

Ⅴ. 41. General linguistics deals with language in general, whereas descriptive linguistics is concerned with one particular language(2 分). The former aims at developing a theory that describes the rules of human language in general while the latter attempts to establish a model that describes the rules of one particular language(2 分). General Linguistics and descriptive linguistics are dependent on each other. In the first place, general linguistics provides descriptive linguistics with a general framework in which any particular language can be described, studied and analyzed(1 分). In the second place, the resulting descriptions of particular languages, in turn, supply empirical evidence which may confirm or refute the model(s) put forward by general linguistics(1 分).

42. Phonetics is a study of speech sounds (1.5 分) while phonology is a study of the sound system of a language(1.5 分). The former deals with the concrete aspects like how sounds are produced by human speech organs, how sounds are transmitted from the speaker's mouth to the listener's ears, how sounds are perceived by the listener, how sounds are classified, and how sounds are described in terms of different criteria(1.5 分). The latter copes with the abstract aspects like whether sounds can differentiate word meaning and how sounds are combined into permissible patterns(1.5 分).

43. There have been many theories of meaning which attempt to seek an answer to the question "What is meaning?". John Lyons mentions six distinguishable and more or less well-known philosophical theories of meaning:

(i) the referential (or denotational) theory ("the meaning of an expression is what it refers to (or denotes), or stands for"; e.g., "Fido" means Fido, "dog" means either the general class of dogs or the essential property which they all share);

(ii) the ideational, or mentalistic theory ("the meaning of an expression is the idea or concept associated with it in the mind of anyone who knows and understands the expression");

(iii) the behaviourist theory ("the meaning of an expression is either the stimulus that evokes it or the response that it evokes, or a combination of both, on particular occasions of utterance");

(iv) the meaning-is-use theory①("the meaning of an expression is determined by, if not identical with, its use in the language");

(v) the verificationist theory ("the meaning of an expression, if it has one, is determined by the verifiability of the sentences, or propositions, containing it");

(vi) the truth-conditional theory ("the meaning of an expression is its contribution to the truth-conditions of the sentences containing it"). (以上六点答出四点即可得满分)

VI. 44. 1) NP→(Det) (AP) N
    2) X→A (B) (C)
    3) T→(L) (M) N
    4) R→ $\begin{cases} (A) \ B \\ C \ (D) \\ E \ F \end{cases}$

45.

	the position of the velum	the presence or the absence of vocal-cord vibration	the place of articulation	the manner of articulation
[b]	oral	voiced	bilabial	plosive
[r]	oral	voiced	post-alveolar	liquid
[n]	nasal	voiced	alveolar	nasal
[k]	oral	voiceless	velar	plosive

46. 1) e   2) f   3) g   4) a
    5) h   6) c   7) b   8) d

47. 1)

```
                    S
         _____|_____
        NP         AUX          VP
        |       ___|___      ___|___
        N     Tense  Perf   V       NP
        |      |      |     |      _|_
                                  Det  N
        |      |      |     |     |   |
       They  Past  have-EN solve the problem
```

---

① The original term was *meaning as use* given by Wittgenstein (1953; cited from Bussmann, 2000: 300), a semantic theory developed by Wittgenstein in connection with ordinary language philosophy according to which the meaning of a linguistic expression is equivalent to its function or use within a known context.

2)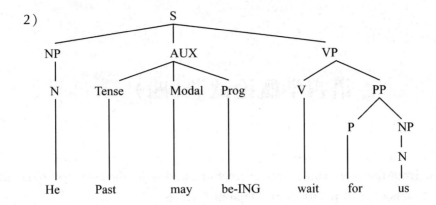

语言学概论试卷(四)

I. Choose from the given choices the correct one and write the corresponding letter in the brackets. (10 points in all, 1 point for each)

1. Language is _____ because every language contains a set of rules which underlie people's actual speech or writing. ( )
   A. vocal   B. arbitrary   C. symbolic   D. a system

2. Of the sub-branches of linguistics, _____ is concerned with the sound system of a language. ( )
   A. phonetics   B. phonology   C. morphology   D. syntax

3. Among the following consonants, _____ is an oral voiced alveolar plosive. ( )
   A. [t]   B. [k]   C. [d]   D. [b]

4. If two sounds are found to be in contrastive distribution, then they are said to be _____. ( )
   A. separate phonemes   B. allophones of the same phoneme
   C. different morphemes   D. allomorphs of the same morpheme

5. Of the suprasegmental features, _____ refers to the phonetic boundary features which may demarcate grammatical units such as morphemes, words or clauses. ( )
   A. stress   B. tone   C. intonation   D. juncture

6. The _____ is defined as the most important part of a word that carries the principal meaning. ( )
   A. free morpheme   B. bound morpheme
   C. root   D. affix

7. Of the word-formation processes, _____ refers to a process of word-formation, in which two or more free morphemes are combined to form a new word. ( )
   A. compounding   B. blending   C. clipping   D. conversion

8. The _____ of an expression is its place in a system of semantic relationships with other expressions in the language. ( )
   A. reference   B. concept   C. sense   D. denotation

9. According to componential analysis, we can analyze a word as a set of _____ with the values: plus (+) or minus (−). ( )

A. sounds B. semantic features
C. phonetic features D. distinctive features

10. Two or more lexical items are _____ when they have the same meaning.　　　　( )

    A. antonyms B. homophones C. hyponyms D. synonyms

II. Fill in each of the following blanks with a word or an expression. (10 points in all, 1 point for each)

11. By saying language is _____, we mean we can't give a sound reason why such a form is pronounced in this way rather than in that way, and why a particular meaning should be indicated by this form rather than by that form.

12. A _____ study of a language is concerned with the historical development of the language over a period of time.

13. A native speaker has several different types of knowledge about his mother tongue. _____ knowledge is a native speaker's intuition about whether a sentence is grammatical or not.

14. Of the three sub-branches of phonetics, _____ phonetics investigates how a sound is perceived by the listener.

15. In English, all the back vowels except [ɑː] are _____.

16. A phoneme is defined as a minimal _____ unit in the sound system of a language.

17. If two sounds can occur in the same environment and the substitution of one sound for the other does not cause a change of meaning, then they are said to be in _____.

18. The constituents which are involved directly in forming a larger constituent are called the _____ of the larger form.

19. Some transformational rules are obligatory and many are optional. The _____ T-rules have to be applied if we want to obtain well-formed sentences.

20. The semantic ambiguity which is caused by ambiguous words rather than by ambiguous structures is called _____ ambiguity.

III. Judge whether each of the following statements is true or false. Write "T" for true (of the ten statements, only ONE is true) or "F" for false in the blank offered after each statement. Give a correct version for each of the false statements. (20 points in all, 2 points for each)

21. According to Chomsky, langue refers to the system of a language.

22. Triphthongs are produced by a glide from one vowel to another rapidly and continuously.

23. The sounds that are in complementary distribution and also phonetically similar are separate phonemes.

24. English linguistics is a kind of general linguistics.

25. Phonetics is the science that deals with the sound system of a language.

26. Acoustic phonetics is concerned with how a sound is produced by the vocal organs.

27. A phoneme is defined as a minimal meaningful unit in the sound system of a language.

28. All bound morphemes are affixes.

29. The word "boy" is neutral in general without any negative sense. However, when a twenty-year-old white man calls a forty-year-old black man "boy", it obviously has a negative connotation reflecting the racist attitude of the speaker.

30. Dynamically, we make structural descriptions of sentences to illustrate the parts of sentences and the relationships among them.

Ⅳ. **Translate the following terms from English into Chinese. (10 points in all, 1 point for each)**

31. representational function
32. TG Grammar
33. nasal cavity
34. allophones
35. infixes
36. backformation
37. theme-rheme theory
38. sense relations
39. signifier and signified
40. The London School

V. Answer the following questions. (20 points in all)

41. How can we decide a minimal pair or a minimal set? (6%)

42. What are the differences between tone languages and intonation languages? (6%)

43. List four morphological rules and give at least one example for each of them. (8%)

VI. Practical work. (30 points in all)

44. Judge whether the following forms are permissible in English. Write "Yes" or "No" on the blank provided after each form. (4%)
    1) /fsem/ _____
    2) /griz/ _____
    3) /sbit/ _____
    4) /mdik/ _____

45. Fill in the following table with "+" or "-": (9%)

	[c]	[r]	[f]
[continuant]			
[anterior]			
[coronal]			

46. Divide the following words into separate morphemes by placing a "+" between each morpheme and the next: (7%)
    Example: bookshelf = book + shelf
    1) weakened = _____
    2) holiday = _____
    3) tourists = _____
    4) television = _____
    5) receiving = _____
    6) children = _____
    7) invisible = _____

47. Draw the deep structure phrase markers for the following two sentences: (10%)
    1) John is not coming.
    2) Mary must have known it.

答 案

Ⅰ. 1–5 DBCAD   6–10 CACBD

Ⅱ. 本项拼写错误、大小写错误、单复数错误均不得分！

11. arbitrary
12. diachronic
13. Syntactic
14. auditory
15. rounded vowels
16. distinctive
17. free variation
18. immediate constituents
19. obligatory
20. lexical

Ⅲ. 21. F：According to Saussure, langue refers to the system of a language.

22. F：Diphthongs are produced by a glide from one vowel to another rapidly and continuously. / Triphthongs are produced by a glide from one vowel to another and then to a third one rapidly and continuously.

23. F：The sounds that are in complementary distribution and also phonetically similar are allophones of the same phoneme.

24. F：English linguistics is a kind of descriptive linguistics.

25. F：Phonology is the science that deals with the sound system of a language. / Phonetics is the science that deals with the speech sounds.

26. F：Articulatory phonetics is concerned with how a sound is produced by the vocal organs. / Acoustic phonetics is concerned with how a sound is transmitted from the speaker's mouth to the listener's ears.

27. F：A phoneme is defined as a minimal distinctive unit in the sound system of a language.

28. F：Bound morphemes are not always affixes.

29. T

30. F：Statically, we make structural descriptions of sentences to illustrate the parts of sentences and the relationships among them.

Ⅳ. 31. 表现功能
32. 转换生成语法
33. 鼻腔
34. 音位变体
35. 中缀
36. 逆生法/逆序造词法
37. 主述位理论
38. 语义关系
39. 能指与所指
40. 伦敦学派

Ⅴ. 41. Technically, a minimal pair should meet three conditions：i) the two forms are different in meaning(2分)；ii) the two forms are different in one sound segment (2分)；and iii) the different sounds occur in the same position of the two strings (2分). If a group of words can satisfy the three conditions, they form a minimal set.

42. Tone languages are those which use pitch to contrast meaning at word level(3

分). Intonation languages are those which use pitch to distinguish meaning at phrase level or sentence level. (3 分)

43. (考生若能答出以下任意四条规则或其他正确的规则,则得 4 分;若举例正确,每例 1 分,四个例子共 4 分)

1) un- + adj. →adj.
2) n. / adj. + -ify→v.
3) v. + -able→adj.
4) adj. + -ly→adv.
5) n. + -ly→adj.
6) in-, il-, ir-, im- + adj. →adj.
7) adj. + -ness→n.
8) v. + -ment→n.
9) v. + -ence/-ance /-ency /-ancy→n.
10) re- + v. →v.
11) en- + adj. / n. →v.
12) adj. / n. + -en→v.
13) dis- + v. →v.
14) adj. + -ize→v.
15) de- + v. →v.
16) n. + -ful→adj.

VI. 44. 1) No   2) Yes   3) No   4) No

45.

	[c]	[r]	[f]
[continuant]	−	+	+
[anterior]	−	−	+
[coronal]	+	+	−

46. 1) weakened = weak + en + ed
2) holiday = holi + day
3) tourists = tour + ist + s
4) television = tele + vis + ion
5) receiving = re + ceiv + ing
6) children = child + r + en
7) invisible = in + vis + ible

47. 1)

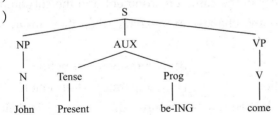

2)

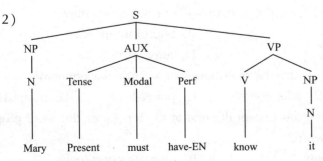

语言学概论试卷（五）

I. **Choose from the given choices the correct one and write the corresponding letter in the brackets. (10 points in all, 1 point for each)**

1. Language is _____ because the primary medium for all languages is sound. ( )
   A. vocal   B. visual   C. auditory   D. symbolic

2. The _____ function refers to the use of the language to communicate knowledge about the world, to report events, to make statements, to give accounts, to explain relationships, to relay messages and so on. ( )
   A. instrumental   B. regulatory
   C. representational   D. interactional

3. According to Saussure, _____ refers to the abstract linguistic system shared by all the members of a speech community. ( )
   A. competence   B. parole   C. performance   D. langue

4. The study of how speech organs produce speech sounds is called _____ phonetics. ( )
   A. auditory   B. articulatory   C. visual   D. acoustic

5. When two sounds can appear in the same environment and the substitution of one for the other does not cause any changes in meaning, then they are in _____. ( )
   A. free variation   B. contrastive distribution
   C. complementary distribution   D. comparative distribution

6. Morphemes can be further divided into subgroups; the _____ is defined as the most important part of a word that carries the principal meaning. ( )
   A. free morpheme   B. bound morpheme
   C. root   D. affix

7. In phonology, _____ are the realizations of a particular phoneme. ( )
   A. allomorphs   B. allophones   C. phones   D. morphs

8. In IC analysis, all the forms except the one at the top (i.e. the word proper) are the _____ of the word. ( )
   A. optional constituents   B. ultimate constituents
   C. immediate constituents   D. constituents

9. Of the word-formation processes, _____ refers to the process of word-formation in which a word is shortened by deleting one or more syllables without any change in the meaning or in the part of speech. ( )
   A. affixation   B. clipping   C. conversion   D. blending
10. The inner layering of a sentence constitutes its _____ structure. ( )
   A. syntagmatic   B. paradigmatic
   C. substitutional   D. hierarchical

II. Fill in each of the following blanks with a word or an expression. (10 points in all, 1 point for each)

11. The description of a language at some point of time (as if it stopped developing) is a _____ study.
12. When the vocal cords are spread apart, voiceless consonants are pronounced because the air stream can pass freely through the glottis into the vocal cavity without vocal-cord _____.
13. Of the sub-branches of linguistics, _____ studies the internal structure of words, and the rules by which words are formed.
14. Semantically speaking, morphemes are grouped into two categories: _____ and affixes.
15. Chomsky's TG Grammar claims that the dynamic study is concerned with both the surface structure and the _____ structure.
16. If the words or phrases within a string have more than one grammatical relation, then the string, though with no change in combination between words, is characteristic of _____ structural ambiguity.
17. Of the design features of language, _____ refers to the phenomenon that there is no motivated relationship between a linguistic form and its meaning.
18. Stops can be divided into _____ (oral stops) and nasals (nasal stops).
19. According to the _____ theory, the meaning of an expression is either the stimulus that evokes it or the response that it evokes, or a combination of both, on particular occasions of utterance.
20. The _____ of an expression is its place in a system of semantic relationships with other expressions in the language.

III. Judge whether each of the following statements is true or false. Write "T" for true (of the ten statements, only ONE is true) or "F" for false in the blank offered after each statement. Give a correct version for each of the false statements. (20 points in all, 2 points for each)

21. Interchangeability refers to the fact that human language can be used to talk about

things that are present or not present, real or not real, and about matters in the past, present or future, or in far-away places.

22. General linguistics attempts to establish a model that describes the rules of one particular language.

23. The description of a language at some point of time is a diachronic study.

24. T-Passive must be applied before T-Negation.

25. The study of how speech organs produce the sounds is called auditory phonetics.

26. Morphs are the realizations of phonemes in general.

27. Derivational affixes serve to indicate grammatical relations, such as number, gender, tense, aspect, case and degree.

28. Deep structures give the forms of sentences.

29. Surface structures are generated by phrase structure rules.

30. The cause is a semantic role which identifies the means of accomplishing the action expressed in the verb.

IV. Translate the following terms from English into Chinese. (10 points in all, 1 point for each)

31. representational function
32. synchronic linguistics
33. morphology
34. front vowels
35. free morphemes
36. affixation
37. competence
38. systemic-functional linguistics
39. syntactic category
40. complementary antonyms

V. Answer the following questions. (20 points in all)

41. What are the differences between competence and performance? (5%)

42. What are the three conditions of a minimal pair? (9%)

43. What are the two ways of studying sentences? (6%)

VI. Practical work. (30 points in all)

44. Write the symbol that corresponds to each of the following phonetic descriptions: (4%)
    1) an alveolar nasal　　　　　　　　　_____
    2) an oral back mid rounded tense vowel　_____
    3) an oral voiceless palatal plosive　　　_____
    4) a bilabial glide　　　　　　　　　　　_____

45. Divide the following words into separate morphemes by placing a "+" between each morpheme and the next: (8%)
    Example: bookshelf = book + shelf
    1) housewife =   5) basically =
    2) television =   6) illogical =
    3) unacceptable =   7) friendship =
    4) work (in "They work in Nanjing.") = 8) unmanly =

46. Match the names of linguistic figures in column A with the schools or theories or works of linguistics in column B: (8%)

Column A	Column B
1) (　) Saussure	a. glossematics
2) (　) Jakobson	b. father of modern linguistics
3) (　) Hjelmslev	c. the Innateness Hypothesis
4) (　) Chomsky	d. the distinctive feature theory

47. Draw the deep structure phrase markers for the following two sentences: (10%)
    1) Can this be true?
    2) What have you been doing?

答 案

I. 1-5 ACDBA　　　　6-10 CBDBD

II. 本项拼写错误、大小写错误、单复数错误均不得分！

　　11. synchronic　　　　　　　　12. vibration
　　13. morphology　　　　　　　　14. root morphemes / roots
　　15. deep　　　　　　　　　　　16. underlying
　　17. arbitrariness　　　　　　　　18. plosives
　　19. behaviorist　　　　　　　　 20. sense

III. 21. F：Displacement refers to the fact that human language can be used to talk about things that are present or not present, real or not real, and about matters in the past, present or future, or in far-away places. / Interchangeability means that any human being can be both a producer and a receiver of messages.

　　22. F：Descriptive linguistics attempts to establish a model that describes the rules of one particular language.

　　23. F：The description of a language at some point of time is a synchronic study.

　　24. T

　　25. F：The study of how speech organs produce the sounds is called articulatory phonetics.

　　26. F：Phones are the realizations of phonemes in general. / Morphs are the realizations of morphemes in general.

　　27. F：Inflectional affixes serve to indicate grammatical relations, such as number, gender, tense, aspect, case and degree.

　　28. F：Surface structures give the forms of sentences. / Deep structures give the meanings of sentences.

　　29. F：Deep structures are generated by phrase structure rules.

　　30. F：The instrument is a semantic role which identifies the means of accomplishing the action expressed in the verb.

IV. 31. 表现功能　　　　　　　　　32. 共时语言学
　　33. 词法/形态学　　　　　　　 34. 前元音
　　35. 自由语素　　　　　　　　　36. 词缀法
　　37. 语言知识　　　　　　　　　38. 系统功能语言学
　　39. 句法范畴　　　　　　　　　40. 互补反义词

V. 41. According to Chomsky(1分), the focus of linguistic theory is to characterize the abstract abilities speakers possess that enable them to produce grammatically correct sentences in a language. This linguistic theory consists of two parts: linguistic competence and linguistic performance. He defines the linguistic competence as one's knowledge of all the linguistic regulation systems(2 分), and the performance as the use of the language in concrete situations(2 分).

42. Technically, a minimal pair should meet three conditions: i) the two forms are different in meaning(3 分); ii) the two forms are different in one sound segment (3 分); and iii) the different sounds occur in the same position of the two strings (3 分).

43. Sentences can be studied in two different ways: statically, we can describe the structures of sentences to illustrate the relationship among the elements of a sentence(3 分); and dynamically, we can study how sentences are generated by syntactic rules(3 分).

Ⅵ. 44. 1)[n]   2)[ɔː]   3)[c]   4)[w]

45. 1) housewife = house + wife
    2) television = tele + vis + ion
    3) unacceptable = un + accept + able
    4) work (in "They work in Nanjing.") = /wɜːk/ + /ɸ/
    5) basically = bas + ic + al + ly
    6) illogical = il + logic + al
    7) friendship = friend + ship
    8) unmanly = un + man + ly

46. 1) b   2) d   3) a   4) c

47. 1)
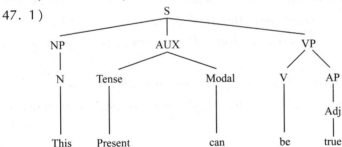

2)
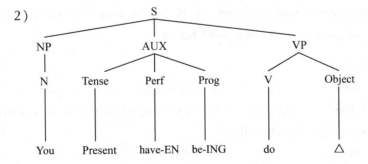

语言学概论试卷(六)

I. **Fill in the following blanks with appropriate words or expressions. (10 points in all, one point for each)**

1. Language is _____ in the sense that there is no intrinsic or logical connection between a linguistic symbol and what the symbol stands for.
2. According to John Lyons, _____ linguistics attempts to establish a model that describes the rules of one particular language.
3. The _____ relation refers to the linear ordering of the words and the phrases within a sentence.
4. The vocal tract is made up of two parts: _____ cavity and _____ cavity.
5. Technically speaking, _____ are minimal distinctive units in the sound system of a language.
6. _____ morphemes are those which cannot occur on their own as separate words. They are always joined with other morphemes to form words.
7. In IC Analysis, the forms at the bottom of a tree-branch diagram are called _____ constituents.
8. If a lexical item has a range of different meanings, it is regarded as a _____.
9. According to Chomsky, _____ is the ideal language user's knowledge of the rules of his language.

II. **Choose the right answer that fits each blank in the sentences from the four choices given. (25 points in all, one point for each)**

1. The sound [v] is a(n) _____. (　　)
   A. oral voiced alveolar affricate　　B. oral voiceless dental liquid
   C. oral voiced labiodental fricative　D. nasal voiced post-alveolar fricative
2. Which of the following is a minimal pair? _____. (　　)
   A. beat and bought　　B. /liːv/ and /fiːl/
   C. /miːt/ and /tiːm/　D. /sit/ and /suːp/
3. The sound [i] can be described as a(n) _____ vowel. (　　)
   A. oral central high unrounded lax　B. nasal front mid rounded tense
   C. oral front high unrounded lax　　D. oral back low rounded tense

4. _____ refer to the sounds produced by raising the back of the tongue to the soft palate. ( )
   A. Velars   B. Palatals   C. Alveo-palatals   D. Glottals
5. If two or more sounds _____, they are in contrastive distribution. ( )
   A. can occur in the same environment and the substitution of one sound for another does not cause a change of meaning
   B. can occur in the same environment and the substitution of one sound for another causes a change of meaning
   C. can never occur in the same environment
   D. can always appear in the same environment
6. Different from intonation languages, tone languages are languages that use pitch to contrast meaning at _____ level. ( )
   A. sentence   B. word   C. phrase   D. phrase or sentence
7. Some new words are created simply by joining the initial letters of several words together. The process involved is called _____. ( )
   A. affixation   B. compounding   C. acronymy   D. blending
8. The sound _____ is an oral voiceless post-alveolar affricate. ( )
   A. [tr]   B. [h]   C. [s]   D. [t]
9. Which of the following is not a minimal pair? _____. ( )
   A. /miːt/ and /met/   B. /fiːl/ and /fel/
   C. /dæns/ and /dɑːns/   D. /beit/ and /bit/
10. _____ is the science that is concerned with the sound system of a language. ( )
    A. Morphology   B. Semantics   C. Phonology   D. Phonetics
11. _____ are the sounds which are produced by bringing the tip of the tongue to the rear part of the alveolar ridge. ( )
    A. Alveolars   B. Post-alveolars   C. Alveo-palatals   D. Palatals
12. In terms of _____, vowels are grouped into tense vowels and lax vowels. ( )
    A. velum state   B. tongue position
    C. tension of the muscles at pharynx   D. lip rounding
13. Phones are the realizations of _____. ( )
    A. phonemes in general   B. a specific phoneme
    C. morphemes in general   D. a particular morpheme
14. The following words contain inflectional affixes except _____. ( )
    A. taller   B. Mary's   C. assignment   D. students
15. According to Chomsky's TG Grammar, in the deep structure of a sentence, verbs always take the _____. ( )
    A. present form   B. base form

C. inflectional affixes D. past form

16. A native speaker usually possesses four types of knowledge about his own language. _____ knowledge is a native speaker's intuition about whether a sentence is grammatical or not. ( )
    A. Semantic   B. Syntactic   C. Morphological   D. Phonological

17. Phonetics has three sub-branches. _____ phonetics is concerned with how a sound is perceived by the vocal organs. ( )
    A. Articulatory   B. Acoustic   C. Auditory   D. Visual

18. Labio-dentals are sounds _____. ( )
    A. formed by bringing the tip of the tongue to the rear part of the alveolar ridge
    B. produced by both lips
    C. produced by the contact between the upper teeth and the lower lip
    D. articulated by raising the tip or the blade of the tongue to the alveolar ridge

19. Allophones are defined as _____. ( )
    A. the realizations of a particular morpheme
    B. the realizations of phonemes in general
    C. minimal distinctive units in the sound system of a language
    D. the realizations of a specific phoneme

20. If _____, then they are said to be in free variation. ( )
    A. two sounds can occur in the same environment and the substitution of one sound for the other does not cause a change of meaning
    B. two sounds can occur in the same environment and the substitution of one sound for the other causes a change of meaning
    C. two sounds can never occur in the same environment
    D. two sounds can occur in contrastive environments

21. If two sounds are _____, they are said to be allophones of the same phoneme. ( )
    A. in contrastive distribution   B. always in free variation
    C. phonetically similar   D. in complementary distribution

22. Conversion refers to the process in which _____. ( )
    A. new words are created simply by changing their parts of speech
    B. a new word is formed by putting an affix to the base
    C. two or more separate words are conjoined to produce a form which is used as a single word
    D. we delete a suffix from an apparently complex form instead of adding a suffix

23. A surface structure is different from a deep structure in that _____. ( )
    A. a deep structure is pronounceable while a surface structure is not
    B. a surface structure is relatively abstract while a deep structure is concrete
    C. a surface structure gives the form of a sentence while a deep structure gives

the meaning of a sentence

D. a deep structure corresponds most closely to the linear arrangement of words as they are pronounced while a surface structure corresponds most closely to the meaningful grouping of words

24. _____ is regarded as the father of modern linguistics. ( )
   A. Mathesius   B. Saussure   C. Halliday   D. Chomsky

25. S_1 entails S_2 in the case of _____ ( )
   A. S_1: I can see a dog.   B. S_1: Pollution is our common foe.
      S_2: I can see an animal. S_2: Pollution is our common enemy.
   C. S_1: The victim was dead.   D. S_1: Tom's car needs repairing.
      S_2: The victim was alive. S_2: Tom has a car.

III. Judge whether each of the following statements is true or false. Write "T" for true or "F" for false in the blank offered after each statement. (15 points in all, one point for each)

1. The sound [p] is an oral voiceless alveolar plosive. _____
2. A diachronic study of a language is concerned with a state of a language at a particular point of time. _____
3. Acoustic phonetics is concerned with how a sound is transmitted from the speaker's mouth to the listener's ears. _____
4. Post-alveolars are different from alveolars in terms of manner of articulation. _____
5. A morpheme is a minimal meaningful unit in the lexical system of a language. _____
6. Derivational affixes serve to indicate grammatical relations. _____
7. According to TG Grammar, to generate sentences, we start with surface structures and then transform them into deep structures. _____
8. A deep structure corresponds most closely to the meaningful grouping of words. _____
9. In the rule T-Affix, the term "affix" refers to the affixes of main verbs. _____
10. The sound [w] is an oral voiced bilabial glide. _____
11. General linguistics deals with the whole human language. _____
12. When two articulators are brought together to form a complete closure which is followed by a sudden release, the sounds are called affricates. _____
13. The sound [æ] can be specified as [−high], [+low], [+front], [−back], [−rounded] and [−tense]. _____
14. Chinese is a tone language. _____
15. Inflectional affixes never cause a change in grammatical class. _____

IV. Answer the following questions. (20 points in all)

1. Explain the interrelations between semantic and structural classifications of morphemes. (6%)
2. How does competence differ from performance? (4%)
3. Define the four terms: phonemes, allophones, morphemes and allomorphs. (4%)
4. How does a surface structure differ from a deep structure? (6%)

V. Practical work. (30 points in all)

1. Write the symbol that corresponds to each of the following phonetic descriptions: (6%)
   1) a voiceless dental fricative   _____
   2) an oral high back lax vowel   _____
   3) a voiceless labio-dental fricative   _____
   4) a bilabial glide   _____
   5) an alveolar nasal   _____
   6) an oral front high tense vowel   _____

2. Analyze the following words by IC Analysis: (5%)
   1) replacements   2) decentralized   3) untruly
   4) disapproval   5) irreplaceable

3. Judge whether the following are minimal pairs by putting "Yes" or "No" on the blank provided: (8%)
   1) /fait/ and /fɔːt/   Yes or No? _____
   2) /ɑːsk/ and /æsk/   Yes or No? _____
   3) bit and bought   Yes or No? _____
   4) /net/ and /ten/   Yes or No? _____
   5) /ˈniːðə/ and /ˈnaɪðə/   Yes or No? _____
   6) /fæt/ and /hæt/   Yes or No? _____
   7) /hai/ and /mai/   Yes or No? _____
   8) /dæns/ and /dɑːns/   Yes or No? _____

4. Draw the deep structure phrase marker and apply necessary transformational rules to generate the following sentence: (11%)
   Has the work been finished?

答 案

Ⅰ. 1. arbitrary 2. descriptive
   3. syntagmatic 4. oral, nasal
   5. phonemes 6. Bound
   7. ultimate 8. polyseme
   9. competence

Ⅱ. 1–5 C A C A B 6–10 B C A C C 11–15 B C A C B
   16–20 B C C D A 21–25 B A C B A

Ⅲ. 1–5 F F T F F 6–10 F F T F T 11–15 T F T T T

Ⅳ. 1. Semantically speaking, morphemes are grouped into roots and affixes. (1.5 分) Structurally speaking, they are divided into free morphemes and bound morphemes. (1.5 分) All free morphemes are roots, but not all roots are free morphemes. (1.5 分) All affixes are bound morphemes, but not all bound morphemes are affixes. (1.5 分)

2. Competence and performance are two terms given by Chomsky. The difference between them can be summarized as follows:
Competence is "the speaker-hearer's knowledge of his language", while performance is "the actual use of language in concrete situations". (2 分) Competence is abstract and not directly observed, while performance is concrete and directly observable. (2 分)

3. Phonemes are minimal distinctive units in the sound system of a language. (1 分) Allophones are the realizations of a particular phoneme (1 分). Morphemes are minimal meaningful units in the grammatical system of a language (1 分). Allomorphs are the realizations of a particular morpheme. (1 分)

4. There are four differences between a surface structure and a deep structure:
(1) A surface structure corresponds most closely to the linear arrangement of words as they are pronounced, but a deep structure corresponds most closely to the meaningful grouping of words. (1.5 分)
(2) A surface structure is relatively concrete, but a deep structure is abstract. (1.5 分)
(3) A surface structure gives the form of a sentence as it is used in communication, but a deep structure gives the meaning of a sentence. (1.5 分)
(4) A surface structure is pronounceable, but a deep structure is not. (1.5 分)

Ⅴ. 1. 1) [θ]   2) [ʊ]   3) [f]   4) [w]   5) [n]   6) [iː]

2.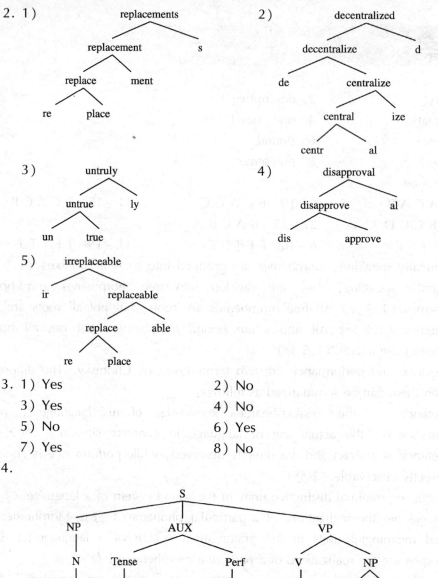

3. 1) Yes   2) No
   3) Yes   4) No
   5) No   6) Yes
   7) Yes   8) No

4.

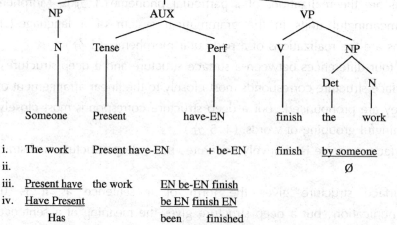

    i. The work   Present have-EN   + be-EN   finish   by someone
    ii.   ø
   iii. Present have   the work   EN be-EN finish
   iv. Have Present   be EN finish EN
        Has   been   finished

(Note: i) T-Passive; ii) T-Agent-deletion; iii) T-Yes/No question; iv) T-Affix)

第四部分

语言学全真试题

2014年1月江苏省高等教育自学考试
27037 语言学概论试卷

I. Choose from the given choices the correct one and write the corresponding letter in the brackets. (10 points in all, 1 point for each)

1. Of the design features, _____ is a feature of all languages that novel utterances are continually being created. ( )
   A. displacement   B. discreteness
   C. arbitrariness   D. productivity

2. The _____ function refers to language used to create imaginary systems, whether these are literary works, philosophical systems or utopian visions on the one hand, or daydreams and idle musings on the other hand. ( )
   A. personal   B. heuristic
   C. imaginative   D. regulatory

3. Chomsky defines the _____ as the use of language in concrete situations. ( )
   A. competence   B. parole   C. performance   D. langue

4. When the vocal cords are nearly touching each other, _____ consonants are produced because the air stream passing through the glottis brings about vocal-cord vibration. ( )
   A. oral   B. voiced   C. nasal   D. voiceless

5. Of the suprasegmental features, _____ refers to the phonetic boundary features which may demarcate grammatical units such as morpheme, word or clause. ( )
   A. juncture   B. stress   C. tone   D. intonation

6. The affixes which interrupt roots (i.e. appear within roots) are called _____. ( )
   A. prefixes   B. infixes
   C. suffixes   D. inflectional affixes

7. In morphology, _____ are the realizations of a particular morpheme. ( )
   A. allomorphs   B. phones   C. morphs   D. allophones

8. In terms of function, affixes fall into two types; _____ affixes can create new words. ( )
   A. inflectional B. functional C. lexical   D. derivational

9. Of the word-formation processes, _____ refers to a process of word-formation in which two or more free morphemes are combined to form a new word. ( )
   A. affixation   B. compounding
   C. conversion   D. blending
10. The constituents which may be present or absent on the right side of the arrow in a phrase structure rule are called _____ constituents. ( )
    A. compulsory   B. ultimate   C. immediate   D. optional

II. Fill in each of the following blanks with a word or an expression. (10 points in all, 1 point for each)

11. A _____ relation describes the vertical dimension of a language. It is a relation between comparable elements at a particular place in structures.
12. Velars are consonants made by bringing the back of the tongue to the _____ palate, or velum.
13. Of the sub-branches of linguistics, _____ studies meaning in use or meaning in context.
14. According to the shape of the lips, we can classify vowels into rounded vowels and _____ vowels.
15. Surface structures are derived from their deep structures by _____ rules.
16. Mathesius's term _____ refers to the transitional part which joins the Theme and the Rheme.
17. Of the design features of language, _____ means that any human being can be both a producer and a receiver of messages.
18. According to the state of the velum, vowels can be divided into two kinds: oral vowels and _____ vowels.
19. According to the _____ theory, the meaning of an expression is its contribution to the truth-conditions of the sentences containing it.
20. Of the three kinds of homonymous words, _____ are the words which are identical orthographically but different phonologically and semantically.

III. Judge whether each of the following statements is true or false. Write "T" for true (of the ten statements, only ONE is true) or "F" for false in the blank offered after each statement. Give a correct version for each of the false statements. (20 points in all, 2 points for each)

21. Displacement refers to the phenomenon that the sounds in a language are meaningfully distinct.
    _____
22. Descriptive linguistics deals with language in general, i.e. the whole human

language.

23. T-Do-insertion is always applied immediately after T-Negation.

24. The description of a language as it changes through time is a synchronic study.

25. When the vocal cords are nearly touching each other, voiceless consonants are produced because the air stream passing through the glottis brings about vocal-cord vibration.

26. When two sounds can appear in the same environment and the substitution of one for the other does not cause any changes in meaning, then they are said to be in complementary distribution.

27. Allomorphs are the realizations of morphemes in general and are the actual forms used to realize morphemes.

28. Surface structures are more abstract.

29. The dynamic study of sentences means that we describe the structures of sentences to illustrate the relationship among the elements of a sentence.

30. A locative refers to the time of the action or state expressed in the verb.

IV. Translate the following terms from English into Chinese. (10 points in all, 1 point for each)

31. imaginative function
32. applied linguistics
33. semantics
34. closing diphthongs
35. derivational affixes
36. backformation
37. actual linguistic behavior
38. traditional grammar
39. structural ambiguity
40. signified

V. Answer the following questions. (20 points in all)

41. What are the differences between microlinguistics and macrolinguistics? (8%)

42. What are the differences between contrastive distribution, complementary distribution and free variation? (6%)

43. What are the differences between syntagmatic, paradigmatic and hierarchical relations. (6%)

VI. Practical work. (30 points in all)

44. Write the symbol that corresponds to each of the following phonetic descriptions: (4%)
    1) a voiced alveo-palatal affricate _____
    2) a nasal high front lax vowel _____
    3) a voiceless dental fricative _____
    4) a bilabial nasal _____

45. Divide the following words into separate morphemes by placing a "+" between each morpheme and the next: (8%)
    Example: bookshelf = book + shelf
    1) television = _____
    2) friendly = _____
    3) strengthen = _____
    4) like (in "I like football.") = _____
    5) disobey = _____
    6) sputnik = _____
    7) oxen = _____
    8) usefulness = _____

46. Match the names of linguistic figures in column A with the schools or theories or works of linguistics in column B: (8%)

Column A	Column B
1) ( ) Mathesius	a. *Coral Gardens and Their Magic*
2) ( ) Chomsky	b. *Syntactic Structure*
3) ( ) Malinowski	c. father of modern linguistics
4) ( ) Saussure	d. the functional sentence perspective

47. Draw the deep structure phrase markers for the following two sentences: (10%)
   1) Were you writing the book?
   2) What could they have achieved?

答 案

Ⅰ. 1-5　DCCBA　　　6-10　BADBD

Ⅱ. 本项拼写错误、大小写错误、单复数错误均不得分!
   11. paradigmatic　　　　　　　12. soft
   13. pragmatics　　　　　　　　14. unrounded
   15. Transformational / T-　　　16. Transition
   17. interchangeability　　　　　18. nasal
   19. truth-conditional　　　　　 20. homographs

Ⅲ. 21. F：Discreteness refers to the phenomenon that the sounds in a language are meaningfully distinct. / Displacement refers to the fact that human language can be used to talk about things that are present or not present, real or not real, and about matters in the past, present or future, or in far-away places.

   22. F：General linguistics deals with language in general, i.e. the whole human language.

   23. T

   24. F：The description of a language as it changes through time is a diachronic study.

   25. F：When the vocal cords are nearly touching each other, voiced consonants are produced because the air stream passing through the glottis brings about vocal-cord vibration.

   26. F：When two sounds can appear in the same environment and the substitution of one for the other does not cause any change in meaning, then they are said to be in free variation.

   27. F：Morphs are the realizations of morphemes in general and are the actual forms used to realize morphemes.

   28. F：Surface structures are more concrete. / Deep structures are more abstract.

   29. F：The static study of sentences means that we describe the structures of sentences to illustrate the relationship among the elements of a sentence.

   30. F：A temporal refers to the time of the action or state expressed in the verb.

Ⅳ. 31. 想象功能　　　　　　　　32. 应用语言学
   33. 语义学　　　　　　　　　 34. 合口双元音

35. 派生词缀
36. 逆生法/逆序造词法
37. 实际语言行为
38. 传统语法
39. 结构歧义
40. 所指

V. 41. The distinction between microlinguistics and macrolinguistics: at its narrowest, microlinguistics studies only the structure of language systems, without regard to anything else(4 分); at its broadest, macrolinguistics deals with everything that is related in any way at all to language and languages(4 分).

42. If two or more sounds can occur in the same environment and the substitution of one sound for another brings about a change of meaning, they are said to be in contrastive distribution(2 分). If two or more sounds never appear in the same environment, that is, each sound only appears in the environments where the other sound never occurs, then they are said to be in complementary distribution (2 分). When two sounds can appear in the same environment and the substitution of one for the other does not cause any change in meaning, then they are said to be in free variation(2 分).

43. Syntagmatic relations refer to the sequential characteristics of speech, seen as a string of constituents in linear order(2 分). Paradigmatic relations refer to the relations between the linguistic elements within a sentence and those outside the sentence(2 分). The inner layering of sentences constitutes their hierarchical structures(2 分).

VI. 44. 1) [dʒ] 2) [i] 3) [θ] 4) [m]

45. 1) television = tele + vis + ion
    2) friendly = friend + ly
    3) strengthen = strength + en
    4) like (in "I like football.") = /laik/ + /? /
    5) disobey = dis + obey
    6) sputnik = sputnik
    7) oxen = ox + en
    8) usefulness = use + ful + ness

46. 1) d 2) b 3) a 4) c

47. 1)

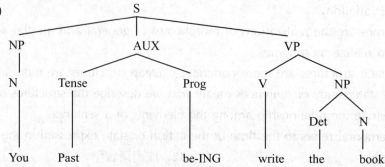

2)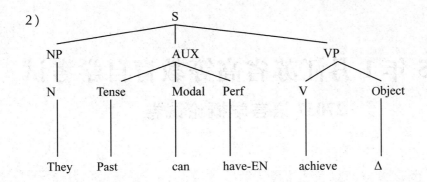

2015年1月江苏省高等教育自学考试
27037 语言学概论试卷

I. **Choose from the given choices the correct one and write the corresponding letter in the brackets. (10 points in all, 1 point for each)**

1. Which of the following is a minimal pair? ( )
   A. /æsk/ and /ɑːsk/   B. /sit/ and /sæd/
   C. bate and bat   D. /liːv/ and /fiːl/
2. The sound [i] can be described as a(n) _____ vowel. ( )
   A. oral central high unrounded lax   B. nasal front mid rounded tense
   C. oral front high unrounded lax   D. oral back low rounded tense
3. The _____ relation is a kind of relation between linguistic forms in a sentence and linguistic forms outside the sentence. ( )
   A. sequential   B. syntagmatic   C. hierarchical   D. paradigmatic
4. The sound _____ is an oral voiceless palatal plosive. ( )
   A. [b]   B. [c]   C. [d]   D. [dr]
5. By _____ knowledge, we refer to a native speaker's intuition about the meaning of language, including meaning of words and meaning of sentences. ( )
   A. semantic   B. phonological   C. morphological   D. syntactic
6. Of the word-formation processes, _____ refers to the process by which words are formed by putting the initial letters of several words together. ( )
   A. blending   B. shortening   C. back-formation   D. acronymy
7. In deriving a surface structure from its deep structure, we need to apply a series of transformational rules. If we want to obtain well-formed sentences, we have to apply _____. ( )
   A. T-Affix   B. T-Imperative   C. T-Passive   D. T-Negation
8. According to Chomsky's TG Grammar, the dynamic study of sentences _____. ( )
   A. is only concerned with one level of structure, i.e. deep structure
   B. deals with two levels of structure: both surface structure and deep structure
   C. deals with neither surface structure nor deep structure
   D. is only concerned with one level of structure, i.e. surface structure
9. The word "beautiful" involves the word-formation process of _____. ( )

A. compounding　　B. blending　　C. affixation　　D. conversion

10. In a hierarchical structure diagram of a sentence, _____ are the constituents of the sentence.　　　　　　　　　　　　　　　　　　　　　　　　(　　)
   A. the forms at the word-level and the phrase-level
   B. the forms connected by the two lines that are branching from the same point
   C. the forms which are always present on the right side of a phrase structure rule
   D. the forms at the word-level

Ⅱ. Fill in each of the following blanks with a word or an expression. (10 points in all, 1 point for each)

11. Language is _____ because the primary medium for all languages is sound.
12. Of the design features of language, _____ refers to the phenomenon that the sounds in a language are meaningfully distinct.
13. The description of a language as it changes through time is a _____ study.
14. The study of the way hearers perceive these sounds is called _____ phonetics.
15. Only when voiceless plosives occur initially in a word or initially in a stressed syllable are they _____.
16. When two sounds can appear in the same environment and the substitution of the one for the other does not cause any changes in meaning, then they are said to be in _____.
17. By _____ morphemes, we refer to those which can exist as individual words, i.e. they can stand alone by themselves.
18. Of the word-formation processes, _____ is a process in which one or more affixes are attached to a root or a base to produce a new word.
19. Of the syntactic relations, _____ relation refers to the sequential characteristics of speech, seen as a string of constituents in linear order.
20. When two words are opposite in meaning, they are _____.

Ⅲ. Judge whether each of the following statements is true or false. Write "T" for true (of the ten statements, only ONE is true) or "F" for false in the blank offered after each statement. Give a correct version for each of the false statements. (20 points in all, 2 points for each)

21. The instrumental function of a language refers to the fact that the language allows speakers to get things done.

22. Phonetics is a study of the sound system of a language.

23. Modern linguistics, in spite of theoretical diversities, is primarily prescriptive.

24. When the vocal cords are nearly touching each other, voiceless consonants are produced because the airstream passing through the glottis brings about vocal-cord vibration.

25. Tone languages are those which use pitch to distinguish meaning at phrase level or sentence level.

26. Phonemes are minimal meaningful units in the sound system of a language.

27. The divisions of morphemes at each step by means of IC Analysis are arbitrary.

28. The constituents which must be present on the right side of the arrow in a phrase structure rule are called optional constituents.

29. T-Passive must be applied after T-Negation.

30. A locative refers to the time of the action or state expressed in the verb.

IV. Translate the following terms from English into Chinese. (10 points in all, 1 point for each)

31. arbitrariness
32. linguistic performance
33. vowel
34. free variation
35. derivational morpheme
36. surface structure
37. mode of discourse
38. gradable antonym
39. Innateness Hypothesis
40. complementary antonym

V. Answer the following questions. (20 points in all)

41. What are the design features of languages? (5 points)

42. How does denotation differ from connotation? Illustrate their difference with examples. (7 points)

43. Why do we say "absolute synonyms are rare or even non-existent"? Illustrate it with examples. (8 points)

VI. Practical work. (30 points in all)

44. Write the symbol that corresponds to each of the following phonetic descriptions: (4 points)

    Example: a voiceless velar plosive   [k]
    1) a voiceless alveo-palatal fricative   _____
    2) a voiced post-alveolar affricate   _____
    3) a voiceless palatal plosive   _____
    4) a mid-front unrounded vowel   _____

45. Divide the following words into separate morphemes by placing a " + " between each morpheme and the next: (8 points)

    Example: bookshelf = book + shelf
    1) disobey = _____
    2) rewrite = _____
    3) yearly = _____
    4) troublesome = _____
    5) talented = _____
    6) lookout = _____
    7) boyishness = _____
    8) disappearance = _____

46. Match the names of linguistic figures in column A with the schools or theories or works of linguistics in column B: (8 points)

Column A	Column B
1) Chomsky ( )	a. The Copenhagen School
2) Jakobson ( )	b. Language Acquisition Device
3) Mathesius ( )	c. Communicative Dynamism
4) Hjelmslev ( )	d. The Distinctive Feature Theory

47. Draw the deep structure phrase markers of the following two sentences: (10 points)

    1) Tim is playing the piano.

2) Johnson could have stolen the wallet.

答 案

I. 1-5　CCDBA　　　　　6-10　DABCA

II. 本项拼写错误、大小写错误、单复数错误均不得分！
11. vocal
12. discreteness
13. diachronic
14. auditory
15. aspirated
16. free variation
17. free
18. derivation / affixation
19. syntagmatic
20. antonyms

III. 21. T
22. F：Phonology is a study of the sound system of a language.
23. F：Modern linguistics, in spite of theoretical diversities, is primarily descriptive.
24. F：When the vocal cords are nearly touching each other, voiced consonants are produced because the air stream passing through the glottis brings about vocal-cord vibration.
25. F：Intonation languages are those which use pitch to distinguish meaning at phrase level or sentence level. / Tone languages are those which use pitch to contrast meaning at word level.
26. F：Phonemes are minimal distinctive units in the sound system of a language.
27. F：The divisions of morphemes at each step by means of IC Analysis are not arbitrary.
28. F：The constituents which must be present on the right side of the arrow in a phrase structure rule are called compulsory constituents. / The constituents which may be present or absent on the right side of the arrow in a phrase structure rule are called optional constituents.
29. F：T-Passive must be applied before T-Negation.
30. F：A temporal refers to the time of the action or state expressed in the verb. / A locative is used to indicate the location of the action or state expressed in the verb.

IV. 31. 任意性
32. 语言行为
33. 元音
34. 自由变异
35. 派生词素
36. 表层结构
37. 语式
38. 等级性反义词
39. 先天主义假说
40. 互补反义词

Ⅴ. 41. The design features of language include 1) productivity, 2) discreteness, 3) displacement, 4) arbitrariness, 5) cultural transmission, 6) duality of double articulation, and 7) interchangeability. 说明：7个特征中只需能正确回答5个特征即可。

42. Generally speaking, meaning can be divided into two different types: denotation and connotation. (1分) The denotative meaning of a linguistic form refers to the person, object, abstract notion, event, or state which the word or sentence denotes. Put in another way, denotative meaning involves the relationship between a linguistic unit and the non-linguistic entities to which it refers. (2分) Or rather, the denotation of a linguistic expression is its dictionary meaning. For example, the denotation of *dog* is its dictionary meaning of "*4-legged flesh-eating animal of many breeds akin to wolf*, etc." (1分)

    By contrast, connotation refers to the emotional associations which are suggested by, or are part of the meaning of a linguistic unit, especially a lexical item. The connotation of a linguistic form has to do with its overtones of meaning, that is, what the linguistic form suggests. (2分) For example, the connotation of the lexical item *December* might include "*bad weather*," "*dark evenings*", "*snow*", or "*parties*" for westerners. (1分)

43. Absolute synonyms are regarded as very rare or even non-existent.

    In the first place, some synonyms have the same denotative meaning but show differences in connotative meaning. (2分) Fox example, *famous* and *notorious* can be treated as synonyms because both of them have the denotative meaning of "*well-known*", but they have different connotation: *famous* has an appreciative meaning (positive value) whereas *notorious* has a pejorative meaning (negative value). (1分)

    In the second place, even when we focus on denotative meaning of words, we may find that some words appear to be synonymous but refer to slightly different sets of concepts or are used in slightly different contexts. (2分) For example, "*salary*" and "*wage*" are two synonymous because both refer to "pay or financial reward given for the work one has done". But they are used in different situations. *Salary* usually pertains to money received by white-collar workers or by executives in managerial positions or by professionals. It is paid monthly. By contrast, *wage* is the amount of money that is regularly paid to someone or to a group of people for a particular type of work, especially manual or unskilled work. (1分)

    Finally, some words are the same in meaning but have different collocations. For example, *charge* and *accuse* have the same denotation, but *charge* collocates with the preposition *with*, while *accuse* collocates with the preposition *of*. (2分)

VI. 44. 1) [ʃ] 2) [dr] 3) [c] 4) [e]

45. a) disobey = dis + obey
 b) rewrite = re + write
 c) yearly = year + ly
 d) troublesome = trouble + some
 e) talented = talent + ed
 f) lookout = look + out
 g) boyishness = boy + ish + ness
 h) disappearance = dis + appear + ance

46. 1) b 2) d 3) c 4) a

47. 1)

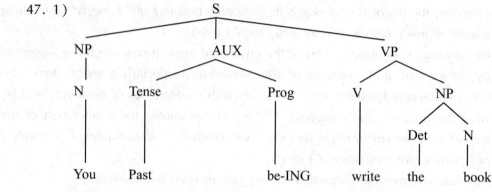

（每个支点 1 分，终端成分 1 分，共 5 分）

2)

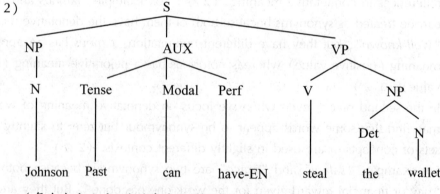

（每个支点 1 分，终端成分 1 分，共 5 分）

References

Akmajian, A., R. Demer & R. M. Harnish, 1979. *Linguistics, an Introduction to Language and Communication*. Mass.: MIT Press.

Aronoff, M. & J. Rees-Miller (eds.), 2001. *The Handbook of Linguistics*. Beijing: Foreign Language Teaching and Research Press; Oxford: Blackwell.

Austin, J. L., 1962/2002. *How to Do Things with Words*. Oxford: Oxford University Press.

Beaugrande, R. De & W. U. Dressler, 1981. *Introduction to Text Linguistics*. London: Longman; Beijing: Foreign Language Teaching and Research Press.

Brown, G. & G. Yule, 1983/2000. *Discourse Analysis*. Cambridge: Cambridge University Press; Beijing: Foreign Language Teaching and University Press.

Bussmann, H., 2000. *Routledge Dictionary of Language and Linguistics*, trans. & ed. Trauth, G. P. and K. Kazzazi. Beijing: Foreign Language Teaching and Research Press; London: Routledge.

Chomsky, N., 1957. *Syntactic Structures*. The Hague: Mouton & Co.

Chomsky, N., 1959. A Review of B. F. Skinner's Verbal Behaviour. *Language*, 35: 26 – 58.

Chomsky, N., 1965. *Aspects of the Theory of Syntax*. Cambridge, Mass.: MIT Press.

Chomsky, N., 1977. *Essays on Forms and Interpretation*. New York: North-Holland.

Coulmas, F., 2001. Sociolinguistics. In Aronoff, M. & J. Rees-Miller (eds.), 2001. *The Handbook of Linguistics*. Beijing: Foreign Language Teaching and Research Press; Oxford: Blackwell.

Crystal, D., 1971. *Linguistics*. Harmondsworth: Penguin.

Crystal, D., 1985. Reprinted in 1991. *A Dictionary of Linguistics and Phonetics*. Oxford: Blackwell.

Davison, D. & G. Harman (eds.), 1972. *Semantics of Natural Language*. Holland: Reidel Publishing Company.

Dittmar, N., 1976. *Sociolinguistics: A Critical Survey of Theory and Application*. London: Edward Arnold.

Eggins, S., 1994. *An Introduction to Systemic Functional Linguistics*. London: Pinter Publishers.

Ellis, R., 1989. *Understanding Second Language Acquisition*. Oxford: Oxford University Press.

Ellis, R., 1997. *Second Language Acquisition*. Oxford: Oxford University Press.
Ferguson, C. A., 1959. Diglossia. *Word*, 15: 325–340.
Ferguson, C. A., 1971. *Language Structure and Language Use*. Stanford: Stanford University Press.
Ferguson, C. A., 1994. Dialect, Register, and Genre: Working Assumptions about Conventionalization. In Biber, D. & E. Finegan (eds.), 1994. *Sociolinguistic Perspectives on Register*. Oxford: Oxford University Press.
Firbas, J., 1964. On Defining the Theme in Functional Sentence Perspective. *Travaux linguistiques de Prague*, Vol. 2:239–256.
Fishman, J. A. (ed.), 1968. *Readings in the Sociology of Language*. The Hague: Mouton.
Foss, Donald J., Thomas G. Bever & Maury Silver, 1981. The Comprehension and Verification of Ambiguous Sentences. *Perception and Psychophysics*, 4: 297–314.
Goffman, E, 1981. *Forms of Talk*. Oxford: Basil Blackwell.
Gordon, E., 1997. Sex, Speech, and Stereotypes: Why Women Use Prestige Forms More than Men. *Language in Society*, 26: 1, 47–63.
Grice, H. P. 1957. Meaning. *Philosophical Review*, 66: 377–388. Reprinted in Rosenberg, J. F. & C. Travis (eds), 1971. *Readings in the Philosophy of Language*. 436–444. New Jersey: Prentice-Hall, Inc.
Groebel, L., 1985. Ambiguity and Second Language Learning. *IRAL*, Vol. XXIII, No. 2: 149–158.
Gumperz, J. J., 1972. Sociolinguistics and Communication in Small Groups. In J. B. Pride & J. Holmes (eds.), 1972. *Sociolinguistics: Selected Readings*. Harmondsworth: Penguin.
Hajicov, E., 1984. Topic and Focus. In P. Sgall (ed.) *Contributions to Functional Syntax. Semantics and Language Comprehension* (*LISEE*, 16). Amsterdam / Philadelphia: John Benjamins: 189–202.
Halliday, M. A. K. & R. Hasan, 1976/2001. *Cohesion in English*. New York: Longman; Beijing: Foreign Language Teaching and Research Press.
Halliday, M. A. K. & R. Hasan, 1985. *Language, Context, and Text: Aspects of Language in a Social-Semiotic Perspective*. Oxford: Oxford University Press.
Halliday, M. A. K., 1967. Notes on Transitivity and Theme in English (part II). *Journal of Linguistics*, No. 3: 199–244.
Halliday, M. A. K., 1973. *Explorations in the Functions of Language*. London: Edward Arnold.
Halliday, M. A. K., 1978. *Language as Social Semiotic*. London: Edward Arnold.
Halliday, M. A. K., 2000. *An Introduction to Functional Grammar* (2nd edition). Beijing: Foreign Language Teaching and Research Press; London: Edward Arnold.
Halliday, M. A. K., A. McIntosh & P. Strevens, 1964. *The Linguistic Sciences and*

Language Teaching. London: Longman.

Hoey, M, 1991. *Patterns of Lexis in Text*. Oxford: Oxford University Press.

Holm, J., 1988. *Pidgins and Creoles*. 2 vols. Cambridge: Cambridge University Press.

Horn, L. R., 1984. Towards a New Taxonomy for Pragmatic Inference: Q-based and R-based Implicature. In Schiffrin, D. (ed.), 1984. *Meaning, Form, and Use in Context: Linguistic Applications*. 11–42. Washington, D. C.: Georgetown University Press.

Hymes, D., 1971. *Language Acquisition: Models and Methods*. New York: Academic Press.

Hymes, D., 1972. On Communicative Competence. In J. B. Pride & J. Holmes (eds.), 1972. *Sociolinguistics: Selected Readings*. Harmondsworth: Penguin.

Krashen, S. D., 1981. *Second Language Acquisition and Second Language Learning*. Oxford: Pergamon Press.

Krashen, S. D., 1982. *Principles and Practice in Second Language Acquisition*. Oxford: Pergamon Press.

Kress, G., Critical Discourse Analysis. In Robert Kaplan (ed.), *Annual Review of Applied Linguistics*, II, 1990, 4.

Lakoff, R., 1973. Language and Woman's Place. *Language in Society*, 2: 45–80.

Leech, G., 1981. *Semantics: The Study of Meaning*. Harmondsworth: Penguin.

Leech, G., 1983. *Principles of Pragmatics*. London: Longman.

Levinson, S. C., 1983/2001. *Pragmatics*. Cambridge: Cambridge University Press; Beijing: Foreign Language Teaching and Research Press.

Levinson, S. C., 1987. Minimization and Conversational Inference. In Verschuren & Bertuccelli-Pape (eds.), 1987. *The Pragmatic Perspective*. 61–129. Amsterdam: John Benjamins.

Lyons, J. (ed.), 1970. *New Horizons in Linguistics*. Harmondsworth: Penguin.

Lyons, J., 1977. *Semantics*, Vol. 2. Cambridge: Cambridge University Press.

Lyons, J., 1981. *Language and Linguistics*. Cambridge: Cambridge University Press.

Lyons, J., 2000. *Linguistic Semantics: An Introduction*. Beijing: Foreign Language Teaching and Research Press; Cambridge: Cambridge University Press.

Mey, J. L., 1993/2001. *Pragmatics: An Introduction*. Oxford: Blackwell Publishers Ltd.; Beijing: Foreign Language Teaching and Research Press.

Newmeyer (ed.), 1988. *Linguistics: The Cambridge Survey*. Vol. 1–4. Cambridge: Cambridge University Press.

Odgen, C. K. & I. A. Richards, 1923. *The Meaning of Meaning*. New York: Harcourt Brace Jovanovich.

Pride, J. B. & J. Holmes (eds.), 1972. *Sociolinguistics: Selected Readings*. Harmondsworth: Penguin.

Richards, J. & T. Rogers, 1986. *Approaches and Methods in Language Teaching*.

Cambridge: Cambridge University Press.

Richards, J. C., 1977. *Error Analysis*. London: Longman.

Sapir, E., 1921/2001. *Language*. New York: Harcourt Brace; Beijing: Foreign Language Teaching and Research Press.

Saussure, F. de, 2001. *Course in General Linguistics*. Trans. R. Harris. Beijing: Foreign Language Teaching and Research Press; London: Gerald Duckworth & Co. Ltd. [originally published in 1916.]

Schiffrin, D. (ed.), 1984. *Meaning, Form, and Use in Context: Linguistic Applications*. Washington, D. C.: Georgetown University Press.

Searle, J. R., 1979/2001. *Expression and Meaning: Studies in the Theory of Speech Acts*. Cambridge: Cambridge University Press; Beijing: Foreign Language Teaching and Research Press.

Shultz, T. R., & R. Pilon, 1973. Development of the Ability to Detect Linguistic Ambiguity. *Child Development*, 44: 728–733.

Skinner, B. F., 1957. *Verbal Behavior*. New York: Appleton-Century-Crofts.

Van Dijk, 1977. *Text and Context*. London: Longman.

Wardhaugh, R., 1979. *Introduction to Linguistics* (2nd ed.). New York: McGraw-Hill Book Company.

Widdonson, H. C., 1979. *Explorations in Applied Linguistics*. Oxford: Oxford University Press.

Wodak, R. (ed.), 1989. *Language, Power and Ideology: Studies in Political Discourse*. London: Benjamins Publishing Company.

Yule, G., 1985/1996/2000. *The Study of Language*. Cambridge: Cambridge University Press; Beijing: Foreign Language Teaching and Research Press.

陈林华.语言学导论.长春:吉林大学出版社,1999.

陈媛.现代语言学.天津:天津大学出版社,2003.

戴炜栋,何兆雄.新编简明英语语言学教程.上海:上海外语教育出版社,2002.

丁言仁,郝克.英语语言学纲要.上海:上海外语教育出版社,2002.

甘世安,杨静.现代语言学精要问答.西安:西安出版社,2002.

何兆熊.新编语用学概要.上海:上海外语教育出版社,2000.

何自然.语用学与英语学习.上海:上海外语教育出版社,1997.

何自然.语用学讲稿.南京:南京师范大学出版社,2003.

何自然,陈新仁.当代语用学.北京:外语教学与研究出版社,2004.

侯国金.英语语言学精要问答与考试指南.武汉:中国地质大学出版社,2000.

胡曙中.英语语篇语言学研究.上海:上海外语教育出版社,2005.

胡壮麟.语言学教程.北京:北京大学出版社,2001.

胡壮麟,李战子.语言学简明教程(英文版).北京:北京大学出版社,2004a.

胡壮麟,李战子.语言学简明教程(中文版).北京:北京大学出版社,2004b.

胡壮麟,朱永生,张德禄.系统功能语法概论.长沙:湖南教育出版社,1989.

胡壮麟,朱永生,张德录,李战子. 系统功能语言学概论. 北京:北京大学出版社,2005.
姜望琪. 语用学——理论与应用. 北京:北京大学出版社,2000.
姜望琪. 当代语用学. 北京:北京大学出版社,2003.
乐眉云. 应用语言学. 南京:南京大学出版社,1994.
李福印. 语义学教程. 上海:上海外语教育出版社,1999.
李福印. 语义学概论. 北京:北京大学出版社,2006.
李洁红. 语言学习题集. 哈尔滨:哈尔滨工业大学出版社,2005.
李悦娥,范宏雅. 话语分析. 上海:上海外语教育出版社,2002.
林晓文. 全国高等教育自学考试速记速查手册(英语专业分册)——现代语言学. 上海:浦东电子出版社,2003.
牛保义. 隐性衔接论,外语教学. 第3期,1998.
牛保义. 英汉语篇含意衔接琐义,外语学刊. 第1期,1999.
刘润清. 西方语言学流派. 北京:外语教学与研究出版社,2002.
刘润清,封宗信. 语言学理论与流派. 南京:南京师范大学出版社,2004.
梅德明. 现代语言学简明教程. 上海:上海外语教育出版社,2003.
石小娟,李炯英. 现代语言学基础教程. 上海:上海交通大学出版社,2004.
王东波. 英语语言学. 济南:山东大学出版社,2003.
王钢. 普通语言学基础. 长沙:湖南教育出版社,1988.
王永祥,支永碧. 英语语言学概论. 南京:南京师范大学出版社,2007.
文秋芳. 英语语言学导论. 南京:江苏教育出版社,1995.
辛斌. 英语篇章的主题连贯性和英语句子的移位转换,山东外语教学. 第3期,1989.
辛斌. 话题与连贯,山东外语教学. 第3期,1998.
辛斌. 语法理论基础. 长春:吉林大学出版社,1995.
辛斌. 批评语言学:理论与应用. 上海:上海外语教育出版社,2005.
杨海英. 现代语言学全国高等教育自学考试标准预测试卷. 北京:学苑出版社,2004.
杨才英. 论语篇的人际意义连贯,中国海洋大学学报. 第2期,2005.
武果. 也谈篇章连贯性,现代外语. 第4期,1987.
张莱湘. 英语语言学笔记精华. 北京:机械工业出版社,2005.
张迈曾. 语言与交际——语言学概论. 天津:南开大学出版社,1998.
张维友. 英语词汇学. 北京:外语教学与研究出版社,1997.
周红红,吴中东. 英语语言学考点测评. 北京:世界图书出版公司,2006.
朱永生,郑立信,苗兴伟. 英汉语篇衔接手段对比研究. 上海:上海外语教育出版社,2001.

附录 I：英语语言学主要专业术语汉英对照表

白板假说 tabula rasa hypothesis
半闭元音 semi-close vowels
半开元音 semi-open vowels
半元音 semivowels
爆破音 plosive
背景/环境 setting
本地话/本国语 vernacular
鼻腔 nasal cavity
鼻腔闭止音 nasal stops
鼻腔辅音 nasal consonant
鼻腔元音 nasal vowel
鼻音 nasal sound
鼻音化 nasality
鼻音化 nasalize
闭元音 close vowels
变项 variable
变音符号/附加符号 diacritical mark
变音符号/附加符号 diacritics
标记法直接成分分析 labeled IC analysis
标准变体 standard variety
标准方言 standard dialect
标准化 standardization
标准语言 standard language
表层结构 surface structure
表层结构歧义 surface structural ambiguity
表达/呈现 representation
表达类 expressives
表情意义 emotive meaning
表述句 constatives
表态类 behabitives
表现功能 representational function

宾语 object
并列句转类法 conversion
并列下义词 co-hyponyms
补语 complement
不带音的/清音的 voiceless
不可分离性 non-detachability
不确定性 indeterminacy
不受时空限制的特性/移位 displacement
不送气 unaspirated
布拉格学派 the Prague School
部分和整体的关系 portion-mass
部分/整体关系 part/whole relationship
裁决类/评判行为类 verdictives
阐述类 representatives
长元音 long vowels
场独立 field independence
场依存 field dependence
超切分特征 suprasegmental feature
成分 constituent
成分分析法 componential analysis
成分关系 constituency
成分结构 constituent structure
成员和集体的关系 member-collection
承诺类 commissives
齿音 dental
齿龈 alveolar ridge
齿龈 teeth ridge
齿龈后音/后齿龈音 post-alveolars
齿龈音(的) alveolar
齿龈硬腭音 alveo-palatal
充分性 adequacy

传统语法 traditional grammar
创造新词 coining
唇音 labial
词干 stem
词根语素 root morpheme
词汇 lexicon
词汇范畴 lexical category
词汇关系 lexical relation
词汇结构 lexical structure
词汇模式 lexical patterning
词汇歧义 lexical ambiguity
词汇衔接 lexical cohesion
词汇学 lexicology
词汇意义 lexical meaning
词汇语素 lexical morpheme
词汇语义学 lexical semantics
词基 base
词素/语素 morpheme
词缀 affix
词缀法 affixation
词缀语素 affixational morpheme
刺激 stimulus
错误分析 Error Analysis
搭配 collocation
搭配意义 collocative meaning
大脑左右半球的侧化 brain lateralization
代码/语码 code
带音化/浊音化 voicing
单元音 monophthong
单元音 pure vowel
单元音 simple vowel
等级关系 hierarchical relation
等级/层次结构 hierarchical structure
等级性反义词 gradable antonyms
等级性反义词 gradable opposites
低层次变体 low variety
低元音 low vowels
地理方言 geographical dialect
地区方言 regional dialects

第二语言习得 Second Language Acquisition
第一语言习得 first language acquisition
调节功能 regulatory function
动机 motivation
短语标记法 phrase markers
短语范畴 phrase/phrasal category
短语结构规则 Phrase Structure rules/PS rules
短元音 short vowel
对比分布 contrastive distribution
对比分析 Contrastive Analysis
对比语言学 contrastive linguistics
多义词 polyseme
多义性/多义现象 polysemy
多语现象 multilingualism
发音部位 place of articulation
发音方式 manner of articulation
发音器官 speech organ
发音系统 vocal tract
发音语音学 articulatory phonetics
反常的 anomalous
反义词 antonym
反义词 opposite（word）
反义关系 antonymy
反应意义 reflected meaning
方括标记法 labeled bracketing
方式准则 maxim of manner
方言 dialect
非词汇范畴 non-lexical category
非规约性 non-conventionality
非规约性间接言语行为 non-conventional indirect speech acts
非同化词 aliens
非言语交际 non-verbal communication
非语言语境/超语言语境 extralinguistic context
非圆唇元音 unrounded vowel
分叉点 branching node
封闭类词 closed class word

符号 symbol
符号的 symbolic
符号三角 semiotic triangle
辅音 consonant
辅音的 consonantal
负面强化 negative reinforcement
负迁移 negative transfer
复合词 compound words
复合法 compounding
复合句 complex sentence
复合元音 complex vowels
复现 reiteration
改变状态的动词 change-of-state verbs
概括过度 overgeneralization
概念 concept
概念功能 ideational function
概念意义 conceptual meaning
干扰 interference
高层次变体 high variety
高元音 high vowels
哥本哈根学派 the Copenhagen School
格 case
个人言语特点/个人习语 idiolect
个性 personality
工具功能 instrumental function
工具性学习动机 instrumental motivation
功能语素 functional morpheme
功能语言教学 Functional Language Teaching
功能语言学 functional linguistics
功能转移 functional shift
共时的 synchronic
共时语言学 synchronic linguistics
构词法 word-formation processes
古英语 old English
关键期 critical period
关键期假说 critical period hypothesis
关联交际原则 communicative principle of relevance
关联理论 relevance theory

关联认知原则 cognitive principle of relevance
关联准则 maxim of relation
关系反义词 relational opposites
规定(语法) prescriptive (grammar)
规约性间接言语行为 conventional indirect speech acts
国际音标 International Phonetic Alphabet
汉藏语系 Sino-Tibetan language family
合适条件 felicity conditions
合作原则 cooperative principle
核心词 head
黑话 argot
横组合关系 syntagmatic relation
宏观社会语言学 macro-sociolinguistics
宏观语言学 macrolinguistics
喉 larynx
后元音 back vowel
后指/下指 cataphora
后缀 suffix
后缀法 suffixation
互补反义词 complementary antonyms
互补分布 complementary distribution
互动功能 interactional function
互换性 interchangeability
滑音 glide
话轮转换 turn-taking
话语/语篇 discourse
话语/语篇分析 discourse analysis
话语 utterance
话语标记 discourse marking
话语标记语 discourse markers
话语意义 utterance meaning
话语指称 discourse deixis
会话分析 conversation analysis
会话含义 conversational implicature
会话语码切换 conversational code-switching
会厌 epiglottis
积极话语分析 positive discourse analysis

计算语言学 computational linguistics
加标记（不加标记）的树形图 labeled (unlabelled) tree diagram
简单句 simple sentence
简洁性 simplicity
交际动力 communicative dynamism (CD)
交际语 lingua franca
交际语言教学 communicative language teaching
交际语言能力 Communicative Competence
接触语言 contact language
结构 construction
结构成分性 structural constituency
结构二重性/结构双重性 duality of structure
结构歧义 structural ambiguity
结构主义 Structuralism
结构主义语言学 structural linguistics
介入性学习动机 integrative motivation
借义词 semantic borrowing
紧元音 tense vowel
禁忌词 taboo word
禁忌语 linguistic taboo
禁忌语 taboo
句法 syntax
句法功能观 functional sentence perspective/FSP
句法规则 syntactic rule
句法类型/句法范畴 syntactic category
句法歧义 syntactic ambiguity
句子语义学 sentence semantics
句子语义学 sentential semantics
具体语言学 specific linguistics
卷舌音 retroflex
开元音 open vowels
可取消性 cancellability/defeasibility
可推导性 calculability
克里奥尔语 creole
克里奥尔语后期连续体 post-creole continuum
空间指称 spatial deixis

空语子 empty morph
口腔 oral cavity
口腔闭止音 oral stops
口腔辅音 oral consonant
口腔音 oral sound
口腔元音 oral vowel
口音 accent
宽式音标 broad transcription
扩展过度 overextension
离散性 discreteness
礼貌原则 politeness principle
俚语 slang
理论语言学 theoretical linguistics
历时语言学 diachronic linguistics
历史比较语言学 comparative historical linguistics
历史语言学 historical linguistics
连词 conjunction
连贯 coherence
连位 transition
连续音的 continuant
连音/音渡 juncture
联想意义 associative meaning
零语子 zero morph
流音 liquid
略写法/截短法 clipping
伦敦学派 the London School
论元/题元 argument
美国结构主义 American Structuralism
描写语言学 descriptive linguistics
明示—推理交际 Ostensive-Inferential Communication
命题 proposition
摩擦音 fricative
母语 mother tongue
母语干扰 mother tongue interference
目标语 target language
内涵 intension
内涵意义 connotative meaning

内在化 internalized
内指 endophora
能产性 productivity
能指 signifier
逆序造词法/逆生法 back-formation
粘着语素 bound morpheme
派生词 derivative
派生词缀 derivational affixes
派生法派生语素 derivational morpheme
判断类动词 verbs of judging
旁流音 lateral liquid
批评性语篇/话语分析 critical discourse analysis
毗邻对 adjacency pairs
毗邻条件 Adjacency Condition
拼缀词 blends
拼缀法 blending
评价理论 evaluative theory
评价意义 evaluative meaning
普遍语法 Universal Grammar
普通语言学 general linguistics
启发功能 heuristic function
前部音的 anterior
前提 prerequisite
前元音 front vowel
前指/回指 anaphora
前置语列 pre-sequence
前缀 prefix
前缀法 prefixation
切分成分/音段 segment
切分特征 segmental feature
清辅音 voiceless consonants
情感意义 affective meaning
情景教学大纲 situational syllabus
情景语境 context of situation
情景语码切换 situational code-switching
情景语言教学 situational language teaching
穷尽性 exhaustiveness
区别性特征 distinctive feature

区别性特征理论 distinctive feature theory
屈折变化 inflection
屈折词缀 inflectional affixes
屈折语素 inflectional morpheme
人称指称 person deixis
人际功能 interpersonal function
人文主义方法 humanistic approach
认知代码法 cognitive code approach
认知心理学 cognitive psychology
认知因素 cognitive factors
任意性 arbitrariness
软腭 soft palate
软腭 velum
软腭音 velar
萨丕尔—沃尔夫假说 Sapir-Whorf hypothesis
塞擦音/破擦音 affricate
塞音/闭止音 stop
三元音 triphthong
删除规则 deletion rule
上唇 upper lip
上义词 general lexical items
上义词 higher terms
上义词 hyperonyms / hypernym
上义词 superordinate
舌齿音 interdentals
舌根 back of tongue
舌尖 tip of tongue
舌面 blade of tongue
舌面音 coronal
社会方言 social dialect
社会方言 sociolect
社会意义 social meaning
社会语言学 sociolinguistics
社会指称 social deixis
深层结构 deep structure
深层结构歧义 underlying structural ambiguity
生成语法 generative grammar
声带 vocal cord
声调语言 tone language

声门 glottis
声门音/喉音 glottal
声学语音学 acoustic phonetics
省略 ellipsis
识别特征 design feature
失语症 aphasia
失语症患者 aphasic
施为句 performatives
时间指称 temporal deixis
实词 content word
实际语言行为 actual linguistic behavior
实体 entity
实体关系（所指对象之间的关系）object relation
使役动词 causative verb
首字母拼音词 acronym
首字母拼音词 acrophone
首字母缩略词 initialism
首字母缩略法 acronymy
输入 input
述位 rheme
述谓结构 predication
述谓结构分析 predication analysis
树形图 tree-branch diagram
数量准则 maxim of quantity
双唇音 bilabial
双位述谓结构 two-place predication
双言现象 diglossia
双语现象 bilingualism
双元音/复合元音 diphthong
松元音 lax vowel
送气 aspiration
所指 signified
所指关系 reference
所指名词 referring expression
所指物 referent
所指衔接 phoric cohesion
特殊性含义 particularized implicatures
替代 substitution

听觉语音学 auditory phonetics
听说法 audio-lingual method
同化 assimilation
同化词 denizen
同化规则 assimilation rule
同形异义词 homograph
同形异义关系 homography
同形异音异义关系 heteronymy
同义词 synonym
同义的 synonymous
同义反复 tautology
同义现象/同义关系 synonymy
同形异义词 homonym
同形异义关系 homonymy
同音异义词 homonym
同音异义关系 homonymy
同音同形异义词 absolute homonym
同音异义词 homophone
同音异义关系 homophony
投射 projection
外来词 borrowed words
外来词 borrowings
外来词 loan word
外延 denotation
外延 extension
外延说 denotational theory
外延意义 denotative meaning
外指 exophora
微观社会语言学 micro-sociolinguistics
微观语言学 microlinguistics
委婉语 euphemism
谓语/谓词 predicate
谓语性形容词 predicative adjectives
文化传递性 cultural transmission
文体意义 stylistic meaning
习得 acquisition
系统 system
系统功能语法 Systemic Functional Grammar
系统功能语言学 Systemic-Functional Linguistics

下层社会方言 basilect
下唇 lower lip
下义词 hyponym
下义词 hyponyms
下义词 specific lexical items
下义词 subordinate
下义关系 hyponymy
先天主义假说 innateness hypothesis
衔接 cohesion
线性结构 linear structure
线性顺序 linear ordering
限定词 determiner
响音 sonorant
想象功能 imaginative function
小舌 uvula
协同发音 coarticulation
心理语言学 psycholinguistics
心理主义/心灵主义 mentalism
心灵说 mentalistic theory
新格赖斯主义 Post-Gricean Theory
行话/黑话 cant
行话 jargon
行使类 exerctives
行为反应说 behaviourist theory
行为主义 behaviorism
形态学/词法 morphology
形态学规则/词法规则 morphological rule
形体关系 form relation
性 gender
性别歧视语 sexist language
虚词 function word
序列规则 sequential rule
叙实动词 factive verbs
宣告类 declarations
循环性 recursiveness
咽 pharynx
咽腔 pharyngeal cavity
严式音标 narrow transcription
言后行为 perlocutionary act

言内行为 locutionary act
言外行为 illocutionary act
言语 parole
言语变体 speech variety
言语交际 verbal communication
言语类型 genre
言语社团 speech community
言语行为 speech act
言语行为理论 Speech Act Theory
验证说 verificationist theory
洋泾浜英语 pidgin
一般性含义 generalized implicatures
一致性 consistency
依存关系 dependency
译借词 translation-loan
意含动词 implicative verbs
意念功能法 notional-functional approach
意念说 ideational theory
意义 meaning
意义 sense
意义成分 components of meaning
意义关系 sense relation
音调/声调 tone
音位 phoneme
音位变体 allophone
音位对立 phonological oppositions
音位规则 phonological rule
音位学/音系学 phonology
音位音标 phonemic transcription
音子 phone
印欧语系 Indo-European language family
应用语言学 applied linguistics
硬腭 hard palate
硬腭音 palatal
幼儿话语 babytalk
语场 field of discourse
语调 intonation
语法翻译法 grammar translation method
语法性 grammaticality

语法意义 grammatical meaning
语际语/过渡语/中介语 interlanguage
语境 context
语境论 contextualism
语码混用 code-mixing
语码切换 code-switching
语篇 text
语篇功能 textual function
语篇性 texture
语式 mode of discourse
语素变体 allomorph
语系 language family
语言 langue
(语言)变体 variety
语言变异 language variation
语言侧化 linguistic lateralization
语言产出 language production
语言风格 styles of speaking
语言干扰 language interference
语言感知 language perception
语言规划 language planning
语言决定论 linguistic determinism
语言理解 language comprehension
语言能力/语言知识 competence
语言能力 linguistic competence
语言迁移 language transfer
语言切换 language-switching
语言社会学 sociology of language
语言文化移入 acculturation
语言习得 language acquisition
语言习得机制 language acquisition device/LAD
语言相对论 linguistic relativism
语言行为潜势 linguistic behaviour potential
语言语境 co-text
语言语境 linguistic context
语言运用/语言行为 linguistic performance
语言运用 performance
语义场 semantic field

语义反常 semantic anomaly
语义关系 semantic relation
语义结构 semantic structure
语义三角 semantic triangle
语义学 semantics
语音特征 phonetic feature
语音学 phonetics
语音音标 phonetic transcription
语用学 pragmatics
语域 register
语旨 tenor of discourse
语子/形素 morph
预设 presupposition
预设触发机制 presupposition trigger
元功能 metafunction
元音 vowel
元音的 vocalic
原始语 protolanguage
圆唇元音 rounded vowel
韵律语音特征 prosody
蕴涵 entailment
真值条件说 truth-conditional theory
正规教育 formal instruction
正面强化 positive reinforcement
正迁移 positive transfer
直接成分 immediate constituents
直接成分分析 Immediate Constituent Analysis/IC Analysis
指称/指示语 deixis
指称说 referential theory
指令类 directives
制定模式 patterning
制约 constraint
质量准则 maxim of quality
中层社会方言 mesolect
中流音 central liquid
中世纪英语 Middle English
中元音 central vowel
中元音 mid vowel

中缀 infix
中缀法 infixation
重复与附加语 iterative and adjunt
重写规则 rewrite rule
重音 stress
主题意义 thematic meaning
主位 theme
铸造新词 coinage
转换规则 transformational rules
转换规则 T-rules
转换生成语法 Transformational-Generative Grammar/TG Grammar
转移/迁移 transfer
浊辅音 voiced consonants
浊音化的 voiced
自我交际 intrapersonal communication
自由变异 free variation
自由语素 free morpheme
自指性功能 personal function
纵聚合关系 paradigmatic relation
阻塞音 obstruant
组成部分和整体的关系 meronymy
最佳关联 optimal relevance
最佳学习年龄 optimum age
最佳应答 preferred second parts
最小对立集 minimal set
最小对立体 minimal pair
最终成分 ultimate constituents

附录Ⅱ：江苏省自学考试英语语言学概论考试大纲

2007-06-11

一、课程性质及其设置目的与要求

（一）课程性质和特点

《英语语言学概论》课程是我省高等教育自学考试英语专业（本科段）的一门重要的专业理论课程，其任务是培养应考者系统地学习英语语言学的基本知识，掌握语言系统内部语言学各分支之间的关系和各分支的重要概念和基本理论，了解语言学在其他学科领域的应用，熟悉现代语言学重要的流派及其代表人物；通过该课程的学习，考生可以从不同的角度了解语言(的性质)，了解语言学习和语言教学，为日后进一步学习语言学、从事语言教学实践和语言学研究打下扎实基础。本课程的特点是：专业术语多，概念多，内容抽象，所以，考生最好在学习本课程之前先学习提高语言读写能力的课程，如高级英语、泛读（三）、写作等，这样可以减少语言障碍，有利于学好语言学的理论知识。

（二）本课程的基本要求

本课程共分为四部分，计十三章。第一部分（一至二章）介绍了语言和语言学；第二部分（三至八章）介绍了语言学的主要分支——语音学、音位学、形态学、句法学、语义学和语用学；第三部分（九至十二章）为跨学科领域与应用——话语分析、社会语言学、心理语言学，以及语言学理论与外语教学；第四部分（十三章）介绍了现代语言学流派。通过对本书的学习，要求应考者对英语语言学有一个全面和正确的了解。具体应达到以下要求：

1. 掌握语言的性质、功能，以及语言学的研究范围、语言学的分支和重要的语言学概念；
2. 掌握语言系统内部语言学各分支之间的关系和各分支的重要概念和基本理论；
3. 了解语言学在其他学科领域的应用；
4. 熟悉现代语言学重要的流派及其代表人物。

（三）本课程与相关课程的联系

英语语言学概论是一门基础理论课程，其涵盖范围很广，既涉及语言系统内部的语音学、音位学、形态学、句法学、语义学和语用学，又涉及许多交叉学科，如话语分析、社会语言学、心理语言学、应用语用学（包括语言学理论与外语教学），以及本教程未涉及的神经认知语言学、计算机语言学、人工智能与机器翻译等。语言学的进一步研究甚至会涉及哲学、逻辑学等领域。

在自考课程中，词汇学与语言学关系最为密切，词汇学的许多概念、理论和研究方法都来源于语言学。高级英语、泛读（三）、写作、翻译等课程则是学好语言学的基础。文学与语言学并非对立的关系，这两个领域的研究方法可以互相补充、互相借鉴，日后无论从事语言学还是文学研究,这两个领域都必须同时涉猎。

二、课程内容与考核目标

第一章 语　　言

（一）课程内容

本章简要介绍了语言的定义、性质和功能。

（二）学习要求

了解语言的定义、性质和功能。

（三）考核知识点和考核要求

1．领会：语言的功能。

2．掌握：语言的定义和性质。

第二章 语　言　学

（一）课程内容

本章介绍了语言学的研究范围、语言学研究的科学程序、语言学的分支和几组重要的区别性概念。

（二）学习要求

通过本章的学习,要求了解语言学的研究范围和语言学研究的科学程序,深刻理解并掌握语言学的分支（语音学、音位学、形态学、句法学、语义学和语用学）的研究对象,掌握语言与言语、语言能力与语言运用、共时与历时、言语与书面语、语言行为潜势与实际语言行为、横组合与纵聚合、言语交际与非言语交际、传统语法与现代语言学等区别性概念。

（三）考核知识点和考核要求

1．掌握：语言学的研究范围,语言学研究的科学程序,语言学的分支（语音学、音位学、形态学、句法学、语义学和语用学）的研究对象。

2．熟练掌握：语言与言语、语言能力与语言运用、共时与历时、言语与书面语、语言行为潜势与实际语言行为、横组合与纵聚合、言语交际与非言语交际、传统语法与现代语言学等区别性概念。

第三章 语　音　学

（一）课程内容

本章介绍了语音学及其分支的定义、发音器官的名称和位置、英语辅音和元音的描述与分类、协同发音与国际语音表以及语音特征。

（二）学习要求

理解并掌握语音学及其分支的定义、发音器官的名称和位置、英语辅音和元音的描述与分类、协同发音与国际语音表以及语音特征。

（三）考核知识点和考核要求

1．领会：发音器官的名称和位置、协同发音与国际语音表。

2．掌握：语音学及其分支的定义。

3．熟练掌握：英语辅音和元音的描述与分类以及语音特征。

第四章 音 位 学

（一）课程内容

本章介绍了语音学和音位学的区别、音位学的重要概念（音位、音子、音位变体、最小对立体、分布类型等）、鉴别音位的原则、区别性特征、音位规则、超切分特征、严式音标和宽式音标等。

（二）学习要求

通过本章的学习，了解并掌握语音学和音位学的区别、音位学的重要概念（音位、音子、音位变体、最小对立体、分布类型等）、鉴别音位的原则、区别性特征、音位规则、超切分特征、严式音标和宽式音标等。

（三）考核知识点和考核要求

1. 领会：语音学和音位学的区别。
2. 掌握：鉴别音位的原则、区别性特征、音位规则、超切分特征、严式音标和宽式音标等。
3. 熟练掌握：音位学的重要概念（音位、音子、音位变体、最小对立体、分布类型等）。

第五章 形 态 学

（一）课程内容

本章介绍了形态学的研究范围、语素的定义、几组重要概念之间的关系或区别（包括词根、词缀、自由语素和粘着语素之间，前缀、后缀和中缀之间，屈折词缀和派生词缀之间，词根、词干和词基之间，语素、语子和语素变体之间，空语子和零语子之间）、直接成分分析、以及构词法。

（二）学习要求

通过本章的学习，了解并掌握形态学的研究范围、语素的定义、几组重要概念之间的关系或区别（包括词根、词缀、自由语素和粘着语素之间，前缀、后缀和中缀之间，屈折词缀和派生词缀之间，词根、词干和词基之间，语素、语子和语素变体之间，空语子和零语子之间）、直接成分分析以及构词法。

（三）考核知识点和考核要求

1. 领会：形态学的研究范围。
2. 掌握：语素的定义以及几组重要概念之间的关系或区别（包括词根、词缀、自由语素和粘着语素之间，前缀、后缀和中缀之间，屈折词缀和派生词缀之间，词根、词干和词基之间，语素、语子和语素变体之间，空语子和零语子之间）。
3. 熟练掌握：直接成分分析方法以及构词法。

第六章 句 法 学

（一）课程内容

本章介绍了句法学的定义、语法与词法和句法之间的联系、三种句法关系（横组合关系、纵聚合关系、等级关系）、分析句法关系的几种方法（直接成分分析、标记法直接成分分析、短语标记法、方括标记法）、成分关系与依存关系的区别、表层结构与深层结构的区别、生成句子深层结构的短语结构规则、将深层结构转化为表层结构的转化规则以及结构歧义现象。

(二) 学习要求

通过本章的学习,了解并掌握句法学的定义、语法与词法和句法之间的联系、三种句法关系(横组合关系、纵聚合关系、等级关系)、分析句法关系的几种方法(直接成分分析、标记法直接成分分析、短语标记法、方括标记法)、成分关系与依存关系的区别、表层结构与深层结构的区别、生成句子深层结构的短语结构规则将深层结构转化为表层结构的转化规则以及结构歧义现象。

(三) 考核知识点和考核要求

1. 领会:句法学的定义、成分关系与依存关系的区别以及结构歧义现象。
2. 熟练掌握:语法与词法和句法之间的联系、三种句法关系(横组合关系、纵聚合关系、等级关系)、分析句法关系的几种方法(直接成分分析、标记法直接成分分析、短语标记法、方括标记法)、表层结构与深层结构的区别、生成句子深层结构的短语结构规则以及将深层结构转化为表层结构的转化规则。

第七章 语 义 学

(一) 课程内容

本章介绍了语义学的定义、语义学的分支、有关意义的理论、语义学的一些重要概念指称/参照、外延、内涵、指称对象、意义、延伸、意图、概念、意义的类型、意义的要素、成分分析理论、语义场理论、词汇关系、决定句子意义的基本因素、句子之间的意义关系以及述位结构理论。

(二) 学习要求

通过本章的学习,了解并掌握语义学的定义、语义学的分支、有关意义的理论、语义学的一些重要概念指称/参照、外延、内涵、指称对象、意义、延伸、意图、概念、意义的类型、意义的要素、成分分析理论、语义场理论、词汇关系、决定句子意义的基本因素、句子之间的意义关系以及述位结构理论。

(三) 考核知识点和考核要求

1. 领会:语义学的定义、语义学的分支、有关意义的理论、语义学的一些重要概念指称/参照、外延、内涵、指称对象、意义、延伸、意图、概念以及述位结构理论。
2. 掌握:意义的类型、意义的要素、成分分析理论、语义场理论、词汇关系、决定句子意义的基本因素。

〔第八—十二章内容不做考核要求〕

第十三章 现代语言学流派

(一) 课程内容

本章重点介绍了索绪尔与现代语言学的关系、欧洲结构主义(布拉格学派、哥本哈根学派)、美国结构主义、乔姆斯基与转换生成语法、伦敦学派、韩礼德与系统功能语法等。

(二) 学习要求

了解并掌握现代语言学影响较大的重要流派:索绪尔与现代语言学的关系、欧洲结构主义(布拉格学派、哥本哈根学派)、美国结构主义、乔姆斯基与转换生成语法、伦敦学派、韩礼德与系统功能语法等。

（三）考核知识点和考核要求

1. 领会：各个语言学流派的特点。
2. 掌握：每个流派的代表人物。

三、有关说明和实施要求

（一）关于"课程内容与考核目标"中的有关说明

在大纲的考核要求中，提出了"领会"、"掌握"、"熟练掌握"等三个能力层次的要求，它们的含义是：

1. 领会：要求应考者能够记忆规定的有关知识点的主要内容，并能够领会和理解规定的有关知识点的内涵与外延，熟悉其内容要点和它们之间的区别与联系，并能根据考核的不同要求，做出正确的解释、说明和阐述。

2. 掌握：要求应考者掌握有关的知识点，正确理解和记忆相关内容的原理、方法和步骤等。

3. 熟练掌握：要求应考者必须掌握的课程中的核心内容和重要知识点。

（二）自学教材

本课程使用教材为《英语语言学概论》，王永祥、支永碧主编，南京师范大学出版社，2007年版。

（三）自学方法的指导

本课程作为一门专业理论课程，综合性强、专业术语和概念多、内容丰富而抽象、理解难度大，应考者在自学过程中应该注意以下几点：

1. 学习前，应仔细阅读课程大纲的第一部分，了解课程的性质、地位和任务，熟悉课程的基本要求以及本课程与有关课程的联系，使以后的学习紧紧围绕课程的基本要求。

2. 在阅读某一章教材内容前，应先认真阅读大纲中该章的考核知识点、自学要求和考核要求，注意对各知识点的能力层次要求，以便在阅读教材时做到心中有数。

3. 阅读教材时，应根据大纲要求，要逐段细读，逐句推敲，集中精力，吃透每个知识点。对基本概念必须深刻理解，基本原理必须牢固掌握，在阅读中遇到个别细节问题不清楚，在不影响继续学习的前提下，可暂时搁置。

4. 学完教材的每一章节内容后，应认真完成教材中的习题和思考题，这一过程可有效地帮助自学者理解、消化和巩固所学的知识，增加分析问题、解决问题的能力。

（四）对社会助学的要求

1. 应熟知考试大纲对课程所提出的总的要求和各章的知识点。
2. 应掌握各知识点要求达到的层次，并深刻理解各知识点的考核要求。
3. 对应考者进行辅导时，应以指定的教材为基础，以考试大纲为依据，不要随意增删内容，以免与考试大纲脱节。
4. 辅导时应对应考者进行学习方法的指导，提倡应考者"认真阅读教材，刻苦钻研教材，主动提出问题，依靠自己学懂"的学习方法。
5. 辅导时要注意基础、突出重点，要帮助应考者对课程内容建立一个整体的概念，对应考者提出的问题，应以启发引导为主。
6. 注意对应考者能力的培养，特别是自学能力的培养，要引导应考者逐步学会独立学习,在自学过程中善于提出问题、分析问题、作出判断和解决问题。

7. 要使应考者了解试题难易与能力层次高低两者不完全是一回事,在各个能力层次中都存在着不同难度的试题。

(五) 关于命题和考试的若干规定

1. 本大纲各章所提到的考核要求中,各条细目都是考试的内容,试题覆盖到章,适当突出重点章节,加大重点内容的覆盖密度。

2. 试卷对不同能力层次要求的试题所占的比例大致是:"领会"20%,"掌握"40%,"熟练掌握"40%。

3. 试题难易程度要合理,可分为四档:易、较易、较难、难,这四档在各份试卷中所占的比例约为 2∶3∶3∶2。

4. 本课程考试试卷可能采用的题型有:填空题、单项选择题、问答题、应用题等类型(见附录题型示例)。

5. 考试方式为闭卷笔试,考试时间为 150 分钟。评分采用百分制,60 分为及格。

附录　题型举例

Ⅰ. Fill in the following blanks with appropriate words or expressions.

　　For example: Deep structures are generated by _____ rules, and surface structures are derived from their deep structures by _____ rules.

　　答案:phrase structure, transformational

Ⅱ. Choose the right answer that fits each blank in the sentences from the four choices given. Write the letter marking the answer in the brackets.

　　For example: The sound [h] is _____.　　　　　　　　　　　　　　(　　)
　　A. a voiceless glottal fricative　　　　B. a voiceless dental plosive
　　C. a voiced alveolar plosive　　　　　D. a voiced velar fricative

　　答案:A

Ⅲ. Answer the following questions.

　　For example: How does a surface structure differ from a deep structure?

　　答案:A surface structure corresponds most closely to the linear arrangement of words as they are pronounced; a deep structure corresponds most closely to the meaningful grouping of words. A surface structure is relatively concrete, but a deep structure is abstract. A surface structure gives the form of a sentence as it is used in communication, but a deep structure gives the meaning of a sentence. A surface structure is pronounceable, but a deep structure is not pronounceable.

Ⅳ. Practical work.

　　For example: Draw the deep structure phrase marker for the following sentence and then apply necessary transformational rules to transform the deep structure into the surface structure:

　　Has the car been repaired?

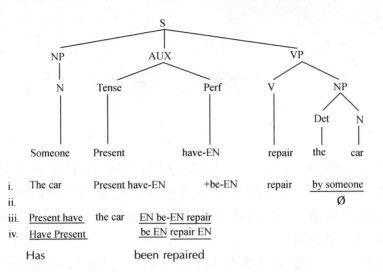

```
       i.    The car      Present have-EN   +be-EN        repair    by someone
      ii.                                                            ∅
     iii.    Present have    the car    EN be-EN repair
      iv.    Have Present               be EN repair EN
              Has                       been repaired
```

(Note：Ⅰ. T-Passive；Ⅱ. T-Agent-deletion；Ⅲ. T-Yes/No question；Ⅳ. T-Affix）

后　记

　　英语语言学理论概念术语繁多,内容抽象难懂,尽管编者花费了一年多的时间对《英语语言学概论》中的重要内容进行了梳理,但仍然不够充分,不够完美,加之我们水平有限,谬误之处在所难免,欢迎读者批评指正,我们一旦发现谬误,一定及时予以修订。

　　为保证质量,本书编者各取所长,密切配合,相互协商,相互审校,相互补充。总体分工大致如下:支永碧(苏州科技学院外国语学院教授)负责编写第一、第二、第四部分和附录,并对全书内容进行补充、修订和审校;王永祥(南京师范大学外国语学院教授,博士生导师)负责编写第三部分,并参与了其他部分的审校工作;王秀凤(大丰市)、李葆春(淮安市)、丁后银(宿迁市,2007年度江苏省教育厅高校哲学社会科学基金项目〔07SJD880080〕)等老师负责该书部分判断题、选择题的编写任务。本书由王永祥、支永碧共同策划,支永碧负责统稿。

编　者